Bernard L. Hyink's

# Politics and Government in California

# Bernard L. Hyink's
# Politics and Government in California

**Seventeenth Edition**

## David H. Provost

California State University, Fresno

**PEARSON**
Longman

New York   San Francisco   Boston
London   Toronto   Sydney   Tokyo   Singapore   Madrid
Mexico City   Munich   Paris   Cape Town   Hong Kong   Montreal

Editor in Chief: Eric Stano
Senior Marketing Manager: Elizabeth Fogarty
Production Manager: Denise Phillip
Project Coordination, Text Design, and Electronic Page Makeup: WestWords, Inc.
Cover Design Manager: Wendy Ann Fredericks
Cover Designer: Base Art Co., Ltd.
Cover Photos: Clockwise from top left: Phil Klein/Corbis; Joseph Dupouy/Alamy;
    David Paul Morris/Getty Images, Inc.; and Mike Dobel/Alamy
Manufacturing Buyer: Roy Pickering
Printer and Binder: R.R. Donnelley & Sons
Cover Printer: Phoenix Color Corporation

For permission to use copyrighted material, grateful acknowledgment is made to the copy-right holders on pp. 2, 3, 11, 13, 16, 17, 18, 26, 31, 38, 39, 41, 42, 45, 50, 71, 79, 96, 106, 107, 111, 117, 119, 134, 135, 144, 145, 147, 158, 170, 172, 173, 179, 183, 194, 197, 203, 204, 210, 214, 220, 227, 230, 241, 242, 243, which are hereby made part of this copyright page.

**Library of Congress Cataloging-in-Publication Data**

Provost, David H.
  Bernard L. Hyink's politics and government in California / David H. Provost.—17th ed.
    p. cm.
  Includes index.
  Rev. ed. of: Politics and government in California / Bernard L. Hyink, David H. Provost.
16. ed. Pearson Longman, c2004.
  1. California—Politics and government—1951– I. Hyink, Bernard L. Politics and govern-ment in California. II. Title.
JK8716.H95 2006
320.9794—dc22

                                    2006016077

Please visit us at www.ablongman.com

ISBN 0–321–43608–3

1 2 3 4 5 6 7 8 9 10—DOC—09 08 07 06

For Nancy

Better Late Than Never

# Contents

# 3

## Politics Into the Twenty-First Century   36

# 4

## Voters, Nominations, and Elections   65

# 5

## Referendum, Initiative, and Recall: Democracy Through Petition   91

# 6

## The Legislature   105

# 7

## The Executive and the Administration    124

# 8

## The Judiciary    143

# 9

## Local Government in California    162

# 10

## Financing California Government    182

# 11

## Economic Growth and the Quality of Life    200

# 12

## Major Political and Social Issues    225

## Epilogue

## Reforms for the Twenty-First Century    253

# Preface

Lights! Camera! Action! These words bring to mind for many a Hollywood sound stage where movies and television programs are taped. For those interested in California politics, however, they can give rise to images of rallies, town meetings and the periodic swarms of television commercials touting (or condemning) candidates and ballot propositions.

The drama that is California is spiced by the incredible variety of ideas, terrain, ethnic groups, economic interests and climate to be found here. As noted in an earlier edition of this book, California is one of the few places in the world where one can go snow skiing in the morning and catch waves on a board in the afternoon. Those living in the Golden State are found tending crops in its rich agricultural industry, working in banks, travel agencies and advertising agencies, in high-tech enterprises and entertainment. They enjoy largely benign temperatures, though Fort Bragg's chilly fog and Death Valley's enervating heat provide contrasts.

As with these factors, the state's politics are also rich in variety. Some of the nation's best known political figures have come from California. They range from noted liberals such as former governor and Chief Justice of the United States Earl Warren to the former governor and later president Ronald Reagan, a strong conservative.

Recent events only illustrate the degree to which California provides rich material for those who seek to supply us with political dramas on television and in movies. In 2003 voters decided to remove from office a governor they had, only months before, handily reelected to a second term. The man they chose to replace him was another in a line of sometimes intriguing personalities, in this case a former body builder and star of action motion pictures. Other "unusual" personalities have prominence in the state. There was George Murphy, best known for his tap dancing ability in Hollywood films in the post-World War II era, chosen to represent California in the United States Senate. There was the curmudgeonly Howard Jarvis who led the revolt that drastically reduced property taxes in 1978. And there was (and still is) Jerry Brown, notable for, among other things, sleeping on the floor and using a Plymouth for trips around Sacramento instead of the governor's limo.

In 2005 another chapter in this colorful history was added. In frustration with his inability to gain agreement from the Democrat-dominated state legislature, Governor Arnold Schwarzenegger pledged a "year of reform" that focused originally on three initiatives designed to make fundamental changes in government. In doing so he aroused an extreme reaction from the state's public employee unions who, in turn, produced a flood of commercials that had two foci: the issues themselves and personal attacks on the governor. By the end of the campaign in November 2005 voters were almost certainly fed up as they endured close to $100 million worth of anti-Arnold ads, not to mention the $80 million spent by the pharmaceutical industry on two other proposals.

These fights seem to have dominated state government and brought much if the policy-making process to a dead stop. Some observers noted that several of the propositions on the November 2005 ballot were so complicated that they should have been dealt with by the legislature. Examples included the aforementioned drug company measures, a proposal to redo (again) the energy regulations that had gone so sour in the crisis in the first years of the twenty-first century, and the technical complexities of budget management (one the governor's targets for reform). Cynics noted that while the legislature ignored these and other pressing policy issues the state needs (infrastructure for rapid transit and roads were frequently mentioned), it could take time to pass legislation that was twice vetoed by the governor making the use of "Redskins" as mascots for high school sports teams unlawful.

If this seems pessimistic, there is much that is not. The state economy has rebounded from the recession of the early 1990s and remains the most productive in the nation. Its agricultural output continues to be the wonder of the world. High-tech has rebounded and is once again among the most innovative to be found anywhere. And, much to the disgust of some, movies produced in the state remain the most popular in the world. Both the good and the not so good are to be found in the following pages. But, for all but the most immune, the one thing not found will be boredom.

The current edition incorporates much that is new while retaining the institutional and procedural information fundamental to an understanding of how government deals with public policy issues. Changes include an updating of demographic and economic information, coverage and analysis of the 2003 recall of the governor and the November 2005 special election. New materials on issues dealing with education, medical marijuana, and transportation are included along with new information on the political processes. As in past editions, every effort has been made to make this the most up-to-date treatment possible of the state, the challenges it faces, and the policies adopted to address them.

As always, many people should be thanked for their assistance in the preparation of this work. We can cite only a few here:

Alan D. Buckley, Santa Monica College
Lawrence L. Giventer, California State University, Stanislaus
Steven Alan Holmes, Bakersfield College
Joseph N. Meyer, Pierce College
Ralph H. Salmi, California State University, San Bernardino
John P. Stead, The Master's College

There were a number of individuals serving in state government offices who provided valuable assistance. Shannon and Ann of state senator Chuck Poochigian's Fresno office will serve as symbols of the many who helped. For his invaluable technical assistance, my thanks to Marc Forestiere of Fresno City College.

David H. Provost

Chapter

# 1

---

# The California Phenomenon

What adjective best describes California? Prosperous, forward looking, eccentric, nuts, laid back, "lala land," sun loving, gross, dazzling? It has been called all these things and many more. And there is a measure of truth in them all, though many outside the state take the image created by Hollywood too seriously. The word the authors prefer is complex. California is many things. It is large cities and small farms. It is forests and deserts. There is a wider range of ethnic groups than can be found anywhere, perhaps anywhere in the world. There are multimillionaires and there are the homeless, the liberals of San Francisco and the conservatives of San Diego. As we have written in other editions of this text, California is a phenomenon, and it is the rich variety of the state, its land and people, that make it such a fascinating place to study. But in order to understand the government and politics of the state we must first gain some knowledge of these people and the resources—economic, cultural, and natural—that make it what it is.

## GEOGRAPHY

California's culture, economy, and polity have been profoundly influenced by its spectacular natural endowments. Stretching along the Pacific Coast for 1,200 miles between the 115th and 124th meridians (comparable to the distance from Charleston, South Carolina, to Boston) with an average width of about 200 miles, California combines the dry heat of the American southwest, the crisp cool air of the soaring Sierra Nevada Mountains, and precipitation from the Pacific to produce (in its natural condition) one of the most ideal climates in the world. There are extremes: Death Valley, 282 feet below sea level, is frequently hotter than any place in North America. Just 60 miles away, Mt. Whitney, one of the highest peaks, is hardly ever free of snow. But the coastal littorals and adjoining foothills are alluringly temperate. (Los Angeles temperatures average 55° F in January and 73° in July with about 40 days of rain each year; San Francisco temperatures average 50° in January and 59° in July with about 65 days of rain.) The warm, dry Central Valley is actually an immense alluvial plain whose fertile soils are irrigated by waters from surrounding mountain lakes and streams.

California's forests, which cover 40 percent of the state, are world renowned for their giant coast redwoods, taller than any other plant or animal life on earth. In addition to being a source of a lucrative timber industry, the forests are crucial for maintaining a sufficient supply of water. Because of the concentration of forests and rivers, Northern California is naturally water-abundant, and Southern California is naturally water-scarce, a situation that has affected the politics of the state in important ways.

The state's geology, dramatized by a history of earthquakes along the San Andreas Fault, has also strongly affected the character of the culture, the economy,

(Courtesy *World West Features*)

'It looks awfully dry here in California. Is there enough water for 21 missions?'

(Dennis Renault, *The Sacramento Bee*)

and the polity. The lure of gold in the eighteenth century and its discovery in the nineteenth was in the first instance largely responsible for making California a part of New Spain and in the second instance a part of the United States of America. Its oil and natural gas deposits have provided a crucial base for industrial development of the state, and their pattern of exploitation in recent years has been one of the most intense political issues, pitting the ecologists and devotees of conservation against the developers and proponents of market-determined growth. Commercially exploitable sources of hard minerals are also a major component of the state's basic economic strength. The water and forests of the state became political battlegrounds in the 1990s when water was diverted from agriculture to preserve fish in the Sacramento Delta and timber interests were at odds with environmentalists, in part over the fate of the famous (or infamous) spotted owl.

## DEMOGRAPHY

### The Indian Genesis

The Indians encountered by the early Spanish explorers of California lived in separate little communities widely dispersed throughout the area and spoke some 135 regional dialects. This highly decentralized pattern and their generally peaceable nature were probably determined by the climate and the abundance of wild fruit, fish, and game. Small communities could happily live off the land without getting in one another's way. Lacking fighting traditions and alliances, they were easily subjugated by a succession of Spanish, Mexican, and Anglo-American regimes. Their numbers declined drastically from about 150,000 at the beginning of the Spanish period to some 16,000 in the 1880s, not so much from deliberate extermination (although there were some notorious massacres during the early American period) as from diseases that were probably the result of their maladaptation to a less natural way of life. Their indigenous cultures were treated with disrespect by their colonial overlords and virtually destroyed. New knowledge of the advances made by California Indians in agriculture, mining, medicine, and trade, not to mention the astronomical observations of Santa Barbara's Chumish, have rendered the old image of the Indian as "grubber in the dirt" obsolete. They had virtually no impact on the evolution of California's political system, but "savages" they were not.

### Hispanic Roots

Upon completing their conquest of Mexico in 1521, the Spaniards under the leadership of Hernando Cortes began a series of explorations up the West Coast in search of the gold-rich "island of Amazons," which, according to a popular Spanish novel, was ruled by a pagan queen, Calafía. Cortes himself got no farther than what is now Baja (Lower) California. Other expeditions followed, most notably that of Juan Rodriquez Cabrillo, who in 1542 explored the coast considerably beyond what is now San Francisco. Actual colonization of the coastal areas north of Mexico, however, was not attempted until the last third of the eighteenth century, when, in fear of Russian encroachment from Alaska and English penetration from Canada, the Spaniards felt impelled to enlarge their empire northward. The Spanish method of colonizing California was essentially what was used in Mexico proper: a combination of the sword and the cross. In 1769 a military force under Gaspar de Portolá and a religious expedition under Fra Junipero Serra were dispatched to "civilize" the natives to the north. (On the East Coast the English settlers had long since driven the Indians back behind the Appalachian mountain range and were on the verge of declaring their independence from Britain.)

The three colonizing institutions used by the Spanish religious and military authorities were missions, military forts, and towns built for civilian settlers. In the *missions*, run by Catholic priests, the indigenous peoples were taught the religion, language, and customs necessary to make them good Spanish subjects. They were provided with food, shelter, and clothing and in exchange were often forced to work as slaves for the missions. The Spanish and Indian settlements that grew up around these missions were the embryos of many of today's cities, San Diego being a notable example. The missions were not always successful in gaining the cooperation of the Indians simply on the basis of economic incentives and religious awe. Some tribes were hostile and had to be subdued by military force; thus the *presidios,* advance outposts protecting the missions, were established. Some of the presidios also attracted settlers and, like San Francisco, grew into cities themselves. The early missions and presidios, having established the feasibility of successful colonization, encouraged the Spanish authorities to sponsor civilian towns, or *pueblos.* Spaniards, Mexicans, and indigenous peoples were recruited as settlers through the offer of land, housing, and supplies. The surplus produce of the settlers would be used to supply the military presidios, and the settlers were subject to military service in emergencies and were required to contribute their labor to public works projects. The vast majority of the Indians lived outside the pueblos but frequently came to town, attracted by the variety of goods and amusements. Limited self-government gradually evolved in the pueblos under an *alcalde* (mayor), appointed by the Spanish military authorities, and a town council, elected in some of the more stable settlements by the citizens themselves.

The indigenous Californians attained their freedom and equality with those of Spanish origin (and a growing population of mixed bloods) in 1822 when Mexico won its independence from Spain, but the entire province *del norte* (to the north) continued to be regarded by the new Republic of Mexico as a colonial appendage. Under the Mexican Secularization Act of 1833 the government seized control of the missions and their lands. Much of the mission property was to have been turned over to the Indians, but governmental instability in Mexico City and the submissiveness of the Indians allowed much of the land to fall into the hands of local politicians. Still, the extension of political democracy during the Mexican period did include the Indians who wanted to become part of the new system.

Although the central government in Mexico City appointed the governor of California, who in turn appointed prefects and subprefects (regional and local administrative officers), the provincial legislature was a popularly elected body with the authority to enact laws concerning commerce, taxes, and education. Moreover, on the local level mayors *(alcaldes),* as well as *ayuntamientos* (town councils), were popularly elected. Given the political turmoil in Mexico City, the Californians were left largely to fend for themselves, and the result in many areas was virtual anarchy.

Thus when westward migrating Anglo-Americans encountered California in the 1830s and 1840s, they found a racially mixed Hispanic society with political traditions of its own, including an evolving democracy with a loose federal structure. However, this rich sociopolitical legacy was not to be integrated as a part of the successor American regime, for the Anglos were by and large contemptuous of the California Mexicans. So the legacy became one of an undercurrent of resentment on the part of the resident Hispanics toward their new overlords and a feeling of alienation from what was once their own land.

## California's Rapid Growth in Population

With more than 37 million people, California is now home to more than 12 percent of the entire U.S. population. More than nine out of every ten Californians live in one of 56 metropolitan areas, making it the state with by far the largest number of cities with a population of 100,000 or more. In recent years the greatest growth has been in the suburbs, with some of the central cities either static or declining in population. The most populous county in the United States is Los Angeles County, with more than 9.7 million inhabitants. Well over half of the growth in the last several years has come from natural increase (births over deaths) with the remaining third from immigration—legal and illegal.

The course of California's political history can be written largely as an answer to the question: When and why did they come to California?

From the time that the early Spanish explorers named the northwest coast of New Spain after the land of dazzling wealth portrayed in a novel by Garcia Ordóñez de Montalvo, California has been a beckoning gleam on the horizon—a "great expectation" to millions of people. Some have envisioned adventure, many have hoped to find material security, and others have dreamed of glamour and bright lights.

Each year since the American whalers and fur trappers began arriving in the early nineteenth century, there have been substantially more arrivals than departures. Thus although the population of the United States has been increasing during the past century at an average rate of 40 percent every 20 years, California's population has nearly doubled every 20 years. But the expansion from fewer than 15,000 in 1846, when the American military authorities took California from Mexico, to over 37 million by 2006 has not come from a steady flow of migrants. There have been periods when immigration was comparatively low, but those demographers who predicted that the 1980s would be one of those periods were wrong. Within every 20-year period, however, there has been at least one stimulus to a major population invasion from other parts of the country. By highlighting these major invasions and the explosive pattern of the state's growth, some of the unique political and governmental problems discussed in the following pages can be better understood.

## Nineteenth-Century Invasions

**The Gold Rush**    The news that James Marshall had struck gold on the banks of the American River in January 1848 brought a rush of adventurous young men, most of whom were between the ages of 18 and 25, almost all unmarried. Not all found gold, however, so they went into lumbering, agriculture, and business—and sent for women. By 1860 the population of California was 380,000, and residents born in other states outnumbered the natives two to one.

**The Railroad Boom**    When the Union Pacific Railroad, built westward from Omaha, was hooked up with the Central Pacific Railroad, built eastward from Sacramento, the trade and migration bottlenecks through the High Sierra passes were cleared. In 1869 the new capitol building was dedicated at Sacramento as if it were a new capitol of the United States. From 1870 to 1880 the resultant increasing land values and commercial expansion stimulated a population rise of nearly 55 percent. This was also the period during which California acquired its large Chinese population, most of whom had been imported into the country by the railroad builders to work as coolie labor. Thousands were laid off in 1876 when the Southern

Pacific completed its line down to Los Angeles, but they later became a permanent and productive part of California's workforce.

## Twentieth-Century Invasions

**The "Black Gold" Rush**   Southern California was found to be rich in oil lands at the turn of the century when oil began to displace coal as the major source of industrial power. The state's oil output increased twelvefold from 1900 to 1910. As the geysers spurted skyward so did property values, attracting real estate developers and land speculators into the Los Angeles area by the thousands.

During this period the agricultural areas were converted from grazing lands to wheat fields, orange groves, and truck gardens requiring a large itinerant labor supply. Further Chinese immigration had been stopped by exclusion acts that grew out of the political turmoil of the latter nineteenth century (see discussion of Kearneyism in Chapter 2), so new labor sources had to be found. Farm organizations waged large publicity campaigns throughout the Midwest and South. "Reduced railroad fares, gaudy pamphlets, and silver-tongued traveling salesmen were all part of the pitch to lure white laborers to the coast."[1] Not enough came to meet the demand, so the farmers and ranchers turned to Japan, Mexico, and the Philippine Islands for cheap labor.

With a developing industrial southland and a broad, central farm belt feeding the thriving commercial area around San Francisco, California looked like a sure investment. Young men and women from the older states, eager to stake out a claim in this mine of many untapped veins, boarded trains at Boston, New York, Philadelphia, and Chicago in confident mood. The state's population jumped to 2.5 million by World War I.

**The Prosperity Push**   Although the population increase slowed during World War I, the prosperous 1920s gave California two million new residents. The value of oil continued to increase. The horse and wagon were pushed to the side of the road by the new gasoline-consuming autos, buses, trucks, and airplanes. California oil producers found the Panama Canal a quick and inexpensive route for shipping oil east to sell at competitive prices. Then, in rapid succession, a series of large new fields was discovered in the Los Angeles area. The Huntington Beach strike in 1920 was followed by the Signal Hill and Santa Fe Springs strikes the next year and the Kettleman Hills bonanza in 1928. People with money to invest descended upon the Southern California area. Refineries were developed to turn the crude oil into gasoline on home grounds. Meanwhile, improved transportation and refrigeration sped California vegetable produce and fancy fruits to Eastern markets, which, in addition to enriching the growers, helped to advertise California.

The most publicity came through the movies and the radio. In snowbound Maine and Minnesota, people heard the radio announcer describe the balmy Rose Bowl weather on New Year's Day, and the local movie screens in Pittsburgh,

---

[1] Kathleen C. Doyle, *Californians: Who, Whence, Whither* (Los Angeles: Haynes Foundation, 1956), p. 29.

Cleveland, and Oskaloosa were animated billboards showing palm trees and movie starlets frolicking in the surf. They used to dream of going to Florida, but now California came to be regarded as the nation's playground or a place to spend one's later years lolling in the sun living on dividends and annuities. The young people came for excitement, the middle-aged came to get in on the ground floor of a sound economic venture, the old came to retire—together they pushed the state's population skyward at a rate of 200,000 a year.

**The Dust Bowl Exodus**    After the stock market crash of 1929, immigration slowed to a trickle. But in the 1930s a huge migrant labor force from Oklahoma, Arkansas, and other prairie states crowded into California. When the dust blew away the topsoil from their small farms and the Great Depression blew away their small savings, they headed west. They heard that there was fruit rotting on the vines in California just waiting to be picked (it was not picked because it could not be sold), and they came to California with their large families because they had nowhere else to go. This time the state's population growth (three times as fast as the nation's) was not an indication of economic health.

**The Siege of the Servicemen**    World War II brought many young men to California who might otherwise never have come. Three hundred thousand servicemen who had been stationed there decided to stay after being discharged. Many others went home, talked about the climate and the oranges, and convinced their families it was worth a try. The process was repeated during the Korean War.

**The Industrial Boom**    World War II, in addition to bringing the servicemen to California, brought heavy industry supported by government subsidies, loans, and cost-plus contracts. The burgeoning of the aircraft industry—Douglas, Hughes, Convair, North American, Lockheed—converted placid suburbs such as Santa Monica and Burbank into humming cities. Allied industries providing parts and supplies to the major aircraft producers were also given impetus. The big steel companies were encouraged by Washington to establish and expand California plants; Henry Kaiser built a huge steel mill in the middle of Fontana's vineyard with the help of a loan from the Reconstruction Finance Corporation. The San Francisco Bay region experienced an industrial revival from the stimulus of wartime shipbuilding. California's oil industry particularly thrived as the state became the fuel station for tankers servicing the Pacific fleet. New electrical supplies, chemicals, and small-tools industries got their start. Civilian employment nearly tripled in manufacturing industries from 1941 to 1945, while other urban employment remained relatively constant. By the end of the war, California's population approached ten million.

Peacetime brought stimulus to California's entertainment industry, especially after television began to make use of Hollywood's talent, facilities, and know-how. Simultaneously, California's infant electronics and plastic industries became giants.

The Korean War and the Cold War gave another fillip to heavy industry (for example, Kaiser's $65 million addition at Fontana) and a demand for a larger urban work force—skilled, semiskilled, and unskilled. The great migration of the 1950s was composed primarily of wage and salary workers, and civilian employment in manufacturing registered a 70 percent gain between 1950 and 1958. Manufacturing displaced the retail and wholesale trades as the top employer. California industry had grown considerably during the previous 20 years. The expanded market in California and rising national freight rates brought many manufacturing plants to the state.

The 1970 census showed that the state added about six million people to the 1960 population, a gain of approximately 38 percent—an average of 1,645 new residents every day. In terms of the labor force, 650 workers were added each day, and the state was having more and more difficulty absorbing them. At the turn of the new decade the state's large aerospace industry had to lay off thousands of workers due to the decrease of governmental contracts, driving the unemployment rate to more than 7 percent in 1970.

## Slow and Go Toward the Twenty-First Century

The growth slowed in the 1970s, due primarily to the slow economy and concerns over the impact of population growth on the environment. But, even so, the absolute growth in population from 1970 to 1980 still totaled more than 3.5 million people— greater than that of any other state.

Since 1964, when California's population of 18 million made it the largest state in the nation, California has grown to over 37 million. Rapid growth in the 1980s (the population grew by 26 percent in the decade) dwindled with the recession of the early 1990s. However, though population growth slowed it was still substantial with some 400,000 more people living in the state each year. The growth was not due to people moving here from other states. Rather it was due to immigrants from other countries combined with natural increase (births over deaths). One estimate, from the Urban Institute of Washington, D.C., is that between 1990 and 1998, California absorbed one million immigrants, many of them entering illegally, drawn to the state by job opportunities. That posed some serious problems for state and local governments (see Chapter 12).

By the mid–1990s a rebounding economy was creating 350,000 new jobs a year and by the end of the decade that figure exceeded 500,000. Once again California was being viewed as the land of opportunity, though the view dimmed by the budget crisis of 2003.

The Census Bureau projects California will have a population of 49.29 million by the year 2025. There is nonetheless a question as to just how many people the state can support. Clogged highways, deteriorating schools, crime-ridden inner cities, overcrowded prisons, and overloaded public services such as libraries and museums that have had their hours cut (or in a few cases eliminated entirely) with others such as hospitals stretched to the breaking point—all these and more point to a state facing major problems. As one environmentalist pointed out, if the population booms of the 1980s were to continue, the state would have 302 million people in it in the year 2092. Energetic and idealistic leadership is required to alert an already concerned population fully as to the seriousness of the situation and mobilize an effective response.

## SOCIOLOGY AND CULTURE

California is a state of great ethnic variety and is becoming more so each year. More than three out of every ten Californians are of Hispanic origin. One out of every 12 is black. Over four million persons of Asian ancestry—more than a third of those living in the United States—live in California. The state's native Indian population (now combined for the first time in the 2000 census with Native Alaskans), is 628,000, more than any other state. Non-white ethnic groups now constitute 46 percent of the population. Los Angeles and San Francisco have become cities with non-white majorities.

The most dramatic increases have been in Asian immigrants, particularly those from Southeast Asia and the Pacific. Between the 1980 census and 1990 census, the Asian/Pacific Islander population grew 127 percent. By 2000 there were 4.2 million and they constituted 12.3 percent of California's population. That made the group the second largest ethnic minority. One in every three Asian/Pacific Islanders in the country lives in California. The largest absolute increase was among Hispanics, bringing their total in 2000 to 10.9 million or 32.9 percent of the population with projections that they will constitute 44 percent of the population by 2030. The slowest-growing group was blacks, who increased to 2.5 million or 7.5 percent.

The most substantial growth, then—from immigration plus reproduction—is among new Californians of foreign ancestry from Asia and Latin America, who are not only visibly distinct from the "Anglo" majority but who also speak different languages. These characteristics are turning California cities into a series of ghettos, not the mythical "melting pot" wherein the immigrants are assimilated into the majority culture, but a collection of little Guadalajaras and little Saigons. The impact on local governments has been enormous. While immigrants have added greatly to the cultural "mix" in the state and have in many ways been major contributors to the state's economy, in other ways they have added to the problems facing the state (see Chapter 12). It is estimated that more than 90 percent of all farm laborers are foreign-born, contributing very significantly to the farm economy (and keeping food prices down), but, on the cost side of the ledger, there were 1.7 million students in 2005 who were designated "English learners" (in other words not proficient in the language) in the state's schools, requiring more intense instruction in the English language. California has certainly been enriched by these newcomers, but there have been at times increases in racial tensions, especially during periods of violence and recession. The targeting of Korean shopkeepers during the 1992 Los Angeles riots is an example. At the end of the 1990s there were repeated examples of tension and discrimination between Hispanics and blacks as well arising out of perceptions that Korean shopkeepers were "ripping off" their black customers with inflated prices. A tide of anti-immigrant fervor during the recession of the early 1990s resulted in voter approval of Proposition 187, which targeted illegal immigrants. It is important to distinguish, as many of those on both sides of the immigration question fail to, between legal and illegal immigrants. While most Californians oppose illegal immigrants, as was shown by their approval of Proposition 187 in 1994 (see Chapter 3), the majority are not opposed to immigrants legally admitted to the country. In the debate over

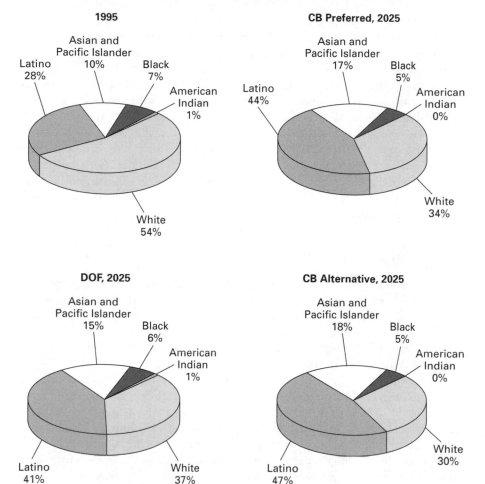

**Figure 1.1**    California Population by Race/Ethnic Distribution. (*Source:* "California Counts," Public Policy Institute, CA, October 1999.)

so-called undocumented workers in 2005 and 2006, Californians were split over proposals to build a 700 mile fence along our southern border and whether such people should be determined to be felons. Most polls indicated an understanding of the role such workers play in key aspects of the state's economy, most notably in agriculture.

Along with the new ethnic complexity is a continuation and further complication of California's renowned religious diversity. Practically every religious group in the world has a visible part of its flock in California. Because of its huge Hispanic population there is a larger proportion of Catholics in California than in the nation at large. The recent influx of refugees from Indochina make it the Buddhist center of the

Americas. Esoteric cults are, as always, at home in California, with religious groups such as the "People's Temple" and the "Jones cult" having made it their headquarters.

The religious groups have much to keep them busy, given the rising incidence of crime; the exploding numbers of youths in violence-prone gangs, often engaged in drug dealing; the high divorce rate; and a whole host of societal ills that have given rise to antisocial behavior.

The state has much to be proud of with its citizens' contributions to music and the arts, in the entertainment field, in scholarship, and in progressive policies adopted by its leaders. California is a wondrous mix of the good, the bad, and the ugly. The glories of its landscape featuring white sand beaches, towering mountains, and awesome deserts are matched by some of the worst smog, most persistent traffic snarls, and increasing displays of gratuitous violence to be found anywhere in the world. The delight of a concert at the Hollywood Bowl is offset by the growing problem of the homeless. And so it goes. All this and more is to be found in California, land of contrasts.

## ECONOMY

With an annual gross output in excess of $1.55 trillion, California would rank eighth in the world if it were a separate nation.[2] With its great economic diversity it has historically been able to weather economic downturns much better than virtually any other state. That proved no longer true in the early 1990s as the nation—and California—were plagued with serious economic woes. In fact, California was slower to come out of the recession than other states, though some aspects—such as tourism, which brought $54.1 billion to the state in 1992—remained relatively strong through the bad times. And agriculture, though briefly damaged by the six-year drought of the late 1980s and early 1990s and a devastating freeze in 1991, rebounded strongly. The economy during this period and through 2002 at times resembled a giant roller coaster. The recession of the early 1990s was followed by the rapid growth of the end of that decade only to be followed by another slow down in 2001. Following the terrorist attacks of September 11, 2001, a key source of economic strength—tourism—took a major hit. Illustrating this was a whopping 22.5 percent drop in commercial air travel at Los Angeles International Airport. Traffic at San Francisco International dropped nearly as much, 17.5 percent. However, by 2005 tourism once again was a major source of strength with the city of Los Angeles recording 24.9 million visitors who spent $12.7 billion, an increase of 8.5 percent over 2004.

Although less than 30 percent of its land area is under cultivation, California consistently leads the nation in gross income from agricultural products ($34.3 billion in 2005). Forty percent of all fruit marketed in the United States is from California, including 85 percent of the grapes and most of the lemons and apricots. Almost every American olive is a California olive, and the same can be said for almonds, artichokes,

---

[2] Actually France barely edged out California for fifth place in 2001 with a gross domestic product of $1.310 trillion.

**TABLE 1.1** Total U.S. Exports (Origin of Movement) via California Top 25 Countries Based on 2004 Dollar Value (in millions of dollars)

| Rank | Country | Value 2001 | Value 2002 | Value 2003 | Value 2004 | % Share 2001 | % Share 2002 | % Share 2003 | % Share 2004 | % Change 2004/2003 |
|---|---|---|---|---|---|---|---|---|---|---|
| | California Total and % share of U.S. Total | 106,777.0 | 92,214.3 | 93,994.9 | 109,967.8 | 14.61 | 13.30 | 12.99 | 13.44 | 16.99 |
| | Total Top 25 Countries and % of California | 99,943.6 | 85,754.6 | 87,481.5 | 101,941.2 | 93.6 | 93.0 | 93.1 | 92.7 | 16.5 |
| 1 | Mexico | 16,343.1 | 16,076.3 | 14,871.8 | 17,239.4 | 15.31 | 17.43 | 15.82 | 15.68 | 15.62 |
| 2 | Japan | 14,635.1 | 11,105.5 | 11,754.7 | 13,323.2 | 13.71 | 12.04 | 12.51 | 12.12 | 13.34 |
| 3 | Canada | 11,816.0 | 10,075.4 | 11,231.6 | 12,111.2 | 11.07 | 10.93 | 11.95 | 11.01 | 7.83 |
| 4 | China | 4,676.1 | 4,482.4 | 5,465.0 | 6,841.8 | 4.38 | 4.86 | 5.81 | 6.22 | 25.19 |
| 5 | Korea | 5,034.9 | 4,711.8 | 4,833.3 | 5,912.1 | 4.72 | 5.11 | 5.14 | 5.38 | 22.32 |
| 6 | Taiwan | 5,664.5 | 5,391.4 | 4,443.0 | 5,362.4 | 5.30 | 5.85 | 4.73 | 4.88 | 20.69 |
| 7 | United Kingdom | 5,588.8 | 4,347.3 | 4,360.0 | 5,206.0 | 5.23 | 4.71 | 4.67 | 4.73 | 19.41 |
| 8 | Hong Kong | 3,934.0 | 3,684.1 | 4,178.9 | 5,117.4 | 3.68 | 4.00 | 4.45 | 4.65 | 22.46 |
| 9 | Singapore | 4,226.8 | 3,298.4 | 3,370.8 | 4,161.4 | 3.96 | 3.58 | 3.59 | 3.78 | 23.46 |
| 10 | Netherlands | 4,318.2 | 3,577.2 | 3,412.2 | 3,813.9 | 4.04 | 3.88 | 3.63 | 3.47 | 11.77 |
| 11 | Germany | 4,657.4 | 3,480.1 | 3,559.7 | 3,682.9 | 4.36 | 3.77 | 3.79 | 3.35 | 3.46 |
| 12 | France | 2,242.0 | 1,885.4 | 1,915.1 | 2,955.1 | 2.10 | 2.04 | 2.04 | 2.69 | 54.31 |
| 13 | Australia | 2,084.5 | 1,910.1 | 1,899.4 | 2,243.2 | 1.95 | 2.07 | 2.02 | 2.04 | 18.10 |
| 14 | Malaysia | 2,554.2 | 1,998.6 | 1,730.8 | 2,002.4 | 2.39 | 2.17 | 1.84 | 1.82 | 15.69 |
| 15 | Belgium | 1,131.7 | 1,244.9 | 1,425.1 | 1,713.7 | 1.06 | 1.35 | 1.52 | 1.56 | 20.25 |

*Source:* U.S. Census Bureau, Foreign Trade Division.

dates, figs, raisins, prunes, walnuts, garlic, nectarines, and persimmons. California leads the nation in the production of 53 crops and livestock products, is second in 14 such products, and third in 6. California farms provide 1.1 million jobs producing 350 different crops. Only Texas exceeds California in hard mineral and oil production, and nearly all of the useful minerals known to humankind have been found in California. Alaska has more timberland, but California's wood products industry is the largest in the nation.

The incredible strength of what is produced by the California economy (and the advantageous location the state enjoys on the Pacific Rim) is demonstrated by the exports that pass through its ports. More specifically, the state leads the nation in the production of computer and electronic products with over $50 billion sold. That constitutes nearly one-third of the production of these in the United States. Tourism fed $82.5 billion into the state's economy in 2004.

The state's economy took several major hits as it neared the end of the twentieth century: loss of defense contracts with the end of the Cold War, the collapse of the "dot com" revolution and even the Northridge earthquake of 1974 played a role.

In 1993 California fought back. In an effort to stem the tide of businesses moving out of the state, the much-maligned workers' compensation system received a major overhaul in 1993 designed to reduce costs to employers and increase benefits to employees.[3] A bipartisan effort led by Speaker Willie Brown and Governor Pete Wilson resulted in significant tax breaks for businesses as well. Both these moves were intended to change an image of the state that had come to be seen as unfriendly to business. As the state looked forward to the twenty-first century, Californians were optimistic. But the recession of 2001 dimmed that feel good feeling. A Field Poll in June 2005 found that just 28 percent thought the state was on the "right track" compared, while 59 percent felt it was on the "wrong track." That compares with just 7 percent who felt the state was on the wrong track in 1992.

Perhaps one factor was the increasing cost of housing in the state. For many it seemed the American dream of owning one's home was slipping away. Late in 2004 the Public Policy Institute of California found that nearly half of those under the age of 35 were thinking of moving to another state. Others, an estimated 350,000, had moved to the relatively less expensive Central Valley. Topping the areas with expensive homes was the Bay Area with Santa Clara County, which reported a median price (half sold for more, half for less) for a single family home of $714,215. A Bay Area home overall averaged $644,000. With a Valley home at just over $300,000 the stimulus to move is apparent. At that, only about a fifth of Californians felt they could afford to buy a home.

The fact that California is at the eastern edge of the Pacific Rim offers opportunities not equaled by any other state. Trade with Asia has been on the rise in recent

---

[3] Under the old system, workers received only 29.5 cents of each dollar contributed to the fund, the rest going to doctors, lawyers, and insurance companies. The changes were estimated to reduce costs by $1.5 billion a year while raising benefits significantly. Later changes ordered by the insurance commissioner were expected to save an additional $500 million.

years. The Port of Los Angeles passed New York Harbor in 1995 to become the country's largest gateway for foreign trade. A large portion of the state's $20 billion in California-made exports travels across the Pacific, with Japan its largest trading partner. Mexico and Canada were the next biggest customers as the influence of the North American Free Trade Agreement (NAFTA) was evident. Still, Asian countries accounted for nearly half of the state's sales abroad in 1998.

## ECOLOGY

The California way of life has been the product of the felicitous balance on this western slice of the continent among nature's various elements (atmosphere, waters, soils, flora and fauna, and topography) and of the belief that California's vastness (158,693 square miles) and its exposure to the great Pacific Ocean would allow the state to accommodate a virtually limitless expansion of human settlements and industry. Nature's profound equilibrium was unlikely to be perturbed; it would simply absorb the marginal alterations made by humans.

However, in recent decades the assumption of an unlimited ecological carrying capacity has been severely eroded along with some of nature's crucial structures. Human settlements have not been evenly dispersed throughout the state but have concentrated with high density in the most climate-attractive locations—the seacoast and the foothills. As these areas were developed, overbuilding at such prize locations has undermined the stability of nature's own retaining walls. Landslides and mudslides have begun to convert intendedly permanent structures into mobile homes and entered them, against their owners' wills, in massive demolition derbies. The limits of the absorptive capacity of the air over densely populated urban areas have been painfully evident to smog sufferers since the late 1940s. Important fish-wildlife-plant ecologies along the seacoast are being destroyed by oil drilling and industrial-residential waste runoff, not to speak of the degradation to recreational assets. Similar assaults are being inflicted on the state's lakes, rivers, and streams by overbuilding or excessive diversion and harnessing of their natural flows for agricultural, industrial, and recreational purposes. The impact of population growth along with industrialization can be seen in the following figures.

- Californians have eliminated 85 percent of old growth redwoods;
- some 91 percent of the wetlands are gone; and
- 99 percent of the grasslands are no more.

On top of that, a federal survey in 1999 found that nearly six in nine fish species are either extinct or on their way to disappearing while of 342 species of land birds found in California, one in five is on an endangered species list.

The discovery that California's ecology has its own priorities and agendas and will fight back—sometimes viciously—if they are not respected has made the management of California's ecology one of the most controversial, if not *the* most controversial, issues in contemporary California politics.

**TABLE 1.2    September 2005 Regional Sales and Price Activity(a)**
**Regional and Condo Sales Data Not Seasonally Adjusted**

|  | Median Price Sep-05 | Percent Change in Price from Prior Month Aug-05 | Percent Change in Price from Prior Year Sep-04 | Percent Change in Sales from Prior Month Aug-05 | Percent Change in Sales from Prior Year Sep-04 |
|---|---|---|---|---|---|
| **Statewide** |  |  |  |  |  |
| Calif. (sf) | $543,980 | −4.4% | 17.3% | 2.9% | 3.9% |
| Calif. (condo) | $424,580 | −1.9% | 14.9% | −11.1% | 4.5% |
| **C.A.R. REGION** |  |  |  |  |  |
| Central Valley | $361,290 | −0.7% | 22.7% | −6.9% | 3.7% |
| High Desert | $312,410 | 2.2% | 31.1% | −2.4% | 22.3% |
| Los Angeles | $560,990 | −0.6% | 22.3% | 2.4% | 8.0% |
| Monterey Regions | $712,800 | −2.0% | 13.4% | 0.7% | −4.8% |
| Monterey County | $680,000 | −1.4% | 18.3% | 2.5% | 4.1% |
| Santa Cruz County | $750,000 | −4.2% | 16.3% | −1.8% | −15.2% |
| Northern California | $434,690 | −1.3% | 16.0% | −11.4% | −11.0% |
| Northern Wine Country | $639,390 | −0.2% | 26.5% | 2.2% | 1.3% |
| Orange County | $708,840 | −1.0% | 11.9% | −11.8% | 19.2% |
| Palm Springs/ Lower Desert | $371,250 | 0.1% | 8.7% | −6.5% | 27.4% |
| Riverside/ San Bernadino | $389,450 | 0.6% | 27.2% | 2.7% | 14.5% |
| Sacramento | $383,920 | −2.7% | 14.5% | −13.2% | −13.9% |
| San Diego | $612,030 | −0.8% | 6.8% | −9.1% | −1.6% |
| San Francisco Bay | $709,980 | −2.8% | 10.5% | −9.7% | −8.5% |
| San Luis Obispo | $602,160 | 6.3% | 24.4% | −9.2% | 30.5% |
| Santa Barbara County | $610,710 | −25.5% | −19.2% | −18.1% | −12.3% |
| Santa Barbara Southern. Coast | $1,475,000 | 11.3% | 55.3% | −36.6% | −34.5% |
| Northern Santa Barbara County | $462,700 | 0.0% | 6.9% | 7.1% | 10.0% |
| Santa Clara | $733,000 | −3.6% | 16.3% | −4.6% | −9.1% |
| Ventura | $678,380 | −1.1% | 10.6% | −13.0% | 14.0% |

*Source:* California Association of Realtors.

## POLITICAL POWER

California's large population alone translates into potent political clout. Following the 2000 census, the 2001 congressional reapportionment gave California 53 seats in the House of Representatives. Just how big that is can be seen by the fact that the next largest delegation in the House, from Texas, is composed of 34.

### States with the Most Electoral Votes

| 1971–1980 | 1981–1990 | 1991–2000 | 2001–2010 |
|---|---|---|---|
| California (45) | California (47) | California (54) | California (55) |
| New York (41) | New York (36) | New York (33) | Texas (34) |
| Texas (27) | Texas (29) | Texas (32) | New York (31) |
| Illinois (26) | Penn. (25) | Florida (25) | Florida (27) |
| Ohio (26) | Illinois (24) | Penn. (23) | Illinois (21) |
| Ohio (25) | Ohio (23) | Illinois (22) | Penn. (21) |

Accordingly, the person favored by California's delegation to the presidential nominating convention of either the Democratic or Republican party has an excellent chance of gaining the presidential or vice-presidential nomination. The Republican party nominated a Californian for president in 1960, 1968, 1972, 1980, and 1984, and in the three previous conventions it nominated a Californian for vice president (one of whom was subsequently chosen to be chief justice of the U.S. Supreme Court). Two of the nominees have been elected president (Richard M. Nixon in 1968 and 1972 and Ronald Reagan in 1980 and 1984). Commenting on the successful 1980 Ronald Reagan election campaign, the noted political historian Theodore White observed that "California is preeminently the nation's political leader, providing its president and its political style."[4] California has been the leader as the nation moves away from the politics of the traditional machines, away from people voting along predictable class, ethnic, and religious lines. Traditionally, the two key elements of the American political system have been its stability and its predictability. But they have never existed in California, and now they are vanishing from the rest of the country as well.

California benefited considerably from the presence of a number of the state's citizens in the higher ranks of the Clinton administration during the president's first term. Leon Panetta served as chief of staff, Warren Christopher and William Perry as secretary of state and secretary of defense respectively, and Laura Tyson was the president's chief economic advisor. Mickey Kantor was, first, top trade negotiator and later secretary of commerce. California concerns were likely to be heard more clearly both because of its electoral college clout and because of the presence of such top advisors to the president. Though there was concern about how much "clout"

---

[4] Theodore H. White, *America in Search of Itself* (New York: Harper & Row, 1982), p. 66.

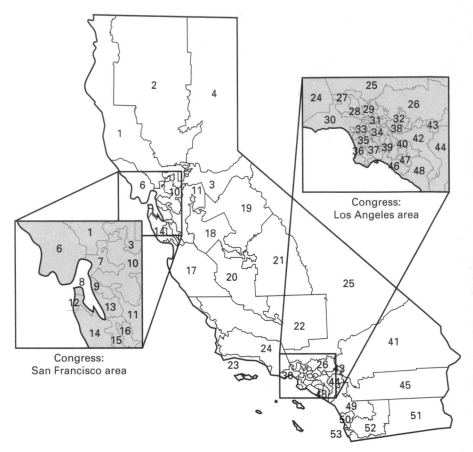

**Figure 1.2**    Map of California Congressional Districts. (Map provided by *California Journal.*)

California would have after all these officials decided to retire, the importance of the Golden State was demonstrated once again with the approach of the 2000 presidential campaign. With its newly moved primary—to the first Tuesday in March—it became a "player" as it had not been in many years. Just how important can be seen by the number of visits made by presidential hopefuls, including some 60 visits by Vice President Gore before 2000 arrived.

That influence continued, somewhat more muted, in the Bush administration in 2001 (Mr. Bush did of course lose the state by 1.3 million votes) with two members of the Cabinet from the state, Norman Mineta as secretary of transportation and, as appropriate for the most productive farming state in the Union, Ann Veneman as secretary of agriculture.

The natural and acquired endowments that make up "the California phenomenon" impart a unique character to the internal politics and government of the Golden State. The sense of excitement about controversies large and small is part of a heady feeling (fantasy? realistic self-concept?) that the way California deals with its increasingly complex political and governmental problems will set the pace for the nation as a whole.

California's role is, of course, that of a state in the federal union that is the United States of America. That role is more circumscribed than in past years, but remains significant nonetheless. It is focused on three major powers.

The first and by far most encompassing is the police power. This is not just the power to catch and punish thieves, murderers, arsonists, and speeders; it involves the state in protecting its citizens' "health, safety, and morals." A few examples will clarify this broad power.

- the inspection of restaurant kitchens to insure cleanliness (no cockroaches!);
- the requirement that drivers and their passengers wear seat belts; and
- prohibiting so-called "blood sports" (no bull fighting allowed).

There are instances when federal and state authorities conflict. An example is over the legality of the use of marijuana for medicinal purposes, approved by the state's voters but opposed by the federal government. (See Chapter 12.)

The second power is more briefly stated and is the power the state possesses over its political subdivisions. Within its sphere of authority it acts much like a unitary system with all power emanating from Sacramento. Thus, cities, counties, school districts, and other governmental entities are creations of the state and receive their power to act from the state.

The last power is quite limited and is over suffrage and elections. Once quite sweeping, it has been reduced by court decisions (no white primary or poll tax), constitutional amendment (the right to vote for women and at age 18) and by congressional actions (no understanding or literacy tests). States retain the power to run elections (there is no federal election machinery) and the right to decide what type, if any, of primary or caucus system they will use and when to hold them.

In the pages that follow, these powers will become evident, from those on elections (Chapters 3 and 4) through the instruments of policy making and local governments (Chapters 5 through 9) to the responses that are made to facilitate state needs and the adoption of public policies (Chapters 11 and 12).

## REVIEW QUESTIONS

Students may find use of the review questions found at the end of each chapter helpful in assuring they have secured a basic understanding of the information contained in them. Page references are provided for the topics.

1. What have been the causes for the waves of immigrants that have come to California since the mid–1800s? (pp. 6–9)
2. It has been said that California is becoming the first "third world state." Explain. (pp. 9–11)
3. Explain the consequences of population growth in the post-World War II era, socially, economically, environmentally, and politically. (pp. 9–17)

# SELECTED WEB SITES ——————

Use of the Internet has been growing geometrically if not exponentially in recent years. The many thousands of web sites include some, at best, of dubious reliability. The authors have selected a few of well-known worth for each chapter that will allow the student to explore topics concerning or related to California politics and government more fully.

A vast amount of information is available through the state Department of Finance (www.dof.ca.gov). Several specific pages are of special interest. The demographics of the state may be found under Demography. Sex, age, and ethnicity/race by cities and counties may be accessed and trends shown. A second site, Financial and Economic Data, cannot be easily summarized. Home prices by city, the consumer price index, wages and salaries, manufacturing—a whole host of information can be obtained here. The California Statistical Abstract, another publication of great usefulness, is also included. For current events, the web site www.rtumble.com is enormously useful in that it reproduces every article concerning California politics and government each day.

# SELECTED REFERENCES ——————

Baldassare, Mark, *A California State of Mind*, Berkeley: University of California Press, 2002.

Barber, Mary Beth, "Can You Make a Buck When Peace Breaks Out?" *California Journal*, January 1994.

——, "Is California Driving Business Out of the State?" *California Journal*, May 1993.

Buck, Claudia, "Business Climate," *California Journal*, February 1998.

Burdick, Eugene, "From Gold Rush to Sun Rush," *New York Times Magazine*, April 14, 1963.

*California Statistical Abstract*, Sacramento: State Printing Office, latest edition.

Editor, "California 2000: The Next Frontier," *California Tomorrow*, Winter 1983.

Field Institute, "Living in California," *California Opinion Index*, July 1981.

Healy, Melissa, "State Leads as Home to Immigrants," *Los Angeles Times*, October 5, 2000.

Kotkin, Joel, and Paul Garbowicz, *California Inc.*, New York: Rawson, Wade, 1982.

*London Economist*, "California, State of the Future," July 1960.

McDonnel, Patrick J., "Immigration to State Slows, Study Finds," *Los Angeles Times*, January 23, 2001.

McWilliams, Carey, ed., *The California Revolution*, New York: Grossman, 1968.

Palmer, Tim, ed., *California's Threatened Environment*, Washington, D.C.: Island Press, 1993.

Quinn, Tony, "The Economy: Gateway to the Pacific," in Thomas Hoeber and Larry Gertson, eds., *California Government and Politics Annual, 1991–1992*, Sacramento: California Journal Press, 1991.

Seidenbaum, Art, *This Is California: Please Keep Out*, New York: Wyden, 1975.

Schrage, Peter, "Golden Moment" in *Paradise Lost*, New York: The New Press, 1998.

Scott, Steve, "Tube Dreams," *California Journal*, July 1997.

U.S. Bureau of the Census, *Census*, Washington, D.C.: Government Printing Office, 2000.

Walters, Dan, *The New California*, 2d ed., Sacramento: California Journal Press, 1992.

Chapter

# 2

---

# The Development of California Politics and Government

From the state that gave you Hiram Johnson, Earl Warren, Richard Nixon, Angela Davis, Ronald Reagan, Cesar Chavez, Jerry Brown, and Howard Jarvis, it seems as if the only thing predictable about California politics is its unpredictability. A multitude of contradictory impulses—some rooted deep in its past, others shaped by visionary dreams of the future, some ruggedly individualistic, others mystically communitarian, some highly rational and pragmatic, others wildly romantic—contend against one another for the soul of the California polity and are reflected in its constitution, its institutions, and its laws. This has always been the case but now more so than ever, for contemporary California is the product of both its inherited paradoxes and its current complexities. Each generation has contributed its own traumas and complications to the character of California.

## THE FORCED BIRTH OF THE GREAT STATE OF CALIFORNIA

California became part of the United States not through an evolutionary expansion of American settlements but through sudden rupture from the mother Hispanic system that nourished its early development. By the 1840s the American government had its eye on the large but weak Mexican province extending up the Pacific Coast toward Canada. Vastly underpopulated (there were estimated to be fewer than 7,000 Mexicans living in the area, only a thousand adult males, and of those only a hundred or so could read and write), its control by Mexico had largely ceased. The United States was in an expansionist mood, and the idea that Americans had a "manifest destiny" to impart the blessings of their civilization to less fortunate peoples became popular.

Failing to buy California from the Mexican government, the U.S. government made efforts to stimulate "independence" movements, which led to the so-called "Bear Flag Revolt" by American settlers in Northern California on June 10, 1846 (they seized some horses belonging to the Mexican governor). Short-lived, it became merely a sideshow to the Mexican-American War (1846–1848).

The Treaty of Guadalupe-Hidalgo formally ended that war on February 2, 1848. Under its terms, Mexico ceded all of what is now California, Arizona, New Mexico, and Texas to the United States. But the end of the war hardly brought peace and quiet. The social, political, and economic conditions of the times were highly volatile and were made worse by the gold rush of 1848 and 1849.

News of James Marshall's discovery of gold on the banks of the American River in January 1848 caused soldiers and sailors to desert, shopkeepers to close their doors, and ranchers to leave their livestock. The non-Indian population quadrupled, reaching 100,000 in 1850. The Hispanic culture was drowned in a flood of young Anglos (most were between 18 and 25 years old) seeking instant wealth.

## A CONSTITUTION AND STATEHOOD

The foundations of the governmental system now operating in the state were instituted in 1849 and 1850 as California joined the Union.

It was not preordained that California would become an American state so soon after it had been taken from Mexico. There was the option of territorial status, which was preferred by the many Southern Californians with strong Mexican ties, since this would allow a looser connection with the United States. But in the more populous North the predominant sentiment was for statehood, and it was the North that controlled the convention that assembled in Monterey in September 1849 to draw up a constitution. The delegates worked quickly, approving the final document in only six weeks. The proposed constitution was largely a prefabricated structure combining planks from the U.S. Constitution and the state constitutions of New York and Iowa. On November 13, 1849, voters (only white males over 21) throughout California ratified the constitution by a nearly unanimous vote of 12,872 to 811 and chose their first governor, Peter H. Burnett, and other state officers, as well as delegates to the U.S. House of Representatives (although California had not yet been admitted to the Union as a state). The state legislature convened and selected two U.S. senators, John Fremont and William Gwinn, to present the California constitution before the Congress and to request admission as a state.

# ECONOMIC AND CLASS CONFLICTS— THE CONSTITUTION OF 1879

Since entering the Union, California's development, though full of surprises, has in the main been in the form of reflections and sometimes magnifications of national trends and traumas. Its responses to the boom and bust cycles in the decades following the Civil War were very much of this character.

An especially severe economic and political reaction to the economic depression of the early 1870s surfaced in California. The thousands of Chinese laborers laid off by the railroad builders upon the completion of the transcontinental lines made the employment situation especially critical and gave a peculiar racist edge to the labor union agitations sparked by the Depression. The Workingmen's Party, under the fiery leadership of a young San Francisco drayman, Denis Kearney, campaigned against the railroad menace and the "Yellow Peril." Labor anger intensified in 1876 and 1877 with the arrival of some 25,000 additional immigrants on ships from China, and there were anti-Chinese riots organized by the unions on the streets of San Francisco. Kearney and his men threatened to take over the state.

In addition to demanding legislation to exclude further Chinese immigration, the Workingmen's Party urged state regulation of the railroads and banks, an equitable system of taxation, an eight-hour day, the abolition of contract labor on public works, compulsory public education, and the direct election of U.S. senators. In combination with the rural Grange, which also disliked the railroads and contended that the existing state constitution allowed the monopolies too much freedom, the Workingmen's Party successfully mobilized popular support for a new constitutional convention.

Voters across the state elected delegates of varied political persuasions to the constitutional convention that convened in September 1878: 51 Workingmen, 11 Republicans, 10 Democrats, 2 Independents, and 78 who identified themselves simply as "nonpartisan." The main division was between people who favored considerable state control over the economy and those who stressed free enterprise. The emerging document, ratified by a slim majority of voters in 1879, was less a reformer's Magna Charta than a bundle of compromises. Still, it did incorporate just enough of Kearney's program to take the steam out of his attempts to polarize the state along class lines.

Rather than being completely new, the constitution of 1879 was in large part an elaboration of the 1849 document, with more specific and detailed provisions. But there were a number of important alterations.

The legislature's power was significantly circumscribed. Whereas previously there had been no restrictions on its financial powers, it was now prevented from appropriating state monies to aid private institutions (including religious schools and hospitals), except homes for the blind, orphans, and the indigent. The governor was given the right to convene special sessions of the legislature in which only the subjects mentioned in his call could be considered. This power could be used with pointed effect when a budget bill was up for passage.

The judicial system was completely reorganized. The state supreme court was expanded to comprise a chief justice and six associate justices. Superior courts created by the legislature were to replace county and district courts.

The Chinese coolie labor problem received special treatment in Article XIX—a concession to the Workingmen's Party delegates. All corporations were prohibited from hiring Chinese, and their employment "except in punishment for crime" was forbidden on any state, county, or municipal project. The importation of contract coolie labor was made illegal, and the legislature was instructed to discourage any further Chinese immigration. (This article was not completely repealed by the voters until 1952, although the courts had earlier found most of the clauses in violation of the U.S. Constitution.)

There were numerous other provisions written into the 1879 constitution to protect nearly every interest represented at the convention. Thus details such as the maximum number of acres of state-owned land to be granted to one settler and whether noncultivated land was to be counted by tax assessors (properly subjects for simple legislative statutes) were included. The result was a bulky and unwieldy document that required amendment very frequently.

## CONSTITUTIONAL REVISION

By 1963 California's constitution had been amended more than 350 times and contained some 80,000 words, becoming the second longest state constitution in the United States. Many of the provisions severely restricted the power of the government to perform its proper functions.

After several unsuccessful attempts at constitutional reform, the state legislature in 1963 appointed a Constitutional Revision Commission made up of 60 leading citizens representing industry, agriculture, education, government, and other civic groups. The recommendations of this Commission, after review by the legislature, were presented to the electorate in a series of constitutional amendments starting in 1966 and continuing through 1980. Most were approved, and the state constitution was reduced to one-third its former length. In addition, several important governmental changes were made, such as the provision for a full-time legislature to replace the former limited terms of legislators. These changes are discussed in following chapters on the legislature, executive, and judiciary.

## THE PROGRESSIVES VERSUS
## THE RAILROAD MAGNATES

In the prosperous 1880s economic power and political power became concentrated in the hands of the railroads' "Big Four": Leland Stanford, Collis Huntington, Charles Crocker, and Mark Hopkins. At the height of their power, according to California historian John Caughey,

> there was hardly an office, from the seats in the United States Senate down through the governorship and the courts to the most inconsiderable town office, in which the right man could not do the railroad a service.[1]

---

[1] John W. Caughey, *California,* 2d ed. (Englewood Cliffs, NJ: Prentice-Hall, 1953), pp. 449–450.

The domination of California politics by the Southern Pacific Railroad went virtually unchallenged from the decline of Kearneyism to the rise of the nationwide Progressive movement at the start of the twentieth century. With the railroad magnates being one of their chief targets, the Progressives, under the national leadership of Theodore Roosevelt and Robert M. La Follette and in California Hiram Johnson, organized themselves into an especially powerful political force in California.

Whereas the railroads brought the Industrial Revolution to the West Coast, and some of its most successful entrepreneurs bequeathed California many of its finest private educational institutions, libraries, and museums, the Progressives brought lasting structural changes into the state's system of politics and government.

The state's first Progressive legislature made such an impact that Theodore Roosevelt called its work "the most comprehensive program of constructive legislation ever passed at a single session of an American Legislature."[2]

## LIVING HIGH BEFORE THE CRASH

The first third of the twentieth century was the period of California's heady adolescence. Much of the lifestyle that was to arouse the rest of the nation's envy (often bitter jealousy) had its origins in this devil-may-care period.

The growth in population slowed somewhat in the immediate postwar period, but the impact of the "black gold" rush continued to increase. As noted earlier, the ease of shipping California's oil to the rest of the nation was enhanced by the construction of the Panama Canal. And of course more and more people were turning from horse-drawn to gasoline-powered transportation. New oil strikes in the 1920s brought more people and with them more development. New preservation techniques meant that California produce could be shipped east as well, a boost to the farmers as well as an enhancement of the state's image.

Postwar prosperity brought popular complacency toward politics and government. The only significant political rivalries of the time were North-South and rural-urban and focused on the issue of legislative reapportionment.

Although in 1900 Southern California had only 20 percent of the state's population, by 1920 it had nearly 40 percent and was continuing to gain rapidly. The population explosion, especially in Los Angeles, threatened the domination of the legislature by the northern and rural interests. The citizens of Los Angeles, outraged when the legislature refused to redraw the state senate after the 1920 census, qualified an initiative constitutional amendment for the ballot to make reapportionment of legislative seats mandatory on the basis of population. Northern and rural interests countered with their own constitutional initiative, which, while requiring a redrawing of assembly districts to reflect the population changes, instituted a "Federal Plan" for California by making the counties the basis for senatorial districts, thereby assuring a greater number of northern and rural senators. The Federal Plan carried the day in the 1926 election. The Southern Californians were not able to change the system in their favor until the 1960s.

---

[2] Ibid., p. 464.

Hyrum Johnson Campaigning. (Courtesy *California State Library*)

The effects of the Great Depression of the 1930s were especially severe in California, because many of the state's major industries—motion picture production, tourism, and olive, date, fig, and citrus growing—were nonessential. Despite the lack of jobs, thousands of persons from other hard-hit areas, particularly the Arkansas-Oklahoma dust bowl, flocked to the "Promised Land." As Wilson, in John Steinbeck's *The Grapes of Wrath*, said:

> Oh, but she's worth it. Why, I seen han'bills how they need folks to pick fruit, an' good wages . . . . An' with them good wages, maybe a fella can get hisself a little piece of land an' work out for extra cash. Why, hell in a couple of years I bet a fella could have a place of his own.

The ranks of the unemployed swelled dangerously. Social and political unrest was rampant. Visionary groups such as the Technocrats vied with religious movements such as the one led by Aimee Semple MacPherson whose vision of heaven was much like Hollywood. However, the period did produce movements with definite political impact. The dormant Progressives revived the Democratic Party, which won the governorship for the first time in 40 years and gained control over the state legislature as well. Culbert Olson, a reformer at heart, had the misfortune of becoming governor during the later stages of the Great Depression. His majorities in the legislature diminished and he was faced with fiscal conservatives from both parties (an "economy block") that frustrated many of his initiatives. He managed to gain approval for improvements in the state's penal system and in the areas of youth correction and mental hygiene.

During Olson's administration the "Yellow Peril" was rediscovered. The result: After Pearl Harbor, pressure was brought on Olson to aid in the evacuation of all Japanese from the state. He disliked the idea but eventually assisted in the federal actions that removed 94,000 Japanese living in the state. That this action might be constructed as prejudice was shown by the fact that only those Germans and Italians actually suspected of espionage and sabotage were evacuated. *All* Japanese, including American citizens, were ordered to relocation centers in other states. The judgment of historians concerning this episode in the state's history is—understandably—harsh. The following comment is typical:

> In retrospect the evacuation of the Japanese appears both cruel and unnecessary. . . . That Olson took no stronger line (opposing it) than he did is clear evidence that even a man of liberal instincts and genuine humanitarianism could be bewildered by the forces set in motion by the waving of "California's Bloody Shirt."[3]

The most lasting effect on California government from the Great Depression was the blurring of the demarcation among spheres of state, local, and national responsibilities. Federal funds were funneled into the state to provide jobs and stimulate business investment. In partnership with the state, superhighways and giant flood and reclamation projects were started, including the Hoover Dam and the Central Valley Project. Grants-in-aid to local social service agencies were provided by Congress, often tied to the local governments' adherence to nationally legislated rules and regulations for their administration. National regulation of business activity reached into the state under the U.S. Supreme Court's increasingly liberal interpretation of the interstate commerce provisions of the federal Constitution as allowing the hand of national authority to extend to firms manufacturing goods that would later be transported for sale across state lines.

## WORLD WAR II: THE NATIONAL GOVERNMENT REVIVES THE CALIFORNIA BOOM

World War II accelerated the enlargement of the national government's role in California. Huge federal subsidies poured into California to support the state's aircraft and other defense-related industries. The revival of the California boom was widely appreciated, but it also had problematical implications. The state's economic well-being was now crucially dependent on decisions made in Washington, D.C. This new situation affected California politics by establishing a common interest between big labor and big business to keep the defense contracts coming in. After the war, particularly in Orange and San Diego counties, labor and business united in sending

---

[3] Robert E. Burke, *Olson's New Deal for California* (Berkeley: University of California Press, 1953), p. 206.

Cold War hard-liners to Congress and electing "moderates" to the state legislature and county councils to preserve an attractive local tax and regulatory climate for the defense industries.

## 1942–1966: ERA OF THE MODERATE PROGRESSIVES

Earl Warren, Goodwin H. "Goodie" Knight, Edmund G. "Pat" Brown—two Republicans and a Democrat, each a strong governor, all part of the popular California fusion of Hiram Johnson progressivism and Franklin D. Roosevelt liberalism—shepherded the state into a position of national leadership for coping with the problems of advanced industrialization and urbanization.

Earl Warren always considered himself a Hiram Johnson Progressive. Entering public service in 1919, he rapidly rose to the position of district attorney of Alameda County. In 1936, still only 45 years old, Warren became chairperson of the Republican State Central Committee and led California's delegation to the Republican National Convention. In 1938 he won the nomination of the Republican, Democratic, and Progressive parties in the primaries for the position of attorney general under Democrat Culbert Olson. So began his successful nonpartisan career.

Warren tried for both the Democratic and Republican gubernatorial nomination in 1942, but Olson led in the Democratic primary. In the general election campaign Warren continued to style himself as a nonpartisan and handily defeated Olson, receiving 57 percent of the vote to Olson's 42 percent. If it is a misfortune that "only men of very loose political affiliations, like Warren, can be elected," commented one analyst, "the blame must be attributed to the (Hiram) Johnson crusade which pounded the ruling party into so many fragments that no one has ever put it together again."[4]

Warren's nonpartisanship paid off spectacularly in 1946 when he won the nomination for governor in both the Republican and Democratic primaries. In 1950 James Roosevelt was able to capture the Democratic nomination, but Warren beat him by more than a million votes in the November general election. Warren had a keen awareness of the controlling features of California politics: the large proportion of independent voters and the necessity for a candidate for governor to appeal to the liberal urban vote as well as to the conservative elements in the state. He followed essentially a middle-of-the-road course, which was displeasing to both the extreme right and the extreme left but was agreeable to the large body of voters in between. He was able to retain the support of both organized labor and the business community.

Warren's ten-year governorship—the longest in California's history—was highlighted by a greatly expanded state welfare program, including old-age pensions, workers' compensation, and mental hospital and prison reforms. His political popularity allowed him to press almost anything he requested through the legislature. The outstanding exception was his compulsory health insurance plan, which, after

---

[4] Raymond Moley, in *The Politics of California: A Book of Readings,* David Farrelly and Ivan Hinderaker eds. (New York: Ronald Press, 1951), p. 220.

determined opposition by the California Medical Association lobby, was defeated in the legislature.

The popular California governor received the Republican vice-presidential nomination in 1948, becoming the running mate of Thomas E. Dewey. He was considered a leading contender for the Republican nomination for president in 1952 until the Eisenhower candidacy was announced. In 1953 Eisenhower appointed Warren chief justice of the U.S. Supreme Court.

The Democrats had to wait four more years for their chance to regain the governorship. Lieutenant Governor Goodie Knight succeeded Warren and won election on his own in 1954. Though he continued many of his predecessor's policies, he failed to be reelected in 1958 when he was forced to run for the U.S. Senate instead so as to give Senator William Knowland the opportunity to run for governor, a game of political musical chairs designed to advance Knowland's presidential aspirations. Both lost.

The beneficiary of this Republican debacle was another political progressive, Attorney General Pat Brown. For the first time since the 1930s, the Democrats were able to take advantage of their 3–2 lead in registration, in part because the cross-filing system now designated clearly which candidates belonged to which party. (For many years newly arrived voters registered Democrat but voted for incumbents, most of whom were Republican. Having come to the state because of the good things it had to offer, they were inclined to keep those in power rather than rock the boat.) The highly pragmatic and nonideological Brown administration was in tune with the mood of the times, and his continuation and gradual expansion of the social-service state erected by his predecessors gave rise to little concerted opposition during his first term. His primary public relations problem was over the issue of the death penalty, which he opposed and most Californians favored. This perceived vulnerability encouraged the entry of the former vice-president, Richard Nixon, narrowly defeated for the presidency by John F. Kennedy in 1960, into the gubernatorial race in 1962. Brown ran stressing his nonideological approach to problem solving (e.g., the state water project, school construction) and clearly was better able to project that nonpartisan image so important in California elections than the highly partisan Nixon. Brown won handily, by 300,000 votes, but at the same time the voters elected a Republican, Thomas Kuchel, to the U.S. Senate, thus demonstrating again the public's nonpartisan mood.

Governors Warren, Knight, and Brown presided over a generally confident California. By the mid–1960s California's per capita income was 20 percent higher than the national average. It consistently led the country in gross income from agricultural products, growing 40 percent of all the fruit marketed in the United States and producing almost as much oil and cotton as Texas. It was the nation's leader in aircraft production and was rapidly gaining on the Eastern industrial states in other heavy manufacturing—steel, fabricated metals, and plant machinery. Almost 90 percent of the 19 million Californians were now living in urban areas, making it the state with the largest number of cities with a population of 100,000 or more.

Industry kept increasing because of the population and resources, and the people kept coming because of the industrial growth. Observers were predicting that by the middle of the 1970s there would be one continuous city from San Diego to

San Francisco. Yet underneath the surface of affluence—in part, a reaction to California's prosperous growth—there were rumblings of doubt and discontent. Many, looking at the increasing air and water pollution, the mudslides and landslides from excessive subdividing of the foothills, the congestion on the freeways, and the overcrowding of parks and beaches, began to wonder whether such continual rapid growth was all good and whether the state and local governments were able to handle it. Some looked at the expansion of government that paralleled the state's economic growth and worried that their freedom of enterprise might be unduly circumscribed. Minority groups began to feel their *relative* deprivation more keenly, as evidenced by the eruption of violence among the blacks in Watts (a pleasant middle-class black community). Students at the University of California launched sit-in campaigns against what they perceived to be the dehumanizing rules and regulations of the vast bureaucracy of the state's multiversity.

The Republican party moved to the political right in 1964, nominating conservative Arizona Senator Barry Goldwater as their presidential candidate. One of his staunchest supporters was motion picture actor Ronald Reagan, who made many speeches (actually the same one, "the speech," many times) urging Goldwater's election and descrying government waste and Democratic policies designed to redistribute the wealth. Lyndon Johnson won easily, both nationally and in California (he carried the state by a huge 1.3 million-vote margin, though he failed to carry Democratic U.S. Senate candidate Pierre Salinger with him; he lost to conservative Republican George Murphy by 300,000 votes). But Reagan's efforts did not go unnoticed. Goldwaterites had gained control of the state's Republican party and Reagan was their man for 1966. When Reagan defeated San Francisco Mayor George Christopher in the Republican primary, Brown supporters were convinced they could once again preempt the political center and win easily. They both underestimated Reagan as a candidate and misjudged the mood of the electorate.

## REAGAN: ANOMALY OR PORTENT OF A CONSERVATIVE TREND?

For the 1966 general election, Reagan competed with the experienced Brown for the middle-American California voter. He purged his rhetoric of some of the more abrasive Goldwaterisms he had thrown around in 1964 and stuck mainly to the standard conservative complaints against excessive government spending and centralization of control in Washington and Sacramento at the expense of private initiative. He also related effectively to the growing citizen concerns about a spread of Watts-type uprisings among disaffected minorities and student demonstrations on campuses. In promising a more efficient system of law enforcement and an investigation of the University of California, he implied that the Brown administration was overzealous in sponsoring civil rights legislation and overpermissive on matters of law and order. Brown was left with little that was new to say and had to content himself with defending his record.

Reagan got 59 percent of the 6,370,000 votes cast. There were only 3,350,000 Republicans registered, as opposed to 4,720,000 Democrats, which means that at

Governor Ronald Reagan and Jesse Unruh Campaigning During the 1970 Election. (Courtesy *Wide World Photo*)

least 300,000 registered Democrats crossed party lines and voted for Reagan. The successful gubernatorial candidate brought into office with him the entire slate of Republican candidates for other state executive offices except attorney general, which was won by incumbent Thomas Lynch. The Republicans also severely cut into the Democratic control of the legislature but not enough to take over either the assembly or the senate.

Reelected in 1970 over the former powerful Speaker of the Assembly Jesse Unruh, Reagan had a full eight years to attempt to reverse the long-established trend toward bigger government and higher taxes. He failed, though the rate of increase slowed markedly. He maintained with some justification that many programs were mandated by law and that Democratic control of the legislature made his efforts much more difficult.

Reagan did succeed in moving the state from some fairly serious red ink into the black during his tenure as governor. He inherited a deficit of $500 million from Brown and left Brown's son, Jerry, with a $350 million surplus in 1974. While Reagan could claim some of the credit, the booming state economy meant higher revenues from income, sales, and business taxes.

During the Reagan years the numbers of employees on the state government payroll stayed relatively constant—a fact the governor rated as possibly his greatest accomplishment in Sacramento. In the final analysis, however, he failed to reduce the role of government, his paramount goal before achieving office.

## EDMUND G. BROWN JR., AND THE POLITICS OF LIMITATION

It was a measure of the younger Brown's keen political instincts that he latched onto the growing popular sentiment in California that defeated his father and brought Reagan into office—the discontent with big government—rather than attempt to resurrect the Progressive-New Deal liberalism of past decades. Edmund G. "Jerry" Brown Jr., added a new element to the state (and national) trend, however, by propounding and symbolically representing the philosophy that the cause of big government lay in society's materialistic appetites and that the whole "more-is-better" approach to life, typified by the California ethos, would have to be reversed if the hope of reducing the size and role of government was to be realized. Brown's counterculture, "small-is-beautiful" approach, however, did not become evident until after his election.

The 1974 election in California mirrored the mood of a country outraged by the antics of Republican President Richard Nixon over Watergate. Democrats won most statewide offices and increased their majorities in the state legislature and the congressional delegation. Alan Cranston won reelection to the Senate by a whopping 1.3 million votes. Still, many were turned off by the scandal and voter turnout was the lowest in 30 years.

Brown cast himself as a crusader against corruption at a time when corruption was very much on the public's mind. As secretary of state he proposed and as candidate for the Democratic nomination for governor he campaigned for Proposition 9, a reform of campaign spending in the 1974 June primary. By so doing he demonstrated his instinct for anticipating the central issues of the day.

The general election campaign between Jerry Brown and his Republican opponent, State Controller Houston Flournoy, turned out to be primarily a popularity contest, one that Brown won, though narrowly, 52–48 percent. That gave him little in the way of a policy "mandate," little leverage over his party or the legislature.

California voters seldom get what they think they will when choosing a governor, but in electing Brown in 1974 they were in for more surprises than usual.

He rejected use of the $1.3 million governor's mansion, opting to sleep on the floor of a rented apartment. He refused use of a Cadillac limousine, preferring a Plymouth Satellite. His inaugural address lasted just seven minutes. And he gave a Suli choir the job of providing the inspirational tone at some official functions. All this and more proved Jerry Brown did indeed march to a different drummer.

## THE 1978 GUBERNATORIAL ELECTION

The outcome of the race for governor was not long in doubt. Facing a relatively colorless candidate in Attorney General Evelle Younger, Brown won going away, 56 percent to 36 percent. But Republicans gained considerable solace from victories by George Deukmejian as the new attorney general and Mike Curb as the new lieutenant governor. In both these contests the California voters showed again their proclivity to split their ballots, with both winners garnering ten-point wins over their opponents.

The most heat in the 1978 election cycle was generated by Proposition 13, the Jarvis-Gann initiative (see Chapter 10). Generated by wildly escalating property taxes and an apparent inability of the state government to take corrective action, the proposition was approved by a 2–1 margin. What proved significant was the reversal by Brown on the issue. A staunch opponent before the vote, he performed one of the most deft feats of political acrobatics ever executed by an American politician the day after the primary election. He announced himself a convert. He would, he proclaimed, implement Proposition 13 in the most humane way possible (using "bailout" funds from the state surplus to cushion the blow on local governments). It may have saved his bid for reelection, since before his conversion he had been trailing slightly in the polls; after his switch he pulled steadily ahead.

## JERRY BROWN'S RECORD

In several fields the Brown governorship made a significant impact, widely regarded as positive. Brown was a strong and effective leader in preserving California's natural environment almost single-handedly saving the California Coastal Commission when it was up for renewal in 1976. He was in the forefront of the effort to attract high-tech industry to the state. He gave active leadership to the search for new sources of energy, stressing solar energy as a means that carried less ecological hazard. Brown also opened high-level government to Californians who had never before been invited to help run the state. Of the approximately 3,000 appointments made by the governor, one-third went to minorities, and one-fourth went to women.

However, Brown made serious missteps in his career as governor. His midterm run for the presidency in 1980 not only took him away from his gubernatorial responsibilities but injured his image as an effective and popular politician.

Probably the most serious error made by Governor Brown was his failure to raise taxes during the last two years of his administration. The recession had caused a sharp decline in state revenues, and at the same time large financial grants were still being transferred to local governments to cover their shortfall caused by Proposition 13. All state surplus funds had been expended, and there was insufficient income to meet current expenses. Indeed, the $1.5 billion deficit that had been accumulated by the time Brown left office proved to be a political disadvantage in his campaign for the U.S. Senate in 1982 and would continue to be a liability to his future political ambitions.

Brown was more at home with ideas of sociocultural change than concrete actions. However, he did expand considerably the scope of government in the regulatory area with several new agencies including the Agricultural Labor Relations Board and the Energy Commission. His governorship is not remembered for highways, dams, and schools built by the state—of which there were virtually no significant new starts during his regime. He is admired more for what he stood for rather than for what he accomplished. A reporter once asked Brown to evaluate his own performance. He replied, "I did it my way."[5]

## REVIEW QUESTIONS

1. The constitution of 1879 was actually a modification of the one adopted just 30 years earlier. Why was it needed and what were the most significant changes made? (pp. 20–23)
2. What caused the adoption of the "Federal Plan" and how did its adoption affect the politics of the state? (p. 24)
3. Governors Olson, Warren, Knight, and Pat Brown had a vision of California government and its role that differed significantly from that of Ronald Reagan. Explain. (pp. 27–31)

## SELECTED WEB SITES

There are few developed sites that cover California's history. There are, of course, sites dealing with narrow aspects to it. As a general site, the Historical Society's is as good as any and better than most. It may be accessed at www.calhist.org. There are other pages or "links" that may be accessed through this site, including ones on California Indians, immigration, a history of San Francisco and counties in the state as well as one dealing with California missions.

---

[5] Editorial, *Los Angeles Times,* January 9, 1983.

# SELECTED REFERENCES

Bollens, John C., and G. Robert Williams, *Jerry Brown in a Plain Brown Wrapper*, Pacific Palisades: Palisades Publishers, 1978.

California Secretary of State, *Statement of Vote*, Sacramento: State Printing Office, issued after each general, primary, and special election.

Cannon, Lou, *Reagan*, New York: Putnam, 1982.

Caughey, John W., *California*, 2d ed., Englewood Cliffs, NJ: Prentice-Hall, 1953.

Chan, Sucheng, and Spencer Olin, *Major Problems in California History*, Boston: Houghton Mifflin, 1997.

Harris, Joseph P., *California Politics*, Palo Alto: Stanford University Press, 1961.

Hill, Gladwin, *Dancing Bear*, New York: Harcourt Brace Jovanovich, 1968.

Katcher, Leo, *Earl Warren: A Political Biography*, New York: McGraw Hill, 1967.

Lorenz, J. D., *Jerry Brown: The Man on a White Horse*, Boston: Houghton Mifflin, 1977.

Mason, Paul, "Constitutional History of California," *Constitution of the United States and the State of California and Other Documents*, Sacramento: State Printing Office, 1973.

Mowry, George E., *The California Progressives*, Berkeley: University of Californa Press, 1951.

Owens, John Robert, Edmond Constantini, and L. Weschle, *California Politics and Parties*, New York: Macmillan, 1970.

Peck, Robert, *Jerry Brown: The Philosopher Prince*, New York: Stein and Day, 1978.

Putnam, Jackson K., *Modern California Politics*, San Francisco: Boyd and Fraser, 1984.

# 3

# Politics Into the Twenty-First Century

A recurring question concerning California politics in the 1980s was: Is the Golden State becoming more conservative? As with so many questions about California, the answer is not easy or simple. At first glance the question itself seems a bit strange. Most people, when they think of California, envision a state and people who are innovative, progressive, and—in the minds of some—even a bit "off the wall" in their approach to life. After all, it was Californians who gave the governorship to a motion picture actor with no previous experience in government an action repeated many years later with the election of Arnold Schwarzenegger. And they followed up by electing a governor whose unorthodox style earned him the title of "Governor Moonbeam." Major experiments from the Progressive era of the early twentieth century to the tax revolt of the late 1970s upheld a tradition of trying new ways of dealing with issues. The fact that in many instances other states followed suit gave California a reputation for leadership that was well deserved.

Was California moving to the right, politically? Has that trend continued? The answer seems to be yes . . . and no . . . and sort of. Evidence of a shift to the right might include voter registration that went from 3–2 Democratic to a much narrower 5–4. Another indicator was the Republican stranglehold on the governor's office, a position they held for 16 straight years. On issues of public safety, including crime, typically an area of strength for Republicans, voters strongly supported "get tough" measures, for example, approval of the Victims Bill of Rights in 1982 and a series of bond issues to construct many new prisons. But in other ways there appeared to be no change at all. Democrats won most statewide offices other than governor and controlled both houses of the state legislature as well as having a comfortable lead in congressional seats. On most social issues other than crime, voters consistently rejected Republican efforts in areas such as abortion rights, gun control, censorship of library holdings and the rights of homosexuals.

From the late 1990s on evidence accumulated indicating the state's designation as "blue" or liberal (the color derived from television maps showing states carried by Republican candidates for the presidency—red—or Democratic candidates—blue— was indeed accurate). Democrats carried the state twice for Bill Clinton and over-whelmingly rejected George W. Bush's candidacy in both 2000 and 2004. Gray Davis ended 16 years of Republican governors in 1998, though his campaign stressed his anti-crime credentials and his service in the Vietnam War, hardly traditional liberal issues. When the voters turned him out of office in 2003 it was not seen as a rejection of liberal policies but of mismanagement. The man chosen to replace him, Arnold Schwarzenegger, was viewed as more moderate than conservative by voters.

On a whole host of issues the people of the state refuse to be easily categorized. They oppose off shore drilling for oil, are overwhelmingly pro-choice on abortion and support extensive services for the disadvantaged. However, they also say they want smaller government, lower taxes, and less government into their private lives. It is this ambivalence that makes California such a fascinating state to study.

Successful California politicians know that there is indeed a political map of the state with definable pockets of deep concern on particular issues. As a start they know that there are at least four regions, defined by socioeconomic characteristics and spe-cial interests. The following is a rough approximation of the major geopolitical areas.

1. **The San Francisco, Berkeley, Oakland Complex,** plus coastal regions up to the Oregon border and down to the Tehachapis (about 22 percent of the state's popu-lation), is predominantly cosmopolitan, intellectual, civil libertarian, internation-alist, and environmentally conscious, with a visible supply of militants who can be mobilized to get out the vote or take to the streets on a variety of issues.

2. **The Southern California Sunbelt,** including Orange, San Diego, and the six other Southern California counties but excluding the city of Los Angeles (about 53 percent of the state's population), is a mostly middle-class and upper-middle-class population comprised of families employed by or indirectly dependent on the research and development and electronics industries of Southern California. The large proportion of engineers, executives, and highly paid blue-collar tech-nicians are for the most part owners of single-family homes and have an intense interest in the property tax, inflation, and other middle-class concerns.

3. **Metropolitan Los Angeles** (about 13 percent of the state's population) is a mélange of black and Chicano ghettos, blue-collar whites, pensioners, media and academic elites, investment and savings-and-loan executives and their middle-income, white-collar entourages. This is a politically volatile area sub-ject to bitter divisions along class and ethnic lines.

4. **The Interior Agricultural Plateau** (about 12 percent of the state's population), dominated by the immense Central Valley, is the breadbasket of California and is highly dependent on government-run hydroelectric, irrigation, and agricultural programs. It is also the area that employs the most migrant Mexican farm work-ers and has been the scene of much labor-agribusiness conflict in recent years.

In recent years a different version of California political regionalism has emerged. An east-west "fault line" is evident with Democrats dominant in coastal counties and Republicans in those inland. San Diego remains slightly Republican but from Los Angeles north Gray Davis carried virtually all coastal counties in 2002. In all of the 18 counties Davis carried, only Imperial was not on the coast. Simon won the other 40, almost all in the interior of the state. Santa Rosa apparently has more in common with Los Angeles than with Los Banos and Riverside more in common with Fresno than with Anaheim. Votes on several propositions on the November 2005 special election ballot reflected this change to an east-west political divide in the state. (See Figure 3.1 as an example.)

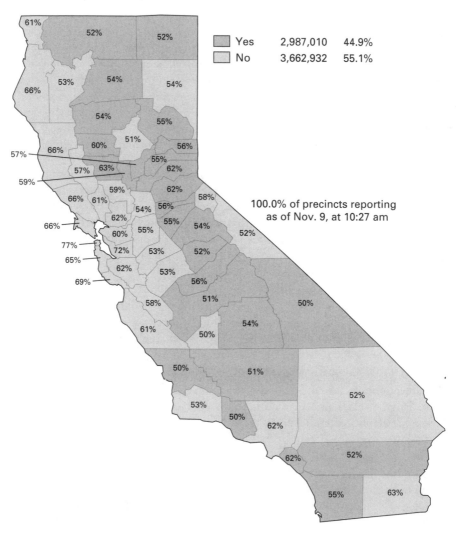

**Figure 3.1**    Special Statewide Election—Proposition 74.

(Tom Meyer, *San Francisco Chronicle*)

Latching onto these diverse and often opposed interests in a way that appeals to a majority of the state's voters is a high political art. Candidates for statewide office must be able to engender confidence on the part of a wide variety of constituents and, more than any of their opponents, must be capable of satisfying (or, at least, of not damaging too greatly) all of their interests. It is no wonder that any successful gubernatorial candidate in California is automatically considered a potential presidential candidate. It is not only that California, being the most populous state, has the most electoral votes in the presidential election but also that anyone able to satisfy California's vast and complex electorate, by that feat alone, acquires the charisma of a master politician.

Analyses of the most recent California elections—who won and how they did it—can therefore tell us even more than what to expect in the form of policy initiative and output from the current set of public officeholders. Such analyses also help us (*and* the officeholders) to understand what the electorate is like and what its various elements most value or oppose.

## ELECTIONS IN THE 1990S

### The Governorship

The 1990s opened with a familiar look in that Republicans, once again, held on to the governorship, this time against truly formidable opposition, former San Francisco mayor Dianne Feinstein. Her no nonsense approach to crime (she favored the death penalty, which outraged many party leaders) went down well with the public, which was in agreement with her by a wide margin. She portrayed herself as a "compassionate liberal," as her record as mayor demonstrated. Her opponent, also a former mayor (San Diego) and United States senator, was Pete Wilson. Though disliked by party conservatives for his pro-choice position on abortion and openness to gun control, he had won the nomination in the belief he had the best chance of getting elected and thwarting another Democratic gerrymander of election districts in 1991. To the voters both candidates appeared to be moderates with few differences between them. The Iraqi invasion of Kuwait may have helped Wilson, a noted hawk on defense issues. In any event he won narrowly in November, 48–46.

In 1994 Wilson's bid for reelection was opposed by a member of California's political dynasty, Kathleen Brown, daughter of one former governor (Pat) and sister of another (Jerry). Wilson first had to fight off an unexpected challenge from multimillionaire Ron Unz who claimed the governor was "too liberal" to be a real Republican. The fall campaign was largely negative with Brown castigating Wilson for the state's poor economy (other states in the West are doing much better) and Wilson responding with his strong support for the death penalty which she opposed (but promised to enforce when elected). Trailing by double digits a year before the election and aided by a rather inept Democratic campaign strategy, Wilson won by double digits (15 points), transforming himself from political road kill into a phoenix rising from the ashes.

The next election cycle in 1998 featured three multimillionaires, two Democrats and one Republican, though the latter was running for United States Senate. If the old expression "money talks" is often true, especially in politics, it was mute this year: all three lost. The lieutenant governor, Gray Davis, spent just $9 million in the Democratic primary to defeat businessman Al Checchi who spent $39 million and Congresswoman Jane Harman whose campaign cost $16 million. Yet after all that cash flowed, Davis won by an astonishing 58 percent of the vote to Checchi's 21 percent and Harman's 20 percent. Davis's campaign slogan, "experience money can't buy," was a not too subtle attack on his rivals who lacked government experience of any kind (Checchi) or in the state (Harman).

The Republican nomination went to Attorney General Dan Lungren, who was considered to be the favorite going in. He was a more dynamic speaker than Davis and was expected to wipe the floor with him in the debates to come. That proved true only in the first debate that took place in the summer when many Californians were on vacation and not watching. Davis stressed his anticrime credentials while Lungren, as A.G., could have (crime was high on the list of things voters saw as important), but did not. Davis was helped by a reenergized labor union movement that had been motivated to defeat Proposition 226 on the June ballot.[1] One other factor entered into Davis's 58–38 victory; he outspent his Republican opponent, taking from him what was normally a GOP advantage.

---

[1]Proposition 226 would have required unions to obtain their members' permission before using their dues for political purposes.

## The United States Senate

The 1992 election had an unprecedented *two* Senate seats up. This was due to Pete Wilson having vacated one to take over as governor. Dubbed the long seat (for a full six-year term) and the short seat (to fill in for the remainder of Wilson's term or two years), these were very different contests. Dianne Feinstein won the short seat easily over little known John Seymour, Wilson's hand-picked replacement. But Barbara Boxer, though seen early on as the clear favorite, had to survive a late surge by conservative television commentator Bruce Herschensohn. The issues were clear. She favored gun control, he opposed it. She supported a woman's right to choose, he did not. He favored drilling for oil off the California coast. She opposed it. In the end she edged him out, 48–43.

Winning the short seat meant Dianne Feinstein had to run again in 1994. Her somewhat surprising opponent was still another multimillionaire, Michael Huffington. It turned out to be the most expensive Senate race up to that time with Huffington spending $29 million (most of that his own money) and $14 million by Feinstein ($2.5 million from her private funds). Many experts felt this should not be close. Feinstein's record in her two years in the Senate was marked by several significant legislative victories. Huffington's record was undistinguished.

Dianne Feinstein. (Photo Courtesy of Senator Feinstein's Office)

The campaign on both sides was quite negative with Huffington characterizing her as a big government-loving liberal while she retorting he had not paid taxes in the state while maintaining a residence in Texas. A very large television blitz brought Huffington into a statistical tie by September and on election day the contest was declared "too close to call." Only when some 700,000 absentee ballots had been counted was Feinstein declared the winner by a scant 166,000 votes out of 7.788 million cast.

In 1998, the so-called "long seat" was up and Boxer was unopposed in the Democratic primary. Her opponent was Matt Fong, the state treasurer and son of long-time Secretary of State March Fong Eu. Fong made it to the finals after a tough battle with another multimillionaire, Daryl Issa. Fong was seen as a moderate or centrist who was more in line with the thinking of voters than the very liberal Boxer ("she never saw a tax increase she didn't like"). However, it was Fong who

Barbara Boxer. (Photo Courtesy of Senator Boxer's Office)

found himself on the defensive when, late in the campaign, a series of television commercials depicted him as an extremist on a number of issues; for example, he was the gun manufacturers' "best friend." These apparently worked as Boxer won by an impressive ten points, 53–43.

## The Propositions

The decade was marked by a number of controversial propositions taken to the voters. Several were approved only to be struck down by the courts, including one in 1992 that would have extended term limits to members of Congress. The Supreme Court held that state-imposed limits for *federal* office are unconstitutional. A special election was held in November 1993 to place before the voters several propositions, one of them quite controversial. It would have provided school vouchers worth $2,600 that would have gone to parents to help them pay for private schools when they felt the public schools were failing. It went down to defeat by a wide margin after critics pointed to a lack of safeguards (anyone, they said, could start a school if they collected 25 warm bodies, even a witches' coven).

Throughout these ten years voters continued to exhibit "get tough on crime" attitudes. They passed measures to lengthen sentences and build more prisons. Perhaps the most dramatic and sweeping was the approval of "Three Strikes and You're Out" in 1994. Stimulated by repeat offenders who killed, the majority of voters sought the means to keep these dangerous criminals off the streets. With a third "strike" such felons were sent to prison for a term of 25 years to life. (For more on this law see Chapter 12.) Another measure on the same ballot proved very controversial, Proposition 187, or the "Save Our State," proposition. Proponents said California needed to send a message to Washington concerning the burden placed on the state by masses of illegal immigrants pouring into California. The cost was estimated at between $1 billion and $1.5 billion a year with the federal government doing little to stem the tide. If implemented, the proposition would have denied the children of illegal immigrants entry into public schools, denied their parents welfare benefits, and allowed them to receive only emergency medical care. It passed handily, 59–41, but was blocked in the courts. Eventually Governor Davis declined to seek its restoration.

Other propositions of note in 1996 include Proposition 196 that abolished the closed primary and introduced in its stead the blanket primary (see Chapter 4). That same year voters approved Proposition 209, the so-called California Civil Rights Initiative (CCRI). Under it all state affirmative action programs were abolished. No longer could state colleges and universities give preferential treatment to minority applicants nor could contracts awarded by the state favor minorities or women. A third measure that proved controversial involved legalization of the medicinal use of marijuana. Anecdotal evidence indicated smoking "pot" alleviated nausea of those undergoing chemotherapy, helped AIDS patients, and reduced pressure in the eye for those suffering from glaucoma. Approved by the voters, none of that has mattered to either the Clinton or Bush administrations who have continued to oppose it. However, in October 2002 the Federal 9th Circuit Court of Appeals in San Francisco ruled the federal government could not, as threatened by U.S.

Attorney General John Ashcroft, revoke a physician's license to prescribe medications if that doctor had recommended marijuana to sick patients. And at the November election that same year the voters of San Francisco approved city growing and selling pot to those in medical need (see Chapter 12).

In 1998 several other propositions of interest were brought before the voters. One, Proposition 227, was designed to significantly reduce or even eliminate bilingual education in public schools. A key statistic in the debate was that only 5 percent of students enrolled in bilingual programs were able to move into mainstream classes each year. Opponents said the one-size-fits-all approach envisioned was simplistic and the one year of English "immersion" was far too short. Despite that, the vote was overwhelmingly in favor of abolition, 61–39.

The last election of the 1990s provided the most expensive battle over a ballot proposition in history, Proposition 5, or the casino gambling initiative. The issue was whether Indian or Native American tribes could run certain kinds of slot machines in their increasingly popular gambling casinos. The state maintained they violated the state constitution, which prohibits games against the house. The tribes countered these casinos were giving them something they had never had since the coming of the white man, financial independence, and that, in turn, meant enhanced self-esteem. The ensuing campaign saw the tribes and their opponents pouring vast amounts of money into the mass media. The tribes spent $68 million to convince the voters they should have the right to have these machines, which, they said, provided them with 75 percent to 85 percent of casino profits. Opponents, led by religious groups, race track owners, and Nevada gambling Meccas spent $30 million to defeat them. Though the proposition was approved, the issue went to the courts, which agreed with the state that the machines were illegal. The question went before the voters the following March, this time as a constitutional amendment, and voters sided once again with the tribes.

## ENTERING THE 2000S

### The Primary Election 2000

There was little drama in the presidential contest on the Democratic side as Vice President Al Gore ran consistently ahead of former New Jersey U.S. Senator Bill Bradley. There was, for a time, a bit more excitement on the Republican side as favorite of the Establishment, Texas Governor George W. Bush, was challenged by Arizona Senator John McCain, a man with a strong record as a war hero (he had been held for years in a Vietnamese prison camp, refusing to be released until his fellow prisoners were) and a sometime maverick on legislative matters, especially campaign finance reform. Though McCain campaigned throughout California, by the time election day arrived, Bush had sown up his party's nomination.

One possible consequence of the McCain candidacy was to motivate conservatives to go to the polls and defeat him. A *Los Angeles Times* exit poll found that 42 percent of those voting described themselves as conservatives while moderates made up 25 percent and liberals 33 percent, this in a state where Democrats outnumber Republicans 5–4. This outpouring of conservatives apparently had an impact on several ballot propositions. One banning gay marriage (Proposition 22) passed 59–41, while another giving prosecutors the say as to whether juveniles accused of crimes would be tried in adult or juvenile court (Proposition 21) passed by the same margin.

On the congressional front, Tom Campbell, a moderate, won the right to face Democratic senator Dianne Feinstein in November.

## The General Election 2000

There was little suspense associated with the presidential contest in California (though a great deal elsewhere, especially in Florida). The polls consistently showed Al Gore with a substantial lead over George W. Bush. In fact, the lead was so great that the Gore campaign spent not one dime on television advertising in the state. The Bush camp, however, vowed not to do what his father had in 1992 when the Republicans gave up on the state early. Millions of dollars were spent in support of his election, but it turned out those polls were indeed accurate and Gore carried the state by some 1.3 million votes, 53.5 percent to 41.7 percent.

The same might be said of the Feinstein-Campbell race. Relatively unknown, Campbell faced a stiff challenge from the beginning against an incumbent who was well-liked and well-respected. Nor were there many hot button issues to separate

(Tom Meyer, *San Francisco Chronicle*)

them since on key social issues they were quite similar. In the end she won reelection easily, 55.9 percent to 36.6 percent.

What interest there was in the election came from several ballot propositions. One involving campaign finance reform is discussed elsewhere (see Chapter 4). An effort to allow state legislators to participate in the state employees retirement system, Proposition 33, was crushed by over 20 points despite the fact these men and women had seen their own retirement system abolished under Proposition 140. Proposition 36 roused a good deal of interest. It proposed solving two problems at once: prison overcrowding and drug addiction. Under this proposition, approved by the voters, a drug addict (not a dealer) is sentenced to one year in a drug treatment program. Proponents argued that this was cost effective and an improvement over the ineffective treatment afforded in prisons. Opponents saw a danger of violent criminals being loosed upon society and no assurance those sentenced to the treatment centers would actually attend. A study from U.C.L.A. in 2006 found support for both positions. Only 24 percent of those ordered into the programs completed them. On the positive side, the study concluded that in the first 30 months of the program, for those completing the process, there were savings from housing of inmates, probation and rearrests of nearly $4 for every dollar spent. That amounted to savings of $173 million over the period. Two other propositions deserve mention. One was a rerun of the school vouchers issue from 1993. It went down again, this time by a no vote of 70 percent. On the other hand, voters liked the idea of reducing the majority needed to approve local school bonds from two-thirds to 55 percent.

## The 2002 Primary

In one sense the 2002 primary election was quite unusual. It featured the sure fire winner in one party's primary spending enormous amounts of money to defeat the leading candidate of the opposition party. Skeptics pointed to the 1966 election where Democrats had desperately wanted one Republican who had never held elective office to defeat a popular mayor of San Francisco, thus assuring reelection of Pat Brown. Beware of what you ask for; you may get it. The Republican victor was, of course, Ronald Reagan who defeated Brown handily in the general election.

Here Gray Davis feared having to face off against the popular mayor of Los Angeles, Richard "Dick" Riordan, a moderate with views on many issues that tended to be similar to those held by the governor. Pro-choice, pro-gun control, a fiscal conservative with strong positions on issues of law and order, Riordan was seen as by far the greatest threat to Davis. The other Republicans, businessman Bill Simon and Secretary of State Bill Jones, were both more conservative and, the thinking went, out of line with mainstream Californians. The attack commercials took statements from Riordan's past to tarnish his image. For example, one advertisement was on abortion. Though supportive on abortion rights for years, he had been quoted a decade earlier as describing the procedure as "murder." In all, the Davis campaign spent $10 million on a television blitz designed to destroy Riordan's candidacy. The strategy worked as Simon, who had trailed badly early on, roared past Riordan to win with 49.3 percent to Riordan's 31.4 and Jones's 17.

With the newly configured legislative districts in place for the first time, it quickly became clear this rearrangement was every bit the "incumbent protection" plan it had been described to be. With little to bring them to the polls, (no contest for governor on the Democratic side, no legislative contests to speak of and no "hot" ballot propositions), vote turnout was a record low of just over a third or 24 percent of those who could have voted if registered. This surprised many who had thought the attacks on the World Trade Center and Pentagon that had unleashed a wave of patriotic enthusiasm would result in many more people going to the polls.

The only significant proposition was one that required gasoline sales tax revenues be spent on transportation rather than going, as it had, into the general fund. That was approved by an overwhelming 70 percent of voters who no doubt did so after repeated encounters with pot holes on the state's highways.

## The General Election 2002

There was little time off between the primary and the general election campaign. Governor Davis fired off salvo after salvo at Simon targeting what was supposedly a Simon strength, his background as a successful businessman. The attacks alleged Simon was associated with several ventures that had failed; that he was under investigation for dubious accounting practices; that his management of a charity had allegedly allowed him to make enormous amounts of money through excessive fees. The announcer's voice over would ask, "If he can't run a business (or charity), how can he run California?" Not too helpful for Simon were the growing Wall Street scandals at WorldCom, Enron, and other big businesses. On top of all that the Internal Revenue Service announced an investigation into a possibly illegal tax evasion practice. Simon with far less money in hand to begin with, started slowly with a Spanish language commercial emphasizing education. Two television commercials poked fun at Davis's seemingly unending fund raising. In one, two cleaning ladies were seen going around the governor's office finding piles of cash everywhere—in drawers, on tables, even on the blades of a ceiling fan. Though humorous, these struck at a potential vulnerability, the impression Davis spent more time raising money than governing the state. An apparent scandal involved the Davis administration in a no-bid contract with the Oracle Corporation that was followed within days by a contribution of $25,000 to the governor's campaign.[2] There was no evidence that Davis himself was involved and, as one writer put it, the governor was faced with being forced to admit his administration was either corrupt or incompetent. He chose incompetence.

---

[2]The Oracle contract had been rushed with unprecedented swiftness though several layers of the bureaucracy in a matter of 22 days. The result was purchase of software with little or no indication that it was wanted or needed. By one estimate, the purchase, which was to save the state millions, was instead to cost anywhere up to $41 million *more* than using current procedures. Then there was the question of need. Of 127 state agencies only eight had responded to a survey. In the aftermath several top administration aides lost their jobs and an assemblyman who had conducted hearings that embarrassed the administration was removed from that committee. The bureaucrats who lost their jobs overrode subordinates who had warned that there had been no time to evaluate the contract and the only evaluation had been by Oracle itself. The contract was voided several months later.

The ongoing theme of the Simon campaign was that Governor Davis followed a "pay to play" policy. If you wanted something from the state government you had to contribute large amounts of money to his campaign. Perhaps typical were allegations contained in a lengthy article in the *San Francisco Chronicle*.[3] The writer cited numerous instances where those who gave the governor contributions, often in six figures, had their requests before the Coastal Commission approved while others who failed to contribute were turned down. Davis, his supporters, and members of the commission vigorously denied any connection between contributions and policy decisions. Still, the public perception that the governor was obsessed with raising campaign funds (he raised a record $68 million from the time he became governor) was reinforced by stories such as these.

The campaign was plagued by several other distractions, among them Simon's refusal to make public his tax returns. Under great pressure and saying he feared invasion of the privacy of family members, he did so though on a limited basis. Reporters, one per outlet, were given up to five hours to study voluminous files—files most reporters found difficult to decipher because they were not tax experts.

More damaging, however, was an action taken by a jury involving allegations of fraud by a Simon family company. After a lengthy trial, the jury awarded the former partner $78 million. This award was later overturned by a judge, but the public perception of Simon had been damaged by the original jury action. Later a charge by Simon that Davis had, four years earlier, accepted a check for his campaign in his lieutenant governor's office (a misdemeanor) blew up in Simon's face when a picture allegedly proving the accusation was shown to have been taken at a home in Santa Monica.

It is not surprising that neither major party candidate turned on the electorate. A Field Poll found both were viewed unfavorably by over half the electorate. One veteran Republican consultant went so far as to describe Simon as "too dumb" to be governor and polls found Davis being viewed by the public as obsessed with fund raising, evasive, lacking in leadership, and untrustworthy. Given this considerable lack of enthusiasm, it was not unexpected when predictions of low turnout and a higher-than-normal vote for third party candidates began to surface. In fact, that is just what happened. Voter participation dropped nearly ten points below the previous low as fewer than half of registered voters bothered to cast ballots.

When the votes were tabulated Davis won by an unimpressive five points, 47–42. Some 10 percent of those who voted chose third party candidates, three times the normal. The *Los Angeles Times* exit poll showed men giving a slight edge to Simon, (47 to 42 for Davis), but women overwhelmingly in support of the governor, 52–37. Simon likewise carried the votes of married couples, 47–43, but lost big time among singles, 53–33.

In the other statewide races Democrats swept the field for the first time since 1882, returning Cruz Bustamante as lieutenant governor, Bill Lockyer as attorney general, and replacing those termed out with other Democrats. The state legislative

---

[3]Lance Williams, "Donors to Davis get Coastal Permits," *San Francisco Chronicle,* October 20, 2002.

"contests" were not real contests in most cases due to reapportionment (see Chapter 6). The only high visibility race involved the congressional seat that had been held by Democrat Gary Condit. He was unseated by a former staff member, Dennis Cardoza, in the primary, and Cardoza was challenged by Richard Monteith, a state senator. As the only truly contested race for Congress in the state, both parties poured large amounts of money into it. The result: Cardoza won by 52–43.

There were unusually few propositions, seven, on the ballot. And none of them roused much fervor among the public. Three bond issues totaling $18.5 billion headed the list and all passed with the largest going to the state's schools. Two others sought to divert money from the general fund to different purposes and one proposed same-day registration for voting. The "diversion" propositions were treated quite differently by the voters who overwhelmingly approved of Proposition 49, a measure strongly supported by Hollywood star Arnold Schwazenegger who contributed $1 million of his own money to the campaign. It sends approximately $495 million a year to local school districts to support after-school programs ranging from tutoring to intramural athletics. The other "diversion" proposal dealt with a variety of subjects from traffic congestion to environmental protection to replacing older school buses deemed unsafe and polluting. Many designated projects were clearly needed, but editorials across the state condemned this as another "pay to play" scheme because a number of the proposed projects were those sponsored by individuals or companies who stood to benefit from the proposition's passage. One example: the initiative would have funded a $120 million light rail line from Los Angeles to an Indian gaming casino. The tribe contributed $500,000 to the campaign. Another: a developer gave $120,000 and stood to gain by improved infrastructure worth $30 million. Total projected cost to the general fund: $1 billion a year. This proposition was drowned at the polls, losing 58–42. The voters reacted negatively to the same day registration proposal, Proposition 52, as well. Urged by backers as a way of increasing vote turnout in a state where it has gotten increasingly poor, those who went to the polls were leery of the potential for fraud (two pieces of junk mail addressed to you would prove you were a resident of the district under this proposition). It went down, 53–47.

## The Primary Election 2004

There was little drama involved in the presidential contests this year. As usual, the selection of the contenders for the presidency had, again, been decided before Californians went to the polls. George W. Bush was not challenged on the Republican side in his search for a second term, and John Kerry, the United States Senator from Massachusetts, won by nearly 4–1 over his last remaining challenger, John Edwards. With virtually all congressional and state legislative seats invulnerable to party challenge (see Chapter 6 on gerrymandering and its consequences), the only "race" to be decided in November was the one for United States Senate between incumbent Barbara Boxer who was unopposed in the Democratic primary and Bill Jones, the former secretary of state. That left the propositions and they for the most part proved less than exciting for most voters. Proposition 56 was a modest exception. It asked that the requirement for approval of the state budget be lowered from two-thirds of each house of the state legislature to 55 percent. That the deadline for passage of the budget had been seldom met (blocked by a minority party with more than one-third of the legislature's members) and that only two other states had such a high hurdle for budget approval, the proponents urged this solution which, they said, would also improve the state's credit rating, lowering borrowing costs. Opponents claimed the change would give a liberal legislature a "blank check" and remove the beneficial requirement there be bipartisan agreement on the budget before it is passed. The voters overwhelmingly bought the opponents' arguments, voting down the proposition by a 34.3–65.7 margin.

The only other issues of note were in two propositions backed by then-movie star now governor Arnold Schwarzenegger. These propositions, the two, 57 and 58, together bundled $15 billion in state debt into a bond to deal with the state deficit (it won with 63.3 of the vote) and placed limits on the state government requiring a balanced budget (yes, 71.1 percent).

## The General Election of 2004

The presidential contest was not exactly that, a contest, as John Kerry easily defeated George W. Bush to secure California's 53 electoral college votes, 54.3–44.4. The race for the United States Senate between Senator Barbra Boxer and Bill Jones did not turn voters on either. He attempted to paint her as soft on issues of national security, logical enough in the wake of the terrorist attacks of 9/11, but nothing seemed to stick. Jones suffered, perhaps belatedly, among the members of the Republican base who never forgave him for his support for tax increases under Governor Wilson in

(Rex Babin, *The Sacramento Bee*)

the 1990s and, perhaps more important, his jumping ship in 2002 to support Arizona Senator John McCain over the Establishment's choice, George W. Bush for the G.O.P. presidential nomination. Whatever the reasons (Jones was woefully underfunded), he lost his bid by the substantial margin of 58–37.7. With virtually all other legislative races for Congress and the state houses decided by redistricting, attention turned to the ballot propositions. In a return to earlier times, there were 16 propositions up for voter consideration. Few roused much interest among the public, though, from a political science point of view, some were significant.

One, Proposition 60, sought to avoid the possibility that a runoff election would have two members of the same party vying for the same partisan office. Voters agreed 67.3–37.7. By way of contrast, Proposition 62 would have had the top two vote getters face off in the general election, even if from the same party. Showing some consistency, voters turned this one down, 45.7–54.3. A more controversial issue for some was found in an effort to change California's three strikes law. (See Chapter 12 for a discussion of this law.) Under the version Governor Wilson signed into law in 1994, the third strike could be for what many would see as a minor offence, though technically a felony. Arguing that 65 percent of those serving "Three Strikes" had been convicted on minor felonies, proponents of Proposition 66 argued the state would save money and relieve prison overcrowding by requiring the third "strike" be for a serious or violent crime. Opponents said judges already had discretion in imposing the third "strike" and relaxing the standard would leave many who are a danger to society—and have demonstrated that by their actions—free to roam the streets. The public apparently agreed and defeated the proposition by a margin of 53.4–46.6.

Finally, Proposition 71 aroused a good deal of interest. It proposed to sell up to $350 million in bonds to provide grants in support of stem cell research. Those in favor argued, with many scientists, that new treatments of diseases such as diabetes, cancer and heart ailments, among many others, might be found through such research. Opponents argued that such research,, which may use human embryos, is considered murder by many and that, in any event, more bonded indebtedness is unwise when private corporations are free to engage in it. The voters sided with the research and approved proposition by 59.1–40.9.

## The Recall Election of 2003

Until 2003 no statewide elected official had ever been recalled—or even faced a recall election. It happened then. Conditions for the recall of Governor Davis came together in what might be described as "a perfect storm." The following were the more significant factors contributing to the storm. The energy crisis of 2001, which resulted in greatly increased power costs for all Californians, and which the governor was perceived to have bungled—first by reacting too slowly and then by signing long-term contracts for energy at the peak of their prices. He was thought to have hidden the extent of the state's financial problems in 2002, the extent of which was revealed only after his reelection. His constant fund raising and soliciting of special interests reinforced the feelings of many that these interests and not those of the people of California were his first concern. The last straw for many may well have been the tripling of car license fees, a measure ordered by Davis to help address the budget deficit, but with the first notices of these substantial hikes reaching the voters the month before the election, many became enraged and the timing for Davis could not have been worse. The campaign to remove Davis was fueled by contributions totaling nearly $2 million and 1.3 million signatures were quickly secured qualifying the recall for a November vote.

The rest of the country had a good laugh at the state's expense when 135 individuals paid the $3,500 filing fee and submitted the required 65 signatures needed to appear on the ballot. Only five or six could be considered serious candidates and not among them were a porn queen, the publisher of *Hustler* magazine, or the diminutive actor, Gary Coleman. Motion picture star of the *Terminator* movies, Arnold Schwarzenegger, announced his candidacy on the Tonight Show with Jay Leno (amid strong rumors his wife, Maria Schriver, was against it). That appearance set the tone for much of his campaign as he generally ignored the usual forums (he skipped all but one of the debates) opting instead to go on such entertainment programs as the *Oprah Winfrey Show*.

Those opposing the recall urged that no Democrat appear on the second part of the ballot where a successor to Davis would be chosen should the recall succeed. However, the lieutenant governor, Cruz Bustamante, broke ranks urging a "no" vote on the recall, but a "yes" for him as the replacement. He especially courted Hispanics and, in what was seen as a major mistake, received several million dollars from Indian gaming interests. He was told by the courts that transfer of this money from a preexisting campaign war chest for this election violated Proposition 34 and he returned the funds, but the damage was done. To many, this was one more indication that special interests controlled the state.

Late allegations published in the *Los Angeles Times* from six women who claimed Schwarzenegger had abused them in past years on movie sets raised hopes in the Davis camp, but on election day the vote was decisive with 55 percent voting to oust Davis. The *Times* exit polls found that, even among women, those most likely to be sensitive to the groping charges, Schwarzenegger had won 42 percent of the vote, well ahead of anyone else.

There are many tidbits of interest but space allows only a quick mention of a few. Among voting groups usually seen as the base of the Democratic Party, Davis fell short. Hispanics who are usually counted on to provide big majorities voted against the recall but only 55–45, and only constituted 11 percent of the vote, far less than opponents of the recall had hoped for. Union households also voted against but barely, 52–48, again far short of expectations.

*Newsweek* magazine titled its coverage of the election "Arnold's Earthquake" and by any measure it was just that, perhaps as much as 8.0 on the political Richter Scale.

## The Special Election of November 2005

Governor Schwarzenegger came into office with a pledge to work with a Democratically controlled state legislature whose members had vigorously opposed the recall that had brought him into office. At first this approach appeared to be working. The governor "smoozed" with Democratic leaders over cigars and talked frequently of "getting along" with the more liberal assembly and state senate. A significant reform of the state's ailing worker's compensation system was an early result. As the months passed, however, the governor became increasingly frustrated with what he perceived to be an unwillingness of the Democratic leadership to make any significant compromises in key areas such as budget reform. His scorn surfaced with public references to those who opposed him as "girlie men" (a term drawn from his motion picture past) who, he said, were unable to resist the pressures of special interests.

This frustration led to the decision to challenge what the governor perceived to be a stranglehold that public employee unions held in Sacramento. What happened next is subject to interpretation. One theory is the governor overestimated his own popularity (or underestimated the power of the special interests he was taking on). A key decision was made when the governor, facing a large budget deficit, asked the education lobby to give up, for one year, $2 billion due the schools with the promise it would be repaid in the following year's budget. Educators agreed and their allies in the legislature went along. Continuing budget problems caused the governor to renege on his pledge and that came back to haunt him in 2005. (Note: the fact that the following budget **added $3 billion** to the education budget and that per student expenditures went above $10,000 for the first time went largely unnoticed.)

As for underestimating the opposition, when Schwarzenegger announced his package of "reform" propositions, he found himself attacked by virtually every public employee union in the state, from teachers to prison guards to police and nurses. Originally, he had thought a campaign war chest of $50 million would be adequate only to find the unions had raised over $80 million to oppose him.

Most of the opposition money went into television commercials that aired early and often, attacking both the specifics of his proposals and the governor himself. "You can't trust him" on education (his failure to repay $2 billion to the schools); he wants to cut fire and police pensions (though this proposal was withdrawn when drafting mistakes were uncovered); he wants to destroy labor unions; and so on. Largely unanswered early, these had their desired effect. The governor's approval ratings sank in the polls. From the mid-60s they dropped to the mid-30s near election time and most Californians did not want to have him serve a second term.

Space does not permit a detailed examination of the propositions. The first one on the ballot was actually not part of Schwarzenegger's "reform" package, but it generated a good deal of heat. It sought to require that the parents of minor girls who became pregnant and opted for an abortion be notified. (If schools could not give an aspirin to a child without parental consent. . . .) Opponents argued a slippery slope that saw an invitation to more and more restrictions on abortions while maintaining most young women did tell their parents in any event.

Proposition 74 was part of the Schwarzenegger reform package. It argued that two years was too short a probationary period for teachers and that tenure laws made it too difficult to fire bad ones. (One commercial cited a teacher who swore at students and showed R rated movies in class and was removed from the classroom only when she agreed to take a payoff of $25,000.) Opponents said the two-years period was perfectly adequate and—in one commercial (inexplicably) counter to most—argued that the proposition would actually make it *more* difficult to fire poor teachers.

Proposition 75, another of the governor's packages, struck at the financial ability of public employee unions to wage campaigns by requiring that any union dues used for political purposes be approved by reach individual member. Proponents said, quite logically, that they should not have their dues used in support of candidates or causes (raising taxes) they opposed. Opponents answered, also with some logic, that this was a "power grab" designed to silence unions while leaving corporate donations unhindered by stockholder objections. Besides, union members had the right under current law to refuse to have their dues used for political purposes.

Proposition 76 was seen by the governor as the pivotal measure. In the face of high deficits and what he saw as the unwillingness of the Democratic legislature to reign in spending, he sought the power to make mid-year cuts when revenues failed to match expenditures. This highly complex proposition (it took over four pages in the voter handbook to display it in all its details) was opposed by many groups who saw this as another "power grab" by the governor who already had the item veto power (see p. 127).

Proposition 77 took dead aim at the legislature. In 2001 Democrats and Republicans had agreed to draw election district lines, as is required following each census, to insure there would be few, if any, that were competitive or capable of being won by either party. The results were obvious. In the election of 2004, there were 153 congressional and state legislative seats up before the voters. The extent to which the redistricting plan of 2001 worked is shown by the fact that not one single district changed party hands. Those backing Proposition 77 simply argued that what the legislature had done was to deny the voters any choices as to who would represent them, an essential element in democracy. Opponents claimed this was simply another "power grab," this time by "politicians," though cynics were inclined to see the true power grab as having been made by incumbents (themselves politicians) in 2001 to secure safe seats for themselves and their parties throughout the decade.

The other propositions were two that dealt with how to meet the needs of senior citizens and the poor who face high drug costs and one that attempted to restore a regulatory system for energy that had existed before the crisis that had developed under deregulation in the early twenty-first century. The two dealing with prescription drugs contrasted one with the other. Proposition 79 had a significant government component with fines for drug companies who failed to produce lower cost prescription medications for seniors and the poor. The other, Proposition 78, was sponsored by the pharmaceutical industry and promised lower cost medications but on a voluntary basis. Both failed after drug companies spent some $80 million in support of 78 and to kill 79. The energy measure also went down, all three perhaps because both were highly controversial and complicated.

The fall in popularity of the governor seemed to have led to voters turning against any and all parts of his "reform" package. (The governor shrugged off his loss of standing, saying even Mother Teresa would have gone down under the kind of personal assault he had endured.)

In the end the failure of all eight propositions was interpreted by some as a sign of voter fatigue, a protest against having so many elections in so short a period of time (not to mention the flood of campaign commercials that seemed unending). This was probably compounded by factors already mentioned: disenchantment with the governor and his style, campaigns for the propositions that were poorly run, and, in the minds of many, propositions that were either badly flawed or on subjects better left to the legislature.

## POLITICAL PARTIES

In the 2004 elections seven organizations had legal status as political parties in California: the Democratic Party, the Republican Party, the American Independent Party, the Libertarian Party, the Green Party, the Reform Party, and the Natural Law Party. Legal status as a political party gives an organization the right to have the names of its candidates for public office printed on the official election ballot. Legal status also obligates a political organization to keep its structure and procedures in conformity with explicit provisions in the Elections Code. Without legal recognition a political organization may still run candidates for office, but their names must be handwritten on the ballot by their supporters on election day.

### Requirements for Legal Status

Legal recognition as a political party in California is conferred upon an organization that either obtains a registration of at least 1 percent of the total number of registered voters or files a petition signed by a number of voters equal to 10 percent of the vote cast for governor in the preceding election. Once recognized, a party continues to appear on the ballot as long as it passes **both** of the following tests: In any gubernatorial election one of its candidates for statewide office must receive at least 2 percent of the vote cast, and it must maintain at least one-fifteenth of 1 percent of the total registration. (The Prohibition Party, the Communist Party and, for the first time since 1968 the Peace and Freedom Party in 2000, are among those organizations that once were on the official ballot but have been disqualified for failing to meet the state requirement. Peace and Freedom requalified in 2003.)

### Formal Structure and Functions

To say that California law is explicit concerning the structure and basic functions of political parties is an understatement. The Election Code goes into such detail that it seems as if the only thing left to the discretion of party leaders themselves is the preparation of a menu to be served convention delegates.[4]

---

[4]For example, "The convention shall be called to order at 10 o'clock . . . by the retiring chairman of the state central committee. It shall at once proceed to the election of a temporary chairman by a roll call read from an alphabetical roll. . . . " (Section 2807) "The convention shall . . . adopt a State platform for its party which shall be made public not later than 6 o'clock in the afternoon of the following day." (Section 2809)

State law provides that every recognized political party must hold its **state convention** at Sacramento once every two years. The convention usually lasts two days. Its principal functions are to draft the state platform and to select presidential elector candidates. The members of the convention consist of all party nominees and holdovers for statewide and congressional offices, and the Republicans add certain party officials to this number.[5]

The day after the state convention has finished its deliberations, the state **central committee** meets, also at Sacramento, to elect the officers of the party's executive committee and to propose certain legislation.

The state central committee is a large body of party leaders composed of all members of the state convention and a number of their appointees. (The Democrats elect additional members by caucus in each assembly district.) The chairpersons of all county central committees and the national committeemen and committeewomen serve as members of the state central committee.

The **executive committee** of each party has the **formal** responsibility to oversee party affairs and campaigns. Occasionally, the committee appoints district campaign committees to assist congressional and state legislative candidates. The day-to-day management of the affairs of the formal party organization is carried out by the chairperson and vice-chairperson. These top offices provide no monetary compensation and have little formal power.

Membership of the executive committee consists of the chairpersons of the 58 county central committees, the co-chairpersons of the 45 congressional districts, the state officeholders, and the elected officers of the state central committee—a group of about 160 persons.

Members of the **county central committees** of the party are chosen by the voters in each county. County committees are elected in the **biennial** partisan primaries for terms of two years. In larger counties they are elected by assembly districts; in smaller counties they are elected by supervisorial districts. In addition to the elected members, party nominees for state offices and incumbents living in the county are ex officio members of the committee. County committees vary in size, but none may have fewer than 21 elected members. The total elected from Los Angeles County is about 250, made up of about 7 elected from each of the assembly districts in the county.

There is very little formal connection between the official state parties and the national organizations. The main link is provided by **national committee members** who serve on the national committee. The national committee's operations are largely devoted to presidential election activities. Because of the manner of selecting national committee members, their ties to their official party organization in California may be tenuous.

## Factional Organizations Within Parties

Hiram Johnson's Progressives, in their move to curb the power of the railroads over state politics in the early twentieth century, sought to enhance the power of the public at the expense of the railroad-dominated parties. The initiative, referendum, and

---

[5]If the party has no holdover incumbents or nominees for a given office, an "appointive delegate" is named by the party committee in the district concerned.

recall, together with cross-filing, were all aspects of this objective (see Chapter 2). Among several restrictions on party leaders was one that led to the development of a number of "unofficial" party organizations that for years played a major role in determining candidates for partisan office. By law, parties were prohibited from making preprimary endorsements, presumably limiting the leadership's power to decide who should run and enhancing the role of the rank-and-file membership.

Cross-filing made it possible for Democrats to "cross over" and run for the Republican nomination and vice versa. The possibility that a single candidate from the opposition might be able to gain the nomination with a bare plurality of the vote, the remainder being split among "regular" party members, was made more likely by the inability of party leaders to endorse in the primary. Then, too, until the mid-1950s primary ballots carried no indication of party affiliation to alert the voters. "Raiding" was therefore easier. The Republicans pioneered in the development of voluntary and unofficial organizations created to prevent this from happening. In 1933 a number of progressive Republicans formed the California Republican Assembly (CRA) to identify, develop, and endorse candidates in primary elections. The Democrats followed in 1953 with the California Democratic Council (CDC). Because they were "unofficial," they were not prohibited from endorsing candidates in primary elections.

Both organizations became deeply involved in taking stands on public issues, the CRA becoming more and more conservative and the CDC increasingly liberal. At times their positions proved so far out of the political mainstream as to be embarrassing to candidates and party leaders. They needed the organizational endorsements and support these groups provided, but they often attempted to distance themselves from the groups' positions. At that, some Republican activists found the CRA too moderate and split, forming the United Republicans of California. More liberal Republicans established the California Republican League.

The influence of these and other unofficial party organizations lessened in the 1970s. The weakness of the state's parties, the tendency of the public to vote for individuals rather than on party lines, the impact of television with its emphasis on personality—all played a role. The reason for the existence of these groups in the first place disappeared in 1984 when a federal judge in San Francisco ruled that the prohibition against preprimary endorsements violated the First Amendment's guarantee of freedom of speech. Upheld by the Federal 9th Circuit Court of Appeals in 1988, this decision has meant that party leaders now may make such endorsements. Republicans have been reluctant to do so, but Democrats have used the primary endorsement power much more generously, including the state party's endorsement of John Van de Kamp over Dianne Feinstein for governor in 1990 (not noticeably very effective).

## Additional Party Groups

Other semiofficial party groups are active in elections from time to time. Young Republicans, Young Democrats, women's party organizations, and university groups have played influential roles within the parties. They may do precinct work, assist at fundraising events, and cover phone banks on election day, and members frequently participate in discussions concerning the positions to be taken by the party and its candidates.

Although these semiofficial or adjunct groups can still play a role in generating support for a party or candidate, the functions they have traditionally performed have grown less important. Walking precincts has, in many cases, given way to the use of direct mail as a principal means of reaching the voter. Stuffing envelopes was a significant—if boring—task in past years. Today, machines perform this same task and much more efficiently. As technology has taken over, many of the routine jobs of campaigning and those who performed these routines have become less and less important to success.

## INTEREST GROUPS

Political parties, and even intraparty factions such as the CDC or CRA, tend to be broad coalitions encompassing a number of different interests and points of view. To be elected, parties need to appeal to many different groups or constituencies. If a party comes to be seen as the "captive" of any one group or narrow ideology, its prospects for victory are likely to disappear. Who, then, speaks for these groups? These are organizations variously called special-interest groups, pressure groups, or vested interests (the last especially if the speaker opposes their goals). Rather than attempting, as parties do, to form electoral coalitions with their inevitable set of compromises (if one group gets all it wants, others will get less than the minimum they will accept and be alienated from the party), interest groups focus on the specific needs of their members. They have an interest in parties and candidates but only as the success of one or the other will affect their goals.

That interest is, however, demonstrated in very concrete ways, and it is here that political action committees (PACs) come in. These organizations are created by special-interest groups for the specific purpose of raising money from supporters, money that is then funneled into the campaigns of candidates likely to be favorably disposed toward the parent group's objectives.

### Special Interests

When the term **interest group** is used, most people probably think of some very large organization such as the AFL-CIO or the National Association of Manufacturers (NAM), and they are right, but only partially. There is an incredible variety of these groups, all dedicated to bring pressure to bear on government in order to achieve at least some of their objectives. (It is that pressure that leads some to prefer the use of **pressure groups** as a more descriptive label for them.) Of course, not all groups qualify as pressure groups because not all try to influence government. Bird-watching societies and model railroad buffs are examples. But thousands of organized groups are registered in Washington, D.C., whose function it is to try to get policies adopted, laws passed, or court decisions made that are favorable to their members.

California has had a long history of special-interest activity, some of it noted in Chapter 2 where the role of railroads in the politics of the late nineteenth century was discussed. One of the ironies of the Progressive Movement's successful campaign to break the power of the Southern Pacific over state government is that in doing so it broke—or severely diminished—the power of political parties. Yet generally it may be said that where parties are weak, pressure groups are strong. Parties can provide protection against pressure group retaliation for an unfavorable vote, but if the parties are weak that protection ceases to exist. If these groups play too influential a role in state politics today, at least some of the blame must rest with Hiram Johnson's Progressives.

Special-interest groups have a bad image, yet they play a constructive role in bringing the views of elements of our society into the political process. For example, there may be no one in the state legislature to present the views of those involved in the wine industry, but groups such as the California Association of Winegrape Growers can and do.

Special interests vary enormously in size, influence, and goals. Some are almost always involved in pressuring government, whereas others do so only rarely. They are numerous. Some 936 lobbyists were registered in Sacramento in 2005. They represented large corporations, farm interests, organized labor, women, churches, environmental interests, doctors, banks, minorities, and small businesses, to mention only a few. From the California Manufacturers Association to the Sierra Club and Burger King to the Mountain Lion Coalition, Mexican-American Political Association, and the California Pistachio Commission, they all take their respective cases before legislative committees, administration boards and, at times, the courts.

One very effective way of gaining "access" to legislators and other elected officials is through making contributions to campaign war chests. That, at the least, guarantees "the returned phone call" when you need to make your case.

It has long been true that the largest contributors category has been business and industry. A surprising new "king of the hill" emerged in 1999—governments, city councils, boards of supervisors, water districts, and school districts. These public agencies, using taxpayer dollars, in the two-year cycle ending December 31, 2001, spent $53 million on lobbying. They were followed by other special interests such as health, manufacturing interests, and finance and insurance. In 2004 a record $213 million was spent by special interests to influence government.

## Citizens' Groups

Organizations of citizens with similar views on a range of public policy issues such as political reforms and improving the environment are also active in the state's political process. In contrast to the special-interest groups, citizens' groups are often broadly based and include members of various occupations and classes. During the past few years citizens' groups have been increasing their membership and carrying more weight with the voters. For example, although the California Taxpayers Association is technically a lobbying group, it performs considerable research toward achieving economy and efficiency in the spending of tax dollars.

Perhaps the best known citizens' group is the League of Women Voters. Born out of the suffragette movement, the League now operates on local, county, state, and national levels. The California League has 15,000 members, most of whom are white homemakers over 30 years old. (Perhaps in deference to "men's lib," the League has now opened its membership to males.) Each member pays annual dues, and this money is divided among each of the four operative levels (national, state, county, and local). The League's main activities include voter services, study programs, and endorsements of legislation (action). Long known for its thorough and unbiased research of issues, the League is widely respected by voters and lawmakers alike. Another well-known nonpartisan citizens' group is Common Cause. Conceived in Washington, D.C., in 1969, Common Cause established its California branch in 1972. Members pay annual dues, which go to the national headquarters. Contributions beyond the regular dues support the state office. Common Cause's program calls for open legislative meetings, lobbying disclosure, conflict-of-interest laws, and public campaign financing. Because its preferred means of change is via the legislature, Common Cause lobbies in Sacramento, using letters of support from its 60,000-plus members as leverage.

Environmentalists have formed some of the most powerful citizens' groups. The Sierra Club is the most prominent, combining thorough research with an effective lobbying team in Sacramento. Other well-known environmental groups include the California Coastal Alliance, Friends of the Earth, and the Environmental Protection Center.

## LOBBYING

The process of lobbying has been described as the art of persuasion. The figures just cited clearly show that lobbying is itself a big business. But who are the lobbyists and how do they ply their trade?

As noted above, in 2005 there were about 936 lobbyists registered in Sacramento, representing virtually any interest imaginable. Some lobbyists are so-called

**TABLE 3.1    California Lobbying Firms**

| Firm | Q4 2004 | Session Total |
|---|---|---|
| 1. Kahl / Pownall Advocates | $1,358,552 | $9,499,559 |
| 2. Nielsen, Merksamer, Parrinello, Mueller & Naylor, Llp | $986,031 | $7,867,430 |
| 3. Flanigan Law Firm, The | $836,069 | $4,872,481 |
| 4. Read & Associates, LLC, Aaron L. | $797,954 | $6,933,315 |
| 5. Rose & Kindel, Inc. | $745,720 | $4,626,243 |
| 6. Platinum Advisors LLC | $735,771 | $6,747,227 |
| 7. Sloat Higgins Jensen & Associates | $669,208 | $5,569,507 |
| 8. Lang, Hansen, O'malley And Miller Governmental Relations | $648,654 | $5,465,338 |
| 9. Manatt, Phelps & Phillips, Llp | $640,757 | $3,643,411 |
| 10. Public Policy Advocates, LLC | $636,716 | $5,308,959 |
| 11. Governmental Advocates, Inc. | $624,218 | $6,278,647 |
| 12. Livingston & Mattesich Law Corporation | $592,007 | $4,937,747 |
| 13. Nossaman, Guthner, Knox & Elliott, Llp | $591,298 | $4,173,387 |
| 14. California Advocates, Inc. | $546,068 | $3,572,283 |
| 15. Capitol Advocacy, LLC | $533,054 | $5,305,375 |

"in-house" lobbyists, individuals who work for and are paid exclusively by a particular organization such as the McDonnell Douglas Corporation or the California Association of Community Colleges. Others are "contract" lobbyists, sometimes referred to as "hired guns," who will and do work for anyone willing to pay their fees. The number of clients may range from two or three to half a hundred or as many as the staff can handle. Kahl/Pownell Advocates employs 15 full-time lobbyists and represents 21 different clients, including the Hertz Corporation, Loma Linda University Medical Center, the New York Stock Exchange, and Reliant Energy. It was, has been for years, the top money maker among lobbying firms with payments from clients totaling over $8.5 million. At the other end of the scale was Melanie Weigner, an in-house lobbyist employed by the Ford Motor Company. Women are making up a larger and larger part of the lobbying corps. In 1977 there were only 44 women registered as lobbyists. In 2005 they accounted for nearly 30 percent. About a third of lobbyists have had some direct experience as members of the legislature or as staff to members of committees. The reason why such individuals are sought out for these jobs may be summed up in one word—access. The first and most important task of any lobbyist is to gain access to the people who hold power over those policies that affect his or her clients. Knowing the governmental ropes—and the players—personally is an enormous advantage when it comes to gaining access.

The definition of a lobbyist is set down in the Political Reform Act of 1974. If someone "communicates directly" and on a regular basis with a government official "for the purpose of influencing legislative or administrative action," he or she is required to register as a lobbyist. The act goes on to define regular access as when there have been more than 25 direct contacts with officials for two consecutive months. Not everyone does register, and the actual number of those engaged in lobbying is almost certainly much higher than the over 900 found on the official roster.

How do these men and women exercise their art of persuasion? There are two basic categories of techniques: direct pressure and indirect pressure. Direct pressure involves attempts to convince government officials to adopt policies supported by the group. Indirect pressure seeks to create a favorable public opinion which, in turn, influences governmental decisions.

The Samish case brought the public's attention to the influence lobbyists had in Sacramento. Artie Samish, a lobbyist for the beer industry, was described in 1949 in *Collier's* magazine as more powerful than the governor of the state. It was alleged he had total control over the Public Morals Committee and his influence only ceased upon his conviction for income tax evasion.

This case led to passage of the Collier Act (in 1949), subsequently amended, which required all lobbyists to register and file monthly reports with the legislature regarding their employers.

It was not until 1973 that further serious efforts were made to regulate lobbying. Led by Common Cause, the People's Lobby, and then Secretary of State Jerry Brown, an initiative was placed on the June 1974 ballot. Proposition 9 was approved by the voters and the new regulations went into effect the following January. The proponents won, arguing that the people had a right to know the sources and uses of special-interest money contributed to their elected representatives.

A lobbyist is prohibited from spending more than $10 a month per legislator—sufficient for two hamburgers and a Coke, said the supporters of the 1974 legislation. The Fair Political Practices Commission (FPPC), created by the Reform Act, has responsibility for enforcing these provisions, including the preparation and processing of the reporting forms and the investigation of all complaints of noncompliance. In cases of violation, the FPPC can subpoena witnesses, issue cease-and-desist orders, and levy fines of up to $2,000. The commission has five members: The chairperson and one member are appointed by the governor, and one member each is appointed by the attorney general, the secretary of state, and the controller. Members serve four-year terms.

Proposition 140 loosened things a bit by pegging the limits on gifts at $250 a year with adjustments for inflation. In 2005 that meant the ceiling had been raised to $340. There is, however, one gaping loophole: overseas trips paid for by nonprofit groups or government entities are excluded from the limit, making expensive—and extensive—trips to Europe, Asia, or other parts of the world another legislative "perk." On a lesser level, but still conducive to good relations, are dinners, lunches, tickets to L.A. Laker games and to amusement parks such as Disneyland.

Just how effective these reforms have been is debatable. There is less socializing of lobbyists with legislators, but the huge amounts of money expended by special interests argue that influence is still a major commodity. And that, of course, is not necessarily a bad thing, given the contributions to the governing process that can be made by lobbyists. Only where abuses occur such as with Artie Samish or the sale of votes uncovered by the F.B.I. "sting" or special interests seriously undermine the general interest should Joe and Jane Public be concerned.

## REVIEW QUESTIONS

1. In what ways may it be said California moved toward the right or became more conservative in the 1980s and early '90s? In what ways did it not? (pp. 36–37)
2. What evidence is there of an east-west split in California politics? (p. 18)
3. What issues tended to dominate the 2002 gubernatorial campaign? (pp. 46–48)
4. Discuss the arguments used in the debates over the following controversial propositions that appeared on the state ballots in this period:
    - Proposition 172 (school vouchers) (p. 42)
    - Proposition 187 (illegal immigration) (p. 43)
    - Proposition 209 (antiaffirmative action) (pp. 43–44)
    - Proposition 215 (medicinal marijuana) (p. 44)
    - Proposition 227 (bilingual education) (p. 44)
    - Proposition 5 (casino gambling) (p. 44)
    - Proposition 77 (reapportionment) (p. 54)
5. A number of organizations have been created to supplement the formal political party structures. What are they and (a) what functions do they perform and (b) why did they come into existence? (pp. 56–57)

6. What functions do pressure groups perform and who are the major players in terms of money spent? How are they regulated? (pp. 60–62)

7. Discuss the reasons underlying the successful recall of Governor Gray Davis. (pp. 51–55)

8. What factors were largely responsible for the defeat of all eight propositions in the 2005 special election? (p. 54)

## SELECTED WEB SITES

There are a great number of web sites dealing with political parties, pressure groups, and politics in California. Many are cited at the end of Chapter 4 where the focus is on campaigns. Here are a few of the sites most often sought.

All political parties authorized to appear on the state ballot have web sites describing their principal beliefs, objectives, often local contacts, etc. They are:

Democratic ca.dem.org
Republican ca.gop.org
Green greens.org/California
Libertarian ca.lp.org
Reform california.reformparty.org
Natural Law natural-law.org/California
American Independent wordpr.com/aip

There are far too many web sites representing interest/pressure groups to allow an extensive listing here. A few illustrations will have to suffice. In each instance the objectives of the group are given and most carry mailing addresses for further information. Examples by interest area include:

**On abortion**
California Abortion and Reproductive Rights League caral.org
Right to Life League of Southern California rtlsc.org

**On business**
California Chamber of Commerce calchamber.com
California Hispanic Chamber of Commerce cchcc.com

**On education**
California Faculty Association calfac.org
California Federation of Teachers cft.org
California Teachers Association cta.org
Home School Association of California hsc.org
California School Boards Association caba.org
California Parent Teachers Association capta.org

**On the environment**
California League of Conservation Voters ecovote.org
Sierra Club sierraclub.org/chapters/ca

**On labor**
California Labor Federation calaborfed.org
United Farm Workers of America ufw.org

**Other issues**

Children Now childrennow.org
Log Cabin Republicans of Orange County (gays) lcroc.org
Christian Coalition of California ccca.org
National Organization for Women of California canow.org
National Rifle Association canra.org

Lists of lobbying organizations active in the state and their web sites are to be found at the secretary of state's site, www.ss.ca.gov, and California Voter Foundation, www.calvoter.org

## SELECTED REFERENCES ─────────

Alchorn, Faith, "Donors Seek Biggest Bang for Their Political Bucks," *Los Angeles Times,* Orange County edition, May 22, 1988.

Baldassare, Mark, Bruce E. Cain, D. E. Appolonio and Jonathan Cohen, "The Season of Our Discontent: Voters' Views on California Elections," *Public Policy Institute of California,* October 2004.

Bastillo, Miguel, "Rise in Absentee Ballots Alters Tactics as Election Day Nears," *Los Angeles Times,* November 3, 2000, p. A3.

Bathen, Sigrid, "Lawyer-Lobbyists Become Big Fish in Capitol Pond," *California Journal,* February 1990.

Borland, John, "Third House Rising," *California Journal,* February 1996.

Brinkerhoff, Noel, "Consultants and Campaigns," *California Journal,* November 2000.

Cook, Gale, "The New Persuaders," *Golden State Report,* November 1987.

Craft, Cynthia, "Gray Davis 'Show Me the Money,'" *California Journal,* May 2001.

Decker, Kathleen, "GOP Beaten at Own Game in States Top Two Contests," *Los Angeles Times,* November 4, 1998.

Gorman, Tom, "State High Court Overturns Indian Gaming Initiative," *Los Angeles Times,* August 24, 1999.

Kindy, Kimberly, "Governments Now Tops in Spending," *Orange County Register,* July 31, 1999.

Napolitan, Joseph, *The Election Game and How to Win It,* 2d ed., New York: Doubleday, 1972.

Nollinger, Mark, "The New Crusaders," *California Journal,* January 1993.

Office of the Secretary of State, *Directory of Lobbyists, Lobbying Firms and Lobbyist Employers, 1999–2000,* Sacramento, 1999.

Price, Charles, "Advocacy in the Age of Term Limits," *California Journal,* November 1993.

Sabato, Larry, *The Rise of Political Consultants,* New York: Basic Books, 1982.

Warren, Jennifer, "Fong Fell Victim to Ad Strategy," *Los Angeles Times,* November 6, 1999.

# Chapter

# 4

# Voters, Nominations, and Elections

The most fundamental question of government is: Who should rule? Although it is generally assumed that in the United States the people rule—that is, we adhere to the principle of popular sovereignty—the U.S. Constitution contains no specific provision guaranteeing the citizen the right to vote or to run for office. Until the 1950s, who could vote had been left up to the states themselves, with the exception that the right of citizens to vote should not be "denied or abridged . . . on account of race, color, or previous condition of servitude" (Fifteenth Amendment) or "on account of sex" (Nineteenth Amendment). However, state governments denied or abridged the right to vote for other reasons.[1] In 17 states the citizen had to be literate (defined differently by the various states), and all states held to a minimum voting age requirement. Some states allowed a person to vote after he or she had lived in the state only six months, and others demanded two years. To vote on certain kinds of issues, such as approving bonds, a half-dozen states have required that the citizen be a property owner.

The provisions in the U.S. Constitution that provide for the popular election of senators and representatives go no further than to require that a state allow the same people to vote for members of Congress as it allows to vote for members of the "most numerous branch of the State legislature." If California's constitution had

---

[1] The Fourteenth Amendment stipulates that the number of a state's representatives in Congress shall be reduced if the state denies the right to vote to any 21-year-old citizen "except for participation in rebellion, or other crime," but this rule has not been invoked.

allowed only dog owners to vote for members of the assembly, it could have established the same requirement for voting in congressional elections.

However, in the past 45 years a far-reaching change has taken place with respect to the legal and constitutional basis of suffrage. Whether by legislation or constitutional amendment, the right to vote has been greatly expanded. Major laws adopted by Congress include the Voting Rights Act of 1965 and its amendments and various civil rights acts, particularly the one adopted in 1964. The age requirement, first established at 18 by the Voting Rights Acts of 1970, was later embedded in the Constitution with adoption of the Twenty-sixth Amendment. Residency requirements have been limited to 30 days by the Supreme Court. The Twenty-fourth Amendment outlawed poll taxes, enfranchising many poor people. In fact, today states have little control over suffrage and not much more over elections.

It has been assumed that the question of who may hold *national* elective office—that is, the presidency, vice-presidency, and congressional seats—was established by the Constitution and that states could not add any further qualifications. That assumption came under challenge when first Colorado and later other states (including California) voted to establish term limits for their elected representatives in Washington, D.C. Ultimately the U.S. Supreme Court ruled term limits on Congress are unconstitutional.

## WHO MAY VOTE?

In November 1972 the voters of California revised Article II of the state constitution to conform to the new provisions of the Twenty-sixth Amendment to the Constitution, the Voting Rights Act of Congress, and court decisions. Article II accords the right to vote in all California elections to any person who meets the following qualifications:

1. **Citizenship.** A voter must be a citizen of the United States. If the voter is not a natural-born American, he or she must have received naturalization papers before registering to vote.
2. **Residence.** The new Article II gives the legislature authority to set the residence requirements for voting. However, the California Supreme Court declared that, under the equal protection clause in both the United States and California constitutions, the state cannot require a citizen to live in the state more than 30 days before being allowed to vote. The legislature then enacted a law that conformed to this decision. Therefore, the present legal requirement is that a voter must live in California, his or her own county, and election precinct only 30 days before the election. The state legislature may reduce this requirement even more if it sees fit.[2]

---

[2] In California counties, a citizen is allowed to vote for president in the November general election even if he or she has been a resident of this state less than the 30 days. The citizen must have been eligible to vote in his or her former state and must appear in person at the office of the county clerk or registrar of voters at least seven days before the election. The citizen is permitted to vote only for the office of president and must formally register to vote in any subsequent elections.

Voters may vote in advance (in person or by mail), provided they have filed an application for an absentee ballot with the county elections official at least seven days before the election.

Before 1976 voters were supposed to have a valid reason (illness, a handicap, living ten or more miles from the polling place, other commitments) for not being able to go to the polls on election day and thus needing to vote by absentee ballot. Under current law any registered voter can request to vote absentee, even one who will mark the ballot in the privacy of his or her own home next door to the polling place. Critics of this procedure argue that it makes it possible for candidates to make campaign pitches in the home and walk out with a vote in his or her pocket.

Absentee ballots were a major factor in the outcome of the Bradley-Deukmejian election for governor in 1982. The state Republican Party sent letters to every Republican household enclosing an application for an absentee ballot and urging a vote for Deukmejian. This effort contributed to the total of 302,000 votes for Deukmejian out of a total of 505,000 absentees—a sufficient margin to overcome the 19,000-vote margin cast for Bradley at the ballot box. And in 1983 San Francisco Mayor Dianne Feinstein made use of the absentee ballot process to defeat a recall election. Use of the absentee ballot has increased greatly in recent years as both major political parties have urged their members to employ it. In 1984 just 6.5 percent of votes cast were absentee; throughout the 1990s it averaged roughly one-fifth. By the 2005 special election the number of ballots cast absentee exceeded 40 percent. And the question being asked by some: Will California follow in the footsteps of Oregon where all voting takes place by mail? Cost savings and convenience make that a real possibility.

3. **Age.** The minimum age for voting throughout the United States is 18. There is no *maximum age*. A centenarian who can get to the polls in person or who can fill out the application for an absentee ballot can continue to vote as he or she has for the previous 80 years.

4. **Special Requirements.** Article II of the California constitution states the legislature "shall provide that no severely mentally deficient person, insane person, person convicted of an infamous crime, no person convicted of embezzlement or misappropriation of public funds, shall exercise the privilege of an elector in this state." Just what an "infamous crime" is or how severe the mental deficiency had to be was left to the voters, who approved Proposition 10 in 1974. That proposition amended Article II, denying the vote to persons "while mentally incompetent or imprisoned or on parole for the conviction of a felony." When someone has finished his or her sentence and has completed the parole period the right to vote is restored.

Before November 1972, Article II required a voter to be able to read the state constitution in the English language and to write his or her name. This was eliminated in the revised version of the Article; furthermore, the Congressional Voting Rights Act of 1970 abolished the literacy qualification throughout the country.

5. **Registration.** A citizen who satisfies all of the qualifications listed cannot merely walk up to the polls on election day and expect to be handed a ballot. To exercise suffrage privileges a citizen must be already registered as a qualified voter with the chief elections administrator of his or her own county. (In most counties this is a duty of the county clerk, but in the counties of Los Angeles, San Francisco, San Diego, San Bernardino, Orange, and Santa Clara the elections official is the registrar of voters.) A person may register at any time except during the 15 days immediately preceding any election. For example, if a prospective new voter fails to register by the end of the thirtieth day preceding the June primary, that voter forfeits any chance of voting in that election and must wait until after balloting day to register for the coming November election. In most counties advance warning of the closing of registration is given by local newspapers and by deputies with the authority to process registrants, sitting at tables placed in front of post offices and supermarkets.

In 1975 the legislature voted to permit registration by mail. California's secretary of state prepared an application form to be uniform throughout the state. Now all that a potential voter has to do is to fill out the form and mail it (postage free) to the county clerk or registrar of voters, who then mails the applicant a card that says he or she is now an officially registered voter. These application forms are made available to political parties or other organizations seeking to get people registered and are kept on hand at many of the state's public offices.

Registration in California is "permanent"; that is, once a citizen is registered, he or she may continue to vote in succeeding elections without reregistering, providing the citizen does not (a) change legal residence to another county, (b) change name, (c) become ineligible because of insanity or serving a sentence for a felony, or (d) change party affiliation.

At the time of registration each voter is asked to indicate the party with which the voter chooses to be affiliated. This answer is indicated on the registration affidavit, and he or she becomes eligible to vote in that party's primary elections. If the voter "declines to state" party preference, he or she may, under the newly adopted open primary system, vote in any one partisan primary.

While efforts to get people registered historically have been seen as the responsibility of the parties, special-interest group organizations, and public interest groups such as the League of Women Voters, a state law adopted in 1976 requires local governments to take action to ensure that eligible residents are registered "at the highest possible level." Just how extensive those efforts needed to be became the issue in a suit brought by Common Cause and the American Civil Liberties Union, among others, in 1988. Citing differences in the percentages of those registered in high- and low-income areas of Los Angeles County, they argued that county officials were not doing enough to encourage low-income and minority citizens to register. Although a "voter outreach" program had been created involving bilingual registrars, with a 24-hour hotline to help people register at 3,500 locations throughout the county, a superior court judge ruled that these steps were insufficient to meet the intent of the law. The California supreme court disagreed, however, and the lower court order was voided. In 1993 a new federal law, the "motor voter law," was passed requiring states to provide opportunities for residents to register to vote when applying for or renewing a driver's license. Proponents touted the likelihood of greater participation in elections while critics pointed to the cost (between $2 million and $5 million a year in California), inconvenience (longer lines at the Department of Motor Vehicles), and an equal likelihood that those so unmotivated to register they had to be collared at the DMV would not vote anyway.

## VOTER PARTICIPATION

Despite extensive efforts to make both registering and voting easier and in the face of expanded "outreach" programs, many Californians, like other Americans, do not vote. Typically, of those who are qualified, *fewer than three out of four bother to register and, of those, 75 percent or fewer go to the polls.*

In the 1996 presidential election, some 65.53 percent of those registered (or, if all those who could have voted if registered are counted, just 52.56 percent) voted. In off-year (nonpresidential) elections such as that in 2002 even fewer vote. That year only 48 percent of registered persons voted (one-third of those eligible). Turnout at primary elections is even worse. In the 2002 primary only 34 percent of the registered voters (or 24 percent of all potential voters) went to the polls. The special election in November 1993 drew just 36.37 percent or an abysmally low 24.74 percent of those eligible, this despite such presumably "hot" issues on the ballot as school vouchers and a sales tax increase. The presidential election of 2004 saw a respectable 76 percent of registered voters (or 57 percent of those eligible go to the polls). Driven by the massive efforts of the public employee unions, turnout of registered voters was 50.1 percent for the special election of 2005, a very high total for an off-year, not regularly scheduled, election.

Why is there so little interest in exercising a right that men and women around the world fight and die to secure? With respect to primaries in presidential election years, many people are discouraged by the fact that decisions on selecting the parties' standard bearers have been reached before Californians have an opportunity to express their preferences. Because the presidential contest is the most visible and glamorous, many are turned off when it becomes apparent that their votes cannot influence the outcome. Then there are those who, in any election, either distrust all politicians ("they're all the same—crooks") or see no differences among candidates; if there are none, why bother? Still others vote only when they are angry, and when they see things going fairly well they tend to stay at home. Finally, there are some, especially in the lower socioeconomic categories, who have in effect "opted out" of the system in the belief that the system does not work—at least for them. For the nonvoter, all those millions spent on television, radio, campaign brochures, and the like are a waste of money. They simply are not paying attention. If the turnouts at national and statewide elections are for many people scandalously low, participation in local contests for seats on a city council, board of supervisors, or school board often falls below 25 percent of even registered voters. For those who pronounce with pride that Americans have the greatest democracy of Earth, they might look at these figures and contrast them with the over 70 percent of Iraqis who voted in December 2005, this where car bombs and suicide bombers threatened voters, something not typical of the election scene here.

## WHO MAY RUN FOR OFFICE?

### Eligibility

The 1964 court ruling in the case of Pierre Salinger, President Kennedy's press secretary who had only shortly before the primary moved to California, shattered the notion that a person is *in*eligible for election to any office for which he or she is not qualified to vote. Specific eligibility requirements are found in the U.S. Constitution for federal offices; in the state constitution and statutes for state senators, members of the assembly, judges of the state courts, county committeepersons, and officers in general law counties and cities; and in local charters for many officers in "home-rule" cities and counties.

California's elected executive officers must be voters and must have resided in the state five years previous to their election. Members of the Board of Equalization, the state's major tax agency, must in addition have resided in their own districts for one year. State senators and assembly members must be voters, and residents of the state for three years and of their district for one year. A ruling of the state supreme court in 1975 held that the residency requirement for candidates seeking local office must be limited to a maximum of 30 days.

### Getting on the Ballot

Any individual who meets the minimum legal qualification for any of the offices listed,[3] or any one of the many other local offices, may have his or her name appear on the ballot at primary election day if at least 60 days before the election the individual files a declaration of candidacy with the county clerk or in municipal elections with the city clerk. The number of sponsors' signatures required varies for different offices but is nominal.

To appear on the primary election ballot of a given party as a candidate for the U.S. Senate or any state executive office, a petition bearing 65 signatures (of registered voters belonging to the party within the constituency of the office sought) must be filed. Aspirants for the U.S. House of Representatives or for the state senate or assembly are required to file a petition carrying at least 40 signatures. At one time a filing fee was also required of all candidates except those running for party county central committees. However, that practice was declared in violation of the Fourteenth Amendment to the federal Constitution by the U.S. Supreme Court. State

---

[3]Except justices of the state supreme court and the district courts of appeal, where the only names appearing on the ballot are those of incumbents whose terms have expired or nominees of the governor in cases in which the incumbent is not running for reelection.

(Dennis Renault, *The Sacramento Bee*)

law now permits waiving of the fee with the collection of additional signatures on nominating petitions.

In 1975 the state supreme court declared the alphabetical listing of candidates on an election ballot unconstitutional. At the same time the court struck down the automatic listing of an incumbent's name at the head of the ballot. As a result, the names of candidates for state and local offices now appear on the basis of a randomized alphabet determined by a public drawing managed by the office of the secretary of state.

A candidate may not run as an independent in the partisan primaries. All contestants must themselves be registered members of a political party. Getting on the ballot in California is simple and relatively inexpensive; getting *elected* is something else!

## PRIMARY ELECTIONS: *THE BLANKET PRIMARY*

The *direct primary* was instituted in California and some other states to give the average voters a say in *nominating* the candidates who will represent their party in the coming general election. It is called "direct" because previously nomination had been indirect—that is, by conventions of party members led by party officials—and the average voters had to take the candidates the party "machine" gave them. Until 1996 it was a partisan primary in that only voters registered in the party could participate in it; it was closed to all others.

The voters changed that at the March 1996 primary when they overwhelmingly approved Proposition 198, which mandated the use of the "blanket primary." This system, employed by fewer than five states in the country, provides the maximum flexibility to voters. All the candidates of all eligible parties for all the offices to be elected are to be found on a single ballot. All registered voters, Republicans, Democrats, and third party members, as well as independents, receive the same ballot. They may choose which party primary they wish to vote in for each of the offices being contested. Thus a Democrat may elect to vote in the Republican primary for governor, the Democratic primary for controller, the Reform primary for United States Senate, and so on. In arguing for this change, proponents stated it was likely to lead to victory for more moderate candidates whose appeal transcended party lines. (One of the proponents was moderate Republican Tom Campbell, who had lost to conservative Bruce Herschensohn in the Republican U.S. Senate primary in 1994.) Opponents took the position that it made no sense to allow Republicans a role in the selection of Democratic candidates and vice versa and the procedure could only further weaken California's already weak political parties. Candidates, they argued, would be even more likely to campaign, not as party members but as individuals, much as they had in the era of cross-filing (see below).

Both major political parties objected to having convention delegates chosen with the "help" of nonmembers and threatened to bar those from the state chosen in this way. Special legislation was passed allowing the secretary of state to code ballots so that just party members would be counted for this function only.

Not satisfied, the major political parties challenged the system before the United States Supreme Court in April 2000 on the grounds that allowing independents and members of opposition parties a role in the selection of another party's candidates violates the right of free association. It makes no sense, they said, to allow Democrats who may hold the balance of power in a close Republican primary the power to determine who the Republican nominee should be. Yet that is precisely what happened in two assembly primaries in Southern California in 2000 where the Republican who *lost* received more *Republican* votes than the winner of the *Republican* primary. Both Governor Gray Davis and Bill Jones who, as secretary of state was the highest ranking Republican elected official in the state, urged the Court not to invalidate the blanket primary, which, they said, had resulted in higher voter participation and the nomination of more moderate candidates. In June 2000 the Court ruled that allowing nonmembers to vote in party elections unconstitutionally violates the right of free association (or not to associate). That left open whether such participation in open primaries where opposition party members may elect to cross over, might be banned. Following the court ruling, the legislature moved quickly to adopt a limited version of the open primary. Under current law those who decline to state a preference may elect to participate in any one party's primary while retaining the ban on "cross over voting."

California's direct primary historically has been held on the first Tuesday following the first Monday in June. However, as noted in Chapter 3, legislative action was taken in 1993 to move the primary in 1996 to the last Tuesday in March to enhance the state's influence in the selection of presidential candidates. As we have seen, the experiment did not work and another effort, spearheaded by state senator Jim Costa, moved the date to the *first* Tuesday in March for the 2000 primary.

The ballot is "longest" in gubernatorial election years (1998, 2002, 2006, and so on) when all state executive offices are open for nomination, as well as all assembly and U.S. House of Representative seats, half the state senate seats, county committee posts, and numerous local offices. The state executive officers serve four-year terms and are not elected in presidential election years (1996, 2000, 2004, and so on).

One of the Progressive reforms (see Chapter 2) designed to weaken political parties was cross-filing. This system allowed a candidate to run not just for his or her own party's nomination but for the nominations of other parties as well. Voters were still restricted to voting in the party in which they were registered but candidates could—and did—file for both (or all) party nominations. If successful, the general election became a formality.

For 40 years it was the political way of life in California for aspirants of state and national office to cross-file. In a majority of the primary contests throughout the state one candidate would capture both major party nominations. For example, in the 1940–1952 period 84 percent of the state senate races and 72 percent of the assembly races were decided in the primaries. Among those who used the cross-filing system to secure the nominations of both parties were Governor Earl Warren and U.S. Senator William Knowland.

Led by the League of Woman Voters, a campaign to abolish cross-filing, described by one political scientist as the greatest barrier to party responsibility yet devised, ultimately succeeded in 1958, though efforts to modify it had been made. In 1954 the party affiliations of the candidates were included on the ballot for the first time. Abbreviations were used (Rep. for Republican, Dem. for Democrat, Proh. for Prohibition) and cross-filing victories dropped dramatically. Today the only way a candidate can duplicate the cross-filing victories of the past is through a write-in campaign. Though eliminated over 40 years ago, its heritage lives on in the present focus on the characteristics of the individual rather than party label that typifies the campaigns of today.

## The Presidential Primary

Voters in the direct primary in presidential election years are given the opportunity to select California's delegates to the national nominating convention of the parties. California is among the great majority of states that have taken the selection of national convention delegates away from the party committees or state party conventions.

California's convention delegates for each party, varying each convention year according to formulas set by the national parties, are selected as a group rather than individually. A Democratic voter, for example, chose among slates of Democrats seeking to be delegates.

In 1972, through a revision of Article II of the state constitution, California voters adopted the "Oregon Type" of presidential primary effective for the 1976 elections. Instead of the presidential candidates having to take the initiative in getting their names on the California ballot, it is now the responsibility of California's secretary of state, who must keep abreast of any political gossip and place on the presidential primary ballot the names of all persons who are "recognized candidates throughout the nation or throughout California for the office of President of the United States." Any candidate whom the secretary of state chooses not to recognize may still get on the ballot by circulating petitions among supporters in California. Furthermore, a person whose name the secretary of state has chosen to put on the ballot may withdraw by filing an affidavit that he or she is not a candidate, as Pat Buchanan did in 2000.

The Democratic Party added further confusion. Its 1972 national convention voted to prohibit winner-take-all primaries. These were primaries in which the candidate with the most votes, even if fewer than half, won all the delegates to the convention. Until then, both parties employed this system. The state's Republican party still does and with the earlier balloting in 2000 succeeded when the state's block of delegates proved quite significant in the selection process. California Democrats have tried several versions of proportional representation. One was winner-take-all by congressional district, but that proved unsatisfactory in that the proportion of the overall popular vote failed to mirror the proportion of delegates won. Currently voters vote directly for the candidates and the number of delegates is determined by the proportion of the popular vote each candidate receives in that district. If there are ten delegates to be chosen and three candidates split the popular vote 40–20–40, the delegates would be apportioned 4–2–4. There is, however, a "threshold" that any candidate must achieve: only those with at least 15 percent of the popular vote in a district can receive delegates.

Although both parties seek to make their delegations broadly representative, the Democrats require that there be an equal number of men and women on each state's delegation. They also mandate that there be Hispanics, blacks, Asians, the disabled, American Indians, gay men, and lesbians in proportion to their presence in the party's membership. If the results of a primary cause any group to be underrepresented, the district delegates must fill so-called at-large and alternate slots in ways that will correct the imbalance.

## The Nonpartisan "Primary"

One state executive officer—the superintendent of public instruction—superior, municipal, and justice court judges, and county elective officers are *elected* at the June primary elections.[4] They appear on the ballot without any party affiliation and may

---

[4] The special provision for the appointment and election of supreme court and district courts of appeal judges is discussed under the court system in Chapter 8.

be voted upon by *all* registered voters. The candidate who receives a majority of the votes for one of these nonpartisan offices is declared elected. If no candidate receives a majority, a runoff is held at the coming November election between the two candidates with the highest number of votes.

Many California voters do not declare their affiliation with any of the legally recognized political parties in this state; at the time of registration they either "decline to state" their party preference or indicate membership in one of the small, unofficial parties. In 1998 for the first time and, as it turned out only time, these Californians were able to vote for candidates for partisan office in the June primary, as well as for candidates for nonpartisan office (as they have in the past). Figures compiled by the office of the secretary of state show that the number of persons declining to state a party affiliation more than tripled between 1976 and 2004, from 490,000 to over 2.2 million and in 2005 to over 18 percent of those registered. Young people in particular show a tendency to register as independents, perhaps out of a sense of disenchantment with political parties.

Municipal officers are elected on a nonpartisan basis. Some municipalities hold their elections on the second Tuesday in March or the second Tuesday in April whereas others combine their elections with the statewide June primary or the November general election.

## THE NOVEMBER GENERAL ELECTION

The final election for partisan offices and those nonpartisan offices for which runoffs are necessary, as well as the vote on most state and county ballot propositions, is held in every even-numbered year on the first Tuesday after the first Monday in November. All registered voters are eligible to vote and receive the same ballots regardless of their party affiliation.

### Presidential Election Years

The ballot is slightly different in alternating general election years. In every presidential election year no state executive offices are filled, but California's presidential electors are chosen.[5] Each party's list of presidential electors is selected at its state convention in its fall meeting preceding the general election. The names of each party's presidential electors do not appear on the general election ballot, however. The ballot contains only the names of the national party candidates for president and vice president, as shown in Figure 4.1. The votes cast for president and vice president are officially counted as votes for the bloc of presidential electors of each party. The electors of the party whose candidates receive the highest vote are declared elected, and they all meet in Sacramento on the first Monday after the second Wednesday in December (as required by an act of Congress) to cast California's entire electoral vote for their party's two candidates. The California law is

---

[5]The number of each state's presidential electors is the same as its total representation in the U.S. Congress (California: 52 representatives and 2 senators).

**OFFICIAL BALLOT / BOLETA OFICIAL**
**CONSOLIDATED PRESIDENTIAL GENERAL ELECTION**
**ELECCIÓN GENERAL PRESIDENCIAL CONSOLIDADA**
**NOVEMBER 2, 2004, FRESNO COUNTY / 2 DE NOVIEMBRE DEL 2004, CONDADO DE FRESNO**

INSTRUCTIONS TO VOTERS: You must use a black pen, blue pen or No. 2 pencil to completely fill in the oval to the left of your choice. Fill in the whole oval, or your vote may not be counted.
INSTRUCCIONES AL ELECTOR: Utilice usted una pluma o bolígrafo de tinta negra o azul, o bien un lápiz No. 2, para llenar completamente el óvalo al lado izquierdo de su preferencia. Llene el óvalo completamente, para que su voto sea contado con seguridad.

**Fill in oval like this** ●          **Llene el óvalo así** ●

**PARTISAN / PARTIDARIOS**

**PRESIDENT AND VICE PRESIDENT**
**PRESIDENTE Y VICEPRESIDENTE**

VOTE FOR ONE PARTY / VOTE POR UN PARTIDO

○ GEORGE W. BUSH (Pres.)          Republican/Republicano
RICHARD CHENEY (V. Pres.)

○ MICHAEL BADNARIK (Pres.)          Libertarian/Libertario
RICHARD CAMPAGNA (V. Pres.)

○ MICHAEL ANTHONY PEROUTKA (Pres.)   American Ind.
CHUCK BALDWIN (V. Pres.)              Ind. Americano

○ LEONARD PELTIER (Pres.)     Peace and Freedom/Paz y Libertad
JANICE JORDAN (V. Pres.)

○ JOHN F. KERRY (Pres.)          Democratic/Demócrata
JOHN EDWARDS (V. Pres.)

○ DAVID COBB (Pres.)          Green/Verde
PAT LAMARCHE (V. Pres.)

○
Write-in

**UNITED STATES SENATOR**
**SENADOR DE LOS ESTADOS UNIDOS**

VOTE FOR ONE          VOTE POR UNO

○ MARSHA FEINLAND     Peace and Freedom/Paz y Libertad
Public School Teacher / Maestra de Escuela Publica

○ BARBARA BOXER          Democratic/Demócrata
U.S. Senator / Senadora de EE UU

○ BILL JONES          Republican/Republicano
Farmer/Businessman / Agricultor/Empresario

○ DON J. GRUNDMANN     American Ind./Ind. Americano
Doctor of Chiropractic / Doctor en Quiropractica

○ JAMES P. "JIM" GRAY          Libertarian/Libertario
Judge / Juez

○
Write-in

**STATE CENTER COMMUNITY COLLEGE DISTRICT**
**DISTRITO DEL INSTITUTO**
**DE LA COMUNIDAD DE STATE CENTER**
**GOVERNING BOARD MEMBER / FIDEICOMISARIO**
**TRUSTEE AREA NO. 3 / ÁREA FIDEICOMISARIA NO. 3**
VOTE FOR ONE          VOTE POR UNO

○ RICARDO ESCOBEDO PAREDES
At Risk Consultant / Consultas para Personas en Riesgo

○ H. RONALD FEAVER
Appointed Incumbent / Titular por Nombramiento

○
Write-in

**STATE CENTER COMMUNITY COLLEGE DISTRICT**
**DISTRITO DEL INSTITUTO**
**DE LA COMUNIDAD DE STATE CENTER**
**GOVERNING BOARD MEMBER / FIDEICOMISARIO**
**TRUSTEE AREA NO. 5 / ÁREA FIDEICOMISARIA NO. 5**
VOTE FOR ONE          VOTE POR UNO

○ PHILLIP J. FORHAN
Incumbent / Titular

○ RICHARD M. CAGLIA
Businessman/Attorney / Empresario/Abogado

○
Write-in

**STATE CENTER COMMUNITY COLLEGE DISTRICT**
**DISTRITO DEL INSTITUTO**
**DE LA COMUNIDAD DE STATE CENTER**
**GOVERNING BOARD MEMBER / FIDEICOMISARIO**
**TRUSTEE AREA NO. 6 / ÁREA FIDEICOMISARIA NO. 6**
VOTE FOR ONE          VOTE POR UNO

○ PATRICK E. "PAT" PATTERSON
Incumbent / Titular

○ PAUL A. DICTOS
Certified Public Accountant / Contador Público Certificado

○
Write-in

**FRESNO UNIFIED SCHOOL DISTRICT**
**DISTRITO ESCOLAR UNIFICADO DE FRESNO**
**GOVERNING BOARD MEMBER, TRUSTEE AREA NO. 2**
**FIDEICOMISARIO, ÁREA FIDEICOMISARIA NO. 2**
VOTE FOR ONE          VOTE POR UNO

○ MANUEL G. NUNEZ
Incumbent / Titular

○ PAUL H. GARCIA
Community Activist / Activista Comunitario

○ JOHN SANTOYA
Education Advocate / Defensor de la Educación

○
Write-in

**FRESNO UNIFIED SCHOOL DISTRICT**
**DISTRITO ESCOLAR UNIFICADO DE FRESNO**
**GOVERNING BOARD MEMBER, TRUSTEE AREA NO. 3**
**FIDEICOMISARIO, ÁREA FIDEICOMISARIA NO. 3**
VOTE FOR ONE          VOTE POR UNO

○ VALERIE F. DAVIS
Teacher/Parent / Maestra/Madre de Familia

○ SILVIA ASTORGA SALCIDO
Appointed Incumbent / Titular por Nombramiento

○ NUEL BROWN
Retired Executive Director / Director Ejecutivo Jubilado

○
Write-in

**KINGS RIVER CONSERVATION DISTRICT**
**DISTRITO DE CONSERVACIÓN DE KINGS RIVER**
**MEMBER, BOARD OF DIRECTORS**
**MIEMBRO DE LA JUNTA DE FIDEICOMISARIOS**
**AT LARGE / DIRECTOR EN GENERAL**
VOTE FOR ONE          VOTE POR UNO

○ EDDIE NIEDERFRANK
Farmer / Agricultor

○ AL QUIST
Appointed Incumbent / Titular por Nombramiento

○ DAVID CEHRS
Hydrologist/Farmer/Professor / Hydrólogo/Agricultor/Profesor

○ JOHN WEDDINGTON
Farmer/Irrigation Specialist / Agricultor/Especialista de Riego

○
Write-in

**NORTH CENTRAL FIRE PROTECTION DISTRICT**
**DISTRITO DE BOMBERO DE NORTH CENTRAL**
**MEMBER, BOARD OF DIRECTORS**
**MIEMBRO DE LA JUNTA DE FIDEICOMISARIOS**
VOTE FOR NO MORE THAN TWO
VOTE POR NO MÁS DE DOS

○ GARY S. HENSON
Retired Fire Fighter / Bombero Jubilado

○ NICK GOOSEV
Farmer / Agricultor

○ RUSTY SOUZA
Incumbent / Titular

○ BOB SHERWOOD
Self Employed / Dueño de Mi Propio Negocio

○ KEN ABRAHAMIAN
Incumbent / Titular

○
Write-in

○
Write-in

**MEASURES SUBMITTED TO VOTERS**
**PROPUESTAS SOMETIDAS A LOS**
**ELECTORES**
**STATE / ESTADO**

1A. PROTECTION OF LOCAL GOVERNMENT REVENUES. Ensures local property tax and sales tax revenues remain with local government thereby safeguarding funding for public safety, health, libraries, parks, and other local services. Provisions can only be suspended if the Governor declares a fiscal necessity and two-thirds of the Legislature concur. Fiscal Impact: Higher local government revenues than otherwise would have been the case, possibly in the billions of dollars annually over time. Any such local revenue impacts would result in decreased resources to the state of similar amounts.

1A. PROTECCIÓN DE LAS RECAUDACIONES DE LOS GOBIERNOS LOCALES. Garantiza que las recaudaciones locales provenientes de los impuestos sobre la propiedad y las ventas permanezcan en los gobiernos locales, salvaguardando por lo tanto el financiamiento de la seguridad pública, la salud, las bibliotecas, los parques y otros servicios locales. Las disposiciones sólo pueden ser suspendidas si el gobernador declara necesidad fiscal y las dos terceras partes de la Legislatura están de acuerdo. Impacto fiscal: Mayores recaudaciones de los gobiernos locales que las que hubiera sido el caso de lo contrario, posiblemente de miles de millones de dólares anuales a lo largo del tiempo. Todos esos impactos sobre las recaudaciones locales resultarían en una reducción de los recursos del estado en cantidades similares.

○ YES, SÍ          ○ NO, NO

**Figure 4.1**    Ballot for California General Election, 2004.

explicit in binding the electors to vote for only the official candidates of their party. However, this has never been enforced, because a federal law permits an elector to vote for a candidate of any party.

## CALIFORNIA'S BALLOT FORM

### "Long" Ballot

A *long ballot* is one that gives voters many things to decide. A state like California—in which there are ten state executives to be elected besides the governor, as well as judges and local government officials, and a host of ballot propositions, initiatives, bond issues, and charter amendments to be approved—may be said to have a very long ballot. Voters in an average precinct who take their suffrage privilege seriously would be obliged to mark over 100 crosses or fill in that many scantron like spaces in the primary and general elections! The voters complain of the ballot's length but are reluctant to part with their privilege of choice among a multitude of officers and ballot propositions.

## "Office Bloc"

The California ballot is divided by office rather than by political party as in some states. Under the heading "Governor," for example, are listed all candidates for that office from all qualified parties. With the office-bloc (in contrast to the party-column) form there is no time saved by voting a straight party ticket. Advocates of tighter party discipline are dissatisfied with the present California ballot; some have urged the institution of the straight-ticket option, in which one punch or one cross placed at the head of a party column is counted as a vote for all candidates of that party.

# THE ADMINISTRATION OF ELECTIONS

## Election Officials

The chief elections officer of the state for the various elections is the secretary of state, and copies of nomination and election petitions must be filed with this officer. The secretary of state also has the major responsibility for ballot specifications and arrangements and certifies and publishes the final vote count. However, the actual preparation of election ballots, selection of voting sites, and counting of votes are the responsibility of the county clerk or the registrar of voters in each county. The county board of supervisors appoints the board of election officials who are the precinct election workers seen at polling places on election day. In municipal elections the city council appoints these workers.

## General Procedures

Voting precincts of an estimated 200–600 voters each are established by the county election officials and are consolidated for local elections. Within each precinct, a polling place is selected and polling booths are erected. The polling place may be in almost any convenient building: a private home, a school, the lobby of an apartment house, or a garage, but not a liquor store or bar. The polls are open from 7 A.M. to 8 P.M. in most counties. As soon as the polls have closed, the precinct boards begin to count the votes (called the first canvass) in the presence of all bystanders. This is usually done at the polling establishments, but provision may be made by county officials for a central counting. The second canvass takes place when county officials—again in public—add together the returns of the individual precincts. The county sends copies of all returns to the secretary of state and stores all ballots for six months, after which time they are destroyed.

Automatic voting machines, at which voters pull a lever to indicate their choice, are being used in a few California counties, including San Francisco. In some counties voting is still done by the old-style rubber stamp on paper ballots, which are counted by hand, but in the majority of counties, including Los Angeles, the voters have marked their ballots by some kind of stylus or marking device, and the ballots are then counted by electronic machines.

The electronic age entered the scene in the twenty-first century with the introduction of electronic voting machines. Faster and "cleaner" than the old paper ballots, these new devices were hailed as the ultimate in balloting. However, questions arose as to accuracy (one machine in North Carolina was set to accept 10,500 ballots when it had a capacity for only 3,005, "losing" some 7,000 votes). While fears of amateurs or others hacking into the voting process appear to have been groundless, the desire to have some means of checking on the accuracy of the count led to demands for some kind of "paper trail" for validation of results. A compromise has been the use of machine-scored ballots using the "fill in the bubble" system beloved by college students taking multiple choice exams.

Still, the advantages of computer voting are evident. One experiment was undertaken in Piedmont where a touch screen system was employed. Using a plastic card coded with ballot information, voters could touch the screen to indicate approval or disapproval of a ballot measure. Instead of the usual three hours needed to tabulate the results, they were ready in 29 minutes. Most counties using the system were enthusiastic and the savings in paper costs over time are significant. Riverside County adopted a similar system for absentee voting over the week prior to the 2000 primary. The reaction of voters was so positive county officials decided to have 4,200 touch screen computers in place for the 2000 general election.

For many years all elections in California were conducted in English; it was against the law for any election official to speak anything but English in a polling place. This prohibition was repealed in 1973 by the California legislature. Then Congress in the Federal Voting Rights Act of 1975 provided that in any state or local subdivision where a significant number of citizens belonged to a non-English-language minority, election materials were to be published in the language of the minority as well as in English. When this law was applied to California, it meant that sample ballots, voters' pamphlets, and instructions at the polling place had to be available in Spanish in 38 counties and in Chinese in San Francisco County. Some 21,000 voters in the city of Valencia in 2000 used the touch screen system with computers loaded with versions of the ballot in Vietnamese, Tagalog, Korean, Spanish, Chinese, and Japanese.

## Special Protections

California's election laws have numerous provisions designed to ensure fair play and guard against fraud. Each detail, from the opening and inspecting of the empty ballot box on election morning to the defacing and destruction of unused and voided ballots, is carefully outlined in the 11,700 sections of the Elections Code. In the case of most offices, election officials must count write-in votes for actual persons. Ballots cast for Mickey Mouse or Superman are ignored. No one may speak to a voter within 100 feet of a polling place about his or her vote. Employers who distrib-

# Caucus

by HüGo

(Courtesy World West Features)

ute political propaganda with the paychecks of their employees are guilty of a misdemeanor. Voting is secret, behind curtains, but a voter may not remain in a polling
booth longer than ten minutes. All business concerns, according to law, must give
their employees sufficient time to vote on election day. There are provisions for chal-
lenging voters at the polls who are suspected of fraudulent voting and for challeng-
ing counts and demanding recounts. Penalties are stiff for voter intimidation or
inducements in the form of money, property, or employment.

## CAMPAIGNS

The process of running for office in California is expensive and arduous. In this age
of advertising message overload, simply getting the voters' attention with a candidate or an argument in support of an issue is a major accomplishment. Sustaining
such attention and building a favorable voter response to a candidacy or a particular

ballot proposition, in the face of opposing candidates and arguments on issues, is a task that has come to require highly specialized skills in itself—the skills of public relations professionals. Few candidates themselves possess the skills, money, or time to manage all of the tasks involved, and so in modern times a new breed of political professional has emerged to take on these duties: the campaign manager. Especially for campaigns in statewide elections, a campaign manager has become virtually indispensable, and campaign management has come to involve so many specialized subtasks that usually entire firms are hired by major candidates and by interest groups for and against ballot measures.

## Campaign Management Firms

For the most part, campaigns prior to World War II were run by party leaders or by the candidates themselves who conducted them largely by "feel," a sense of what worked, what appealed to the voters. As dramatically portrayed in such motion pictures as *The Candidate* and *Power,* that is no longer the case. The rise of political consultants began in California in 1933 when the husband and wife team of Whitaker and Baxter formed the first campaign management firm. It is not surprising that what has since become a national phenomenon began in California. The state's weak political parties meant that many of the traditional means of conducting campaigns were not available. The lack of patronage with its accompanying stimulus to party loyalty was one factor. Patronage elsewhere provided a ready army of campaign workers on whom candidates could depend, but the Progressive reforms of the early twentieth century had virtually eliminated it in California. The prohibition against party endorsements in primary elections and in all nonpartisan races left official party organizations out of the process. Cross-filing had a similar effect even in partisan contests (see pages 73–74).

Ballot propositions, often involving important public issues, were proposed and opposed usually with little or no reference to party. With parties to a considerable degree foreclosed by law from their traditional roles, campaign management firms took on many of the functions that parties performed elsewhere. Even the size of the state played a role. With a rapidly growing population, campaigns necessarily and increasingly came to depend on newspapers and later radio and television to reach the voters. These firms provided the expertise needed. Some might even argue that Californians' penchant for being entertained, arising from the influence of Hollywood and the television industry, enhanced the opportunities for campaign management firms with their emphasis on dramatic, attention-getting political messages. Whatever the reasons, they have come to play an extremely important role in any statewide race as well as many city and county campaigns.

Darry Sragow and Dan Schnur, Sal Russo and Eileen Padberg are hardly household names, but their organizations and others like them have a great deal to say about the style and substance of campaigns in California. What the public learns about candidates and issues is heavily influenced by how they decide campaigns should be conducted. Their decisions, in turn, are based on what they believe will help most in ensuring that their client, the candidate, wins. That means using public opinion polling.

## Polling

Even those who pay little attention to politics know about polls. They measure public attitudes and opinions on a wide variety of questions. Which candidate is ahead? What do people think about the death penalty or higher taxes or abortion? What few people realize is that what they see in the newspapers or hear about on radio or television is only the tip of a very large iceberg. Most polls are intended solely for the eyes of those who pay for them. How effective is a series of beer commercials? What image do people have of a particular industry? What do they think of a candidate's character? Ability? No major national or large statewide campaign is without the services of a professional polling organization. One nationally prominent campaign manager, Joseph Napolitan, has said: "I personally would no more try to run a campaign without adequate polls than I would try to sail the Atlantic without a compass."

Polls are generally conducted by telephone, with the interviewer following a carefully prepared script. Questions are framed in as neutral a way as possible to avoid bias. Those asking the questions are trained to use vocal intonations that do not invite a particular response. "Do you (really) think this is a good idea?" Use of a word or tone implying skepticism may well result in skewed results, making the poll worthless. In a survey of general opinion, a proper sample must be used. Percentages of the overall population, male and female, by income and education levels, ethnicity, religion, and the like are reflected in the sample of people interviewed.

Polls serve several functions. A *benchmark poll* is taken before the campaign begins. It may be designed to identify those issues of most interest to the voters because that will vary from place to place and race to race. Getting and keeping the voter's attention requires a focus on what he or she is interested in. Another function of such a poll may be to identify the candidate's strengths and weaknesses, the strengths to be emphasized in the campaign, the weaknesses countered. If a candidate is seen as uncaring or abrasive, television commercials may show him or her sitting with—and smiling at—a group of the elderly, for example.

A rather different kind of poll involves what are called *focus groups*. A small number of people representative of the group the candidate hopes to influence views a television commercial before it airs. Is the message clear? Is the announcer believable? Do the pictures help or hinder the message? In the past commercials have been drastically altered and even dropped altogether after measuring the reactions of such focus groups.

While national polling organizations such as Gallup and Harris conduct opinion surveys in California, several state-based polls have earned the respect of professionals. The California Poll, under the leadership of Mervin Field since its inception over 45 years ago, is considered by many to be the best. The *Los Angeles Times* also gets high marks for its polling, as does a relative newcomer, the Public Policy Institute of California.

## Television

The importance of television in waging a statewide or regional campaign cannot be overemphasized. Virtually every home has one or more sets; most of us watch what is on them several hours a day. When we add the fact that up to 70 percent of the public gets all or most of its news from television, the formula for success seems apparent: Be seen on "the tube" as much and as favorably as possible.

The staple of television advertising is the 30-second commercial. It is long enough to get the candidate's name, the office being contested, and a slogan included, but not so long that "channel surfing" sets in. With so little time, commercials are carefully crafted to insure maximum impact. That, more often than not, means the use of "visuals" to enhance the image of the person running. The candidate sits in a classroom smiling at—and being smiled at—by a group of children, properly balanced by sex and ethnicity. He obviously loves kids and wants the best possible education for them. The classroom has a prominently displayed American flag, and on the blackboard there may be some arithmetic problems, the scene symbolizing patriotism and an endorsement of "basic" education. In agricultural areas a farmer with a red tractor substitutes for the children and classroom, but there is a similar message: The candidate knows and supports agriculture. With name identification so important in local contests, the 30-second commercial can make the candidate seem familiar to the voters. A catchy slogan ("She gets things done") or Deukmejian's in 1986 ("Great Governor, Great State") is likely to stick in the viewer's mind when going to the polls.

The subject matter of a television commercial is influenced by those benchmark polls at the beginning of a campaign. How it is presented may be changed after review by a focus group. Then the question becomes when to air it. This decision is the province of the "media buyers." Not all commercials "sell" equally well in all time slots. Some are designed to appeal primarily to a sports-oriented audience and may be shown during football games. Others target those who watch soap operas. Older citizens, blue-collar workers, ethnic minorities—all are "targets" of specially created commercials.

The potential impact of the Hispanic vote led to a greater use of Spanish language television in the 2005 special election campaigns. Expenditures more than tripled between 2003 and 2005, from $2.2 million to $7.3 million with a large portion of those funds going to the #1 Spanish language network, Univision, which, with its sister network Telefutura, controls about 90 percent of the Hispanic market in large parts of the state. Not all the focus on television rests with commercials, however. While commercials can be effective, coverage obtained on local newscasts has several advantages, not the least of which is credibility. The viewer is likely to assume that if a reporter from Channel XYZ thinks a candidate is worth covering, he or she must have a genuine chance of winning. In one notable case, a candidate ran a commercial in which he was interviewed by several "reporters" (really actors) just to create this impression. A second advantage is of course cost. Compared with a single local television commercial in Los Angeles next to *CSI* or *American Idol,* which can run as much as $50,000, (one Los Angeles station charged $110,000 for a spot next to the hit show *Designing Women* in the special election of 2005; there were no takers) such free coverage is a bargain. Attractive as it is, however, there are some disadvantages. When the candidate buys commercial time, he or she is sure of being seen. When "free" time is given, the candidate may be preempted by a major international incident or even a particularly spectacular fire or traffic accident. And to get the station news editor's attention often means setting up "photo opportunities": Situations in which the candidate can be filmed in colorful and telegenic settings such as visiting a hospital and chatting with patients to underscore support for health insurance or backpacking in the Sierra Nevadas to demonstrate a commitment to wilderness preservation.

The availability of "free" time has shrunk in recent years and nearly disappeared in 1998. A study of news coverage of the gubernatorial race in 1998 by the Annenberg School for Communications at the University of Southern California found that less than one-third of 1 percent of local news time in five major markets (Los Angeles, San Diego, Sacramento, Bakersfield, and San Francisco) was devoted to it. In a comparison used by the study's authors, all local stations each day broadcast a total of more than 100 hours of news, sports, and weather but only 19 minutes a day on the governor's contest. Almost all campaign communication was forced to be paid. It should be noted the governorship race was the "best" covered by television news.

## Radio Comes Back

The use of radio in campaigns declined precipitously in the late 1950s with the advent of television, but in recent years it has made a comeback and now forms an integral part of most well-developed strategies. Several factors have made radio attractive in the 1980s and 1990s. One is cost. Preparing a radio commercial is much less expensive than preparing and running one for television. When buying time on television, a campaign pays for the entire market served. If running for Congress or the state legislature in San Francisco or San Diego or Los Angeles, that means paying to reach a large majority of viewers who cannot vote for the candidate in any event. They live outside the district. Because of its low cost, radio makes this financially bearable. Another advantage is a greater ability to target particular audiences. While television viewers tend to change channels fairly frequently in search of their favorite programs, radio listeners are much more likely to be loyal to one or two stations. What kinds of people listen to which stations is well-documented through periodic surveys, though often common sense is an adequate guide. If the music featured is of the "oldies but goodies" variety, a particular type of person is likely to be tuned in. The same is true of rock 'n' roll, classical, country-western, and so on. Spanish-language stations are an obvious example, and talk radio has its own clientele. For each, a different type of message can be prepared, keyed to that audience's interests. Radio has yet another advantage: The content of what is being communicated is better remembered than on television. And a low-cost, 60-second commercial, which allows more to be said, becomes feasible.

Radio is present almost everywhere. Most homes have several—in the family room, the kitchen, the bedrooms. Portables are carried to sporting events, parks, and beaches. Most cars have one, and for those caught up in urban rush hour traffic, radio is an ever-present companion—a companion through which the campaign message can be delivered.

## Direct Mail

Of all the means of communicating with the electorate, direct mail may have made the greatest advances in recent years. Mailing campaign brochures ensures hitting the targeted audience—and only that audience—every time. These mailings are carefully designed for maximum positive effect. They are usually colorful in order to attract attention, they make extensive use of pictures showing the candidate with members of the target group, they employ a good deal of what is called white space, which contains no printing, thus reducing the amount of reading required, and they prominently display the name of the person running on both front and back so that even if the brochure is tossed away immediately the name will be remembered.

The first uses of direct mail employed a single brochure sent to all voters. Today, different mailers are sent to different groups. A student of voting age may receive a mailer specifically created to appeal to student concerns, whereas other brochures, quite different in focus, will go to union members or those who rent apartments. Clinton Reilly, the prominent San Francisco political consultant, described one contest in which 33 different mailers were employed in a single campaign. By using computer-generated mailing lists based on 160 categories, it is possible to identify all single women living in apartments in the Richmond area and send them a brochure designed to appeal specifically to them. Or the prospective audience can be gays with college degrees living in condominiums in Laguna Beach.

Particularly helpful in this process is a system first developed in 1978 called PRIZM. The underlying assumption of the PRIZM system is that people with similar interests tend to live in clusters. By identifying what kinds of people live where, it is possible to develop campaign messages for those living in such clusters. A few of the many categories used in the system include: "furs and station wagons" (well-educated, affluent, mobile professionals with teenage children living in the suburbs); "shotguns and pickups" (small-town, outdoors-loving, blue-collar workers with school-age children); "Bohemian mix" (integrated singles neighborhoods with generally well-fixed residents, heavy with academics, writers, and artists); and "Hispanic mix" (urban, densely populated bilingual Latino neighborhoods with large families of small children, and a high percentage of new immigrants). Knowing that central Los Angeles is high in the "Hispanic mix" or that many communities in the Central Valley have concentrations of those in the "shotguns and pickups" category makes targeting, especially through television, which is less selective than radio or direct mail, more effective.

A different kind of direct mail is the *slate mailer*. These are the often multicolored brochures that flood into mail boxes the weeks before an election urging support of this candidate or opposition to that proposition. They use imagery that implies they are official party organizations. An example is one that used a title "Your Republican Voter Guide" and had a picture of Ronald Reagan on the front along with the outline of an elephant. It had no official standing and was, in fact, a series of endorsements that had been paid for by those endorsed. Endorsements for statewide office run as high as $100,000. The law requires that these are acknowledged on the brochure but standard practice has been to place the disclaimer, in tiny print, on the back of the brochure at the bottom. The voters, convinced this was deceitful, approved Proposition 34, which required that the brochures carry disclaimers in bold face print. This was challenged in state court on the grounds that the larger print took up space that could be used for political expression. It should be noted there are slate mailers that do not charge for their endorsements. These are sent to special groups such as gun owners, teachers, union members, and the like with the intent to get those candidates favorable to the group's goals elected to office.

## Print Media

A long-time favorite means of reaching the voter, newspapers have been considered less important as the role of electronic media has grown. As noted earlier, most of us get most of our news from television; even those who read the papers tend to turn to the sports or entertainment sections, bypassing any "hard" news about politics. Newspapers continue to play a significant role, however. Opinion leaders are more likely to depend on them because coverage of issues is given in some depth, whereas television, with its time limitations, tends toward what former CBS news anchor Dan Rather has called "headline reading." One study pointed out that the entire script of a half-hour national newscast can be printed on two-thirds of the front page of the *New York Times*. Therefore, the opinions of those more likely to influence others are affected by newspaper coverage.

Newspaper endorsements are still sought, especially in races in which the candidates are not well-known or, as in most local elections, the cue of party label is absent. The influence of such publications as the *Los Angeles Times*, the Sacramento, Modesto, and Fresno *Bees*, the *San Diego Union*, the *Orange County Register*, and the *San Francisco Chronicle* on such races is considerable. Organizational endorsements are also valued. Police and fire associations; ethnic groups such as the National Association for the Advancement of Colored People (NAACP) and the Mexican-American Political Association (MAPA); professional and economic organizations such as the California State Employees Association (CSEA), California Teachers Association (CTA), and the California Farm Bureau Federation; and environmentalist groups such as the Sierra Club regularly urge their members to support candidates for office. Traditional newspaper advertisements featuring slogans and candidate positions are generally less effective than advertisements listing support for a candidate from several major groups. For voters who know little about the qualifications and positions of the contestants, such endorsements provide a handy guide when voting.

## The Dark Side

American politics has long had its perversions. Mudslinging was not invented in the mid-twentieth century. Modern means of communication have simply made it more evident and, it must be added, more sophisticated. Negative campaigning, which emphasizes the faults of the opponent rather than one's own virtues, is not necessarily dirty. Condemning a policy position or vote cast is part of the give and take of politics, though some believe that so much negative campaigning may help to account for declining voter participation.

Critics of modern campaigning point to two major areas of concern: the tendency toward oversimplification and an increasing use of the half-truth or outright lie in the scramble for votes. The first criticism arises from the impact of television with its focus on short, snappy "bites." A serious address on tax policy may be summarized in a single sentence alleging a "taxpayer ripoff," ignoring the careful analysis that led to it. Speechwriters know this and include such "bites" in their scripts to secure time on television newscasts. The more outrageous and simplistic the statement, the better the chance it will make it on the air.

The second point critics make centers on what most consider dirty politics. Direct mail has been used to make slashing attacks on opponents, attacks that may have no basis in fact. An example is a mailer sent out just before the June 1982 primary. In a hotly contested race to gain the Democratic nomination in a Southern California congressional district composed largely of Hispanics, one candidate sent a mailer accusing his opponent of not being married to the woman with whom he had lived for over 25 years. Among Hispanics with their strong sense of family, this was a devastating charge—and one that was totally false. Sent over the last weekend before the election, it caused what had been a fairly large lead virtually to disappear, though the victim of this smear did manage to pull out a narrow victory. At the height of the special election campaign of 2005, a mailer sent targeting black voters that endorsed the pharmaceutical industry's drug prescription plan for seniors and the poor. Pictures of a dozen black legislators were featured, implying support. In actuality, many supported a rival proposition opposed by the industry. One black legislator described this tactic as "political skullduggery."

Political messages, both in print and on radio and television, regularly resort to highly selective use of facts, uses that are at the least misleading and at worst involve out and out lies. Which applies to the following, chosen from the 2005 special election campaign?

- A teacher's statement supporting Governor Schwarzenegger's *budget cutting* Proposition 76, claiming it would "free up" more funds for schools.
- Two anti-Proposition 77 commercials that warned of a "power grab by politicians" seeking to change the way election district lines are drawn when the state legislature, composed of politicians, had created districts so safe no one could challenge the incumbents, thus taking choice away from the voters and seen by many as a true "power grab."
- Some television commercials did not even bother to say what was in the targeted proposition, relying on emotion-laden words to encourage a certain vote. Several commercials on radio and television warned of the influence of "special interests" when labor unions or businesses themselves paid for the ads, qualifying as a special interests.

The last type obviously is less a distortion than the first two, but can hardly be said to be educational. Though used only by implication in 2005, some seemed to portray a contest between good and evil with not a single reference to the proposition being praised or attacked.

Earlier examples that could be cited include a 1998 mailer that asserted an opponent was facing "voter fraud, tax fraud, conspiracy, and perjury charges." Only by reading the fine print inside did one learn these "charges" had not been levied by some government agency, but by the candidate's opponent, the one sending the mailer.

The "truth boxes" or "ad watches" found in some newspapers that analyze television commercials for the accuracy of their assertions are useful antidotes when hyperbole or distortion goes too far.

## Controls on Campaign Contributions and Spending

California has strict laws requiring detailed disclosure of money received and spent by candidates for state and local office, by committees acting on their behalf, and by committees supporting or opposing ballot propositions. The purpose of these laws, according to the Political Reform Act of 1974, is to assure "that the voters may be fully informed and improper practices may be inhibited." The Reform Act, a legislative initiative passed by California voters during the height of national furor over the Watergate scandals, also attempted to put limits on campaign expenditures under the premise that "state and local government should serve all citizens equally without regard to their wealth."[6]

California is easily the most expensive state in which to run for office. The number of people to be reached, their great mobility, and the geographic extent of the state all combine to make the use of television, radio, and direct mail virtually mandatory in statewide contests and in many regional and municipal campaigns as well. All this costs a great deal, and these costs have been increasing at a rate many candidates find alarming. Statewide campaigns are of course the most expensive, at least when there is some possibility that either of the major contenders might win. In the general election campaign of 1986, the two major party candidates together spent $15.7 million. In 1998, Gray Davis and Dan Lungren spent a total of $52.5 million, an increase of $21 million in just four years. In 2002 Gray Davis and Bill Simon approached spending $100 million.

Many legislators had grown weary of having to spend so much time on fund raising and were also sensitive to the bad press they had received because of it. For several years, California Common Cause and the League of Women Voters have been pressing for reforms to curb the influence of big money in elections, including the financing of campaigns. A 1983 California law allowed individuals to contribute to the party of their choice with a nondeductible donation at the time they pay their income taxes. However, this has proved an inadequate incentive. As a result, several bills have been introduced in the legislature—all unsuccessful—to allow donations to political parties to be deducted from taxes and for such funds to be given to candidates on a matching basis.

Public concern with what was perceived to be too great an influence by special interests on elections and policy making has led to several propositions being placed on the ballot to curb campaign contributions. Two approved in 1988 were struck

---

[6]*Political Reform Act of 1974* (Sacramento: State Printing Office, 1974), p. 5.

down by the courts for several reasons, one being that the larger vote getter pre-empted the second only to see that proposition largely voided as well as unfair to challengers in limiting the period for fund raising.

In 1996 the voters approved Proposition 208, another attempt at campaign finance reform. It set voluntary limits on spending that varied with the office sought. For example, a candidate could spend up to $150,000 running for the assembly in the primary and up to $200,000 in the general election. Gubernatorial candidates were limited to $6 million in the primary and $8 million in the general. (It is worth noting for comparison purposes that this is less than one-third of the amount actu-ally spent by the gubernatorial candidates in the 1998 general election.) However, once again the courts intervened, a federal judge holding that these limits were too low and violated the First Amendment by preventing effective communication between candidates and the public. Contribution limits were also voided. Public concerns over special interest influence remained. A Field Poll taken late in 1999 found 70 percent of the public believed special interests had more influence on legis-lators than the voters.

In 2000 voters tried again, passing Proposition 34 by a wide margin. This again set limits on fund raising and "voluntary limits" on expenditures, the latter modeled after federal law that has passed muster before the United State Supreme Court. The limits were in each instance higher than those in Proposition 208. For example, in 208 the limit of $200,000 in the general election for the assembly was by Proposition 34 raised to $700,000. The gubernatorial limit of $8 million in 208 was upped to $10 million, still, however, quite short of what had been spent in the 1998 campaign. Of course these were voluntary, but the inducements to abide by them were felt by many to be rather pallid. They included being identified on the voter pamphlet as having done so and being made eligible to purchase space on the pamphlet for a statement in support of the candidacy. Along with spending limits came contribution limits. For governor, an individual could give no more than $20,000, for assembly member $3,000. Both of these are higher than under 208 and contributions to political parties rather than candidates were not limited at all.

There was one loophole in Proposition 34—or at least one that the state Fair Political Practices Commission placed in it. The commission held that the contribu-tion limits did not apply to campaign committees set up before January 1, 2001. That is, at least for now, an enormous advantage to incumbents whose committees had over challenger committees that were not. A report in June 2002 said that legis-lators had held 240 fund raisers in the first six months of that year with most having a tab of $1,000. Assembly Speaker Herb Wesson of Los Angeles topped the list with two fund raisers, one in Sacramento that cost $25,000 a head and the other in Los Angeles with a tab of $10,000. The record to date involved a golf tournament. Cost to participate? $30,000.

The more normal activities still take place, of course. But these fund raisers place a considerable burden on lobbyists' employers and their pocketbooks. Yet if the game is to be played, if you are to benefit from "the returned phone call" or by having "access" to key legislative leaders, these "voluntary" contributions are a price that has to be paid.

# REVIEW QUESTIONS

1. What are the qualifications needed to vote in California's elections? (pp. 66–68)
2. Democrats and Republicans do not employ the same procedures in the selection of delegates to their respective presidential nominating conventions. How do they differ and what impact was expected from moving the primary to early March from its previous date in June? (p. 74)
3. What are the various kinds of polls and what functions do each fulfill? (p. 81)
4. What are the advantages and disadvantages in using television, radio, direct mail, and newspapers in campaigns? Which are the most effective in "targeting"? (pp. 82–85)
5. Public concern with the rising cost of election campaigns is related to the influence perceived to be brought on the legislative process by special interests. Explain. (pp. 87–88)

# SELECTED WEB SITES

As with political parties and pressure groups, there are many web sites devoted to tracking elections, providing information on candidates and their backgrounds, and for incumbents, their voting records. Financial records provide information on major contributors. In addition, there is a growing number of sites sponsored by individual candidates.

Campaign finance information, including the sources of contributions, may be found on the secretary of state's web site, www.ss.ca.gov. Other sites dealing with this subject include the Center for Public Integrity at www.publicintegrity.org, National Institute on Money in State Politics, www.followthemoney.org, the Center for Responsive Politics at www.opensecrets.org and www.electiontrack.com.

Following politics and government in California has been made easier with the creation of Rough and Tumble, www.rtumble.com, a site that provides a review of all stories on the subject every day. Articles from newspapers across the state and nation are reproduced. Other specific sites include www.latimes.com, www.sfgate.com (the *San Francisco Examiner and Chronicle*), www.merccenter.com (*San Jose Mercury News*), www.hotco.com (the *Contra Costa Times*), www.ocregister.com (*Orange County Register*), www.sacbee.com (the *Sacramento Bee*), www.around the capitol.com for "campaign gossip" and other items of interest concerning Sacramento politics.

# SELECTED REFERENCES

Borland, John, "Let the Games Begin," *California Journal,* November 1996.
Campaigning in California" *California Journal,* current ed., Sacramento: California Journal Press, no date.
Cook, Gale, "Mail Order Voters Tip the Balance in Close Elections," *California Journal,* February 1991.
Guber, Susan, *How to Win Your 1st Election,* Del Rey Beach, FL: St. Lucie's Press, 1997.
Martin, Hugo, "Campaign Smear Victims Left With Little Protection," *Los Angeles Times,* April 8, 1999.
Ostrom, Mary Anne, "State Focuses on Update of Flawed Punch Cards," *San Jose Mercury News,* November 22, 2000.

Padmanabhan, Sekhar, "Calls for Cash: They Keep Coming," *California Journal,* August 1999.

Salladay, Robert, "Fund Raising Hits Pay Dirt: Politicians Go for the Gold," *San Francisco Chronicle,* August 22, 1999.

Savage, David G., "Justices Reject State's 'Blanket Primary' Law," *Los Angeles Times,* June 27, 2000.

Trent, Judith, and Robert V. Friedenberg, *Political Campaign Communication,* New York; Praeger, 2000.

Zeigler, Richard, "Few Citizens Make Decisions for Everyone," *California Journal,* November 1990.

Chapter

# 5

---

# Referendum, Initiative, and Recall: Democracy Through Petition

Proposition 13, the Jarvis-Gann initiative passed in 1978 limiting property taxes, brought nationwide attention to the importance of the petition process for direct democracy in California. Under this procedure the people themselves make their own laws rather than relying solely on legislative bodies for the formulation of public policy. Furthermore, by means of the recall petition voters may remove from office any elected official before the expiration of the term. For over 90 years Californians have been making major governmental decisions at almost every election.

Popular petition for legislation and the recall of elected officials, along with the direct primary and cross-filing, were part of the reform program sponsored by the Progressives to rid the state of control by political bosses and the railroad machine. In California the movement was championed by the Direct Legislation League, headed by the prominent Los Angeles physician John Randolph Haynes. At the instigation of Haynes and his associates, petition devices were adopted in several cities, including Los Angeles and San Francisco, from 1902 to 1910. The election campaign of the Progressives in 1910 contained the promise to institute a statewide initiative and referendum system. Upon election Governor Hiram Johnson sponsored a series of constitutional amendments that, when approved by the voters in 1911, extended the initiative, referendum, and recall to the state and to local governments that had not yet adopted the system. California is now among 17 states where both initiative and referendum may be employed on a statewide basis. Only

19 states, including California, allow for the recall of both state and local elected officials.[1] Though often controversial, the processes of direct democracy remain popular. A poll taken late in 2005 found that 48 percent of those questioned believed the public made better decisions on policy issues than elected officials. Only 30 percent thought officials did a better job. With specific reference to the initiative, however, only 10 percent indicated they were "very satisfied" with the way it was being used, the most often expressed complaint being that special interests were too influential in the process. A huge 83 percent supported some version of the indirect initiative (see below).

## REFERENDUM BY PETITION

Referendum by petition is used to prevent laws already passed by the legislature and signed by the governor (or passed over the governor's veto) from going into effect. This should not be confused with the so-called compulsory referendum, whereby constitutional amendments and bond issues passed by the legislature must always be approved by the people in order to become law. Referendum by petition is a popular device for *interrupting* the normal legislative process. Any law passed by the legislature may be held up on referendum, "except urgency statutes, statutes calling elections, and statutes providing for tax levies or appropriations for usual current expenses of the State."[2]

### Procedure

To prevent a statute from taking effect, a petition bearing the signatures of registered voters amounting to at least 5 percent of the vote cast for governor in the last election must be filed with the secretary of state. The filing must take place within a 90-day period after the enactment of the bill at a regular session or 91 days after a special session. If the petition qualifies, the act to which it refers is not enforced until the next election when the people have a chance to accept or reject it.

Before each election, voters receive in the mail (along with their sample ballot) a booklet containing all of the ballot propositions with arguments pro and con. These arguments are written by legislators or citizens whom the presiding officer of the senate or assembly has designated as a legitimate spokesperson for each side. At the polls a majority of "yes" votes allows the measure to become law; a majority of "no" votes defeats the measure.

### Extent Used

During the first 30 years of its use in California, the popular referendum was applied to 34 legislative acts. Twenty-one of them were voted down by the people. During the next 40 years and until 1982 only one referendum proposition appeared on the

---

[1] *The Book of the States, 1998–99* (Lexington, KY: Council of State Governments, 1998).
[2] Constitution of the State of California, Article II, section 9.

ballot: a legislative act that exempted nonprofit private and religious schools from the property tax was held up by a referendum petition only to be approved by the voters at the 1952 election. In 1982 Republicans registered their protest of the Democrat-controlled Reapportionment Act of 1980 by placing three referendum measures on the June 1982 ballot. All three were approved by the voters, and thus the Democratic reapportionment plans for congressional, state senate, and state assembly districts were invalidated. In the same election, another referendum measure that would authorize a peripheral canal across the Sacramento-San Joaquin delta was disapproved by the voters.

At the 2000 primary the referendum by petition was used by insurance companies to invalidate two recently adopted laws that would have allowed "third party suits" against them for failure to deal with claims in good faith. The interesting slant in this case involved the companies seeking to *void* these laws by placing on the ballot propositions that would *ratify* them. The strategy was based on history that showed that a "no" vote was likely to succeed where those on that side substantially outspent the "yes" side. The insurance companies did just that, spending over $50 million and successfully canceling the laws by a 2–1 margin.

The short time limit given referendum petition circulation before a legislative statute goes into operation has made the referendum much more difficult to qualify than an initiative. Thus those who disagree with legislative policy find the direct initiative a more suitable and feasible means to employ.

## DIRECT INITIATIVE

Through the direct-initiative method, groups of people (often organized interest groups) originate and pass laws and constitutional amendments without recourse to the legislature. No subjects are exempted from the direct initiative. The only constitutional restriction is that a given initiative proposal must deal with only one main subject.[3] The governor may not veto an initiative measure.

### Procedure

The sponsors of a direct initiative may draft their proposal as either a statute or a constitutional amendment. However, under the 1966 revision of the state constitution the petition for a constitutional amendment must be signed by a number of registered voters equal to at least 8 percent of the vote cast for all candidates for governor in the last gubernatorial election; the required number of signatures for a statutory initiative, on the other hand, is 5 percent of the total votes in the last gubernatorial election. (In 2006, the number of signatures required to qualify a constitutional amendment was 598,105 and for a statutory initiative it was 373,846.) Despite this fact, more direct initiatives have been constitutional amendments than

---

[3] A motion to disqualify the Jarvis-Gann initiative on the basis that it covered more than one subject was denied by the courts.

statutes, because constitutional amendments, once enacted, are more difficult to amend or repeal, because they require a two-thirds majority vote of both houses of the legislature and a subsequent majority vote of the electorate for any constitutional change. A statutory initiative may be amended or repealed by a *simple* majority vote of the legislature and an approval by the electors unless the statutory initiative permits amendment or repeal without their approval.

The draft of a proposed initiative is sent to the secretary of state for recording and is then referred to the attorney general, who must approve the official title and add a brief description of the initiative. A maximum of 150 days is allowed for sponsors to secure the required number of signatures. Once the necessary signatures are secured, the petition is transmitted to the secretary of state for final verification of the signatures and placement on the ballot.

The title of the initiative measure, its summary, which is prepared by the legislative analyst, its complete text, and its arguments pro and con appear in the ballot booklet and is sent to all registered voters in advance of the election. If the measure receives a majority affirmative vote, it becomes law. A law thus passed may not be amended or repealed by the legislature (unless so provided in the measure) without approval by the voters. In the event that conflicting initiative measures appear on the same ballot and are passed, the one receiving the highest vote becomes law.

## Extent Used

During the first four decades of initiative activity (1912–1950) some 40–70 initiative petitions were circulated in every ten-year period, slightly more than half of them qualified for the ballot, and about one-third were approved by the voters. In the 1950s and 1960s only 55 initiatives were proposed, with 21 qualifying for the ballot, and only 5 were approved. However, beginning in 1970 California experienced a tremendous increase in the use of the initiative, because numerous ballot measures have been proposed by elected officials, special-interest groups, citizen organizations, and citizens with pet projects trying to reform government and the way of life. The peak for initiatives up until now came in 1988 and 1990 when 12 and 13 appeared on the respective November ballots. The explosion in the use of the direct initiative is shown by the following figures: in the 1960s there were 47 initiative petitions circulated, 16 qualified for ballot, and 6 were approved. In the 1990s, 333 were circulated, 49 qualified, and 16 were approved. The trend continued in 2000 with 65 circulated, 11 qualified, and 3 approved. This flood is even greater when local measures are added. San Francisco is notorious for placing a dozen or two measures before the voters. In 1993, for example, residents found Proposition BB, which asked approval for a police officer to carry a ventriloquist's dummy with him while on patrol. The dummy won.

Initiatives have covered an extremely wide range of subjects over the years. One early use dealt with Prohibition. More recently there have been initiatives concerning possession and use of marijuana, limitations on affirmative action, extension of the death penalty, gun control, clear-cutting of forests, taxes on tobacco products, English as the state's official language, physician-assisted death, casino gambling, abortion, and term limits for elected officials, to mention only a few of the controversial propositions.

# INITIATIVE AND REFERENDUM
# IN COUNTIES AND CITIES

## Procedure

As already noted, the initiative and referendum as petition devices were adopted by cities before they were instituted by the state and included in the state constitution. As revised in 1966, the state constitution now provides that "initiative and referendum powers may be exercised by the electors of each city or county under procedures that the legislature shall provide." This section does not affect a city having a charter.[4] Under present legislative requirements most cities and counties are prevented by state law from requiring more than 15 percent of their electors' signatures to qualify an initiative or more than 10 percent to qualify a referendum. The usual practice is for local governments to require signatures equal to 10 percent of the vote in the last general election for initiative petitions. The time allowed for securing signatures is longer than that for statewide petitions. Completed local petitions may be presented to city councils and county boards of supervisors for their action. If the proposal is approved, a direct vote of the electors is not necessary. Many of the noncontroversial measures are adopted in this manner. In most jurisdictions financial matters and public works are not subject to popular petition.

## Extent Used

The referendum and initiative have been more frequently used on a statewide basis than locally. On the local level they have been used more often in the more populous cities and counties. The rule at work seems to be that there is less need for direct legislation when government is close to the people.

Worthy of special note was the 2002 general election in San Francisco. With 19 local propositions, one regional proposition, and seven state issues to be voted on, along with the election of statewide officials, members of Congress, state legislators and local officials, the voter pamphlet (which in San Francisco may carry paid ballot arguments on local issues) was well over 300 pages. This is truly a test of endurance as well as of citizenship.

Subjects put before local voters by petitioners have included police officers' and fire-fighters' salaries and pensions, garbage and refuse collections, and regulation of liquor establishments and dance halls. Other topics have included bond issues, policies toward the homeless, water policy, and issues involving public power. At the special election of 2005, San Francisco voters voted to ban all handguns from the city as well as possession or sale of ammunition.

# EVALUATION OF THE INITIATIVE AND REFERENDUM

California's experience with direct-legislation devices, especially in recent years, has highlighted many features unforeseen by the Progressives who championed the 1911 constitutional amendments. Much could not be foreseen, because the "great game of

---

[4]Constitution of the State of California, Article II, section 11.

politics" has been transformed dramatically since the days of Hiram Johnson and the Lincoln-Roosevelt league. Thus some of the criticisms against the initiative and referendum are new and cannot be dismissed by reference to the standard theories of democratic government and popular sovereignty. Other criticisms, however, are perennial, recurring each time the matter comes up for discussion. Yet a balanced evaluation must grant the possibility that even the old criticisms may assume a new validity with changing conditions. The arguments, pro and con, are discussed in the following areas of concern.

## Voter Confusion

A long list of complicated fiscal, administrative, and technical matters frequently confronts voters as ballot initiatives. Many do not have the time, the training, or the inclination to cast informed votes on such issues as judicial procedures, insurance practices, and reapportionment of legislative districts, or attempt to understand the intricacies of environmental protection, all of which have appeared on the California ballot. To add to the confusion, there has been an expanded use of what are termed "counter-initiatives" in recent years. A proposition dealing with a subject such as campaign finance reform is placed on the ballot. A second proposition dealing with that subject is put on the same ballot, typically, though not always, with the intent of confusing the voters, who, in their confusion, vote "no" on both. Intended or not, that was the effect in 2005 when the pharmaceutical industry placed a second measure of

"The woods are full of 'em." (Bastion, *San Francisco Chronicle*)

the ballot to compete with one sponsored by consumer groups designed to address the high cost of drugs for seniors and the poor. Whatever the intent, both lost.

The voter pamphlet (occasionally more like a book) the voters receive in the mail before each election can help, but it is often written in legalese and its very size, with many pages devoted to the texts of the propositions in small print, is daunting. For the November 1990 election, voters were asked to read 222 pages of material before casting their ballots! The arguments given are so at odds with one another (at times from highly respected experts on *both* sides) and are at times so guilty of hyperbole the voters are turned off. Thirty-second television commercials proclaim a great future or an unprecedented disaster, this on the same proposition. The 1986 toxic waste disposal proposition, Proposition 65, was going to clean up the environment and make it safe or it would drive farmers out of business. In 1996, proponents of Proposition 215, which attempted to legalize the medicinal use of marijuana, argued its usefulness in relieving suffering from AIDS, radiation treatments for cancer, and the pressure on the eye from glaucoma. Opponents claimed it was a back door attempt to legalize general use of the drug and would lead to greater use of hard drugs such as cocaine and heroin.

In rebuttal to the argument that citizens are asked to vote on measures that are too complicated for them to be able to evaluate wisely, it is contended that the experience is good for them: It contributes to their civic education. In answer to the charge that in initiative and referendum campaigns voters are made captives of the public relations consultants hired by pressure groups, it can be observed that misleading advertising is not a problem exclusive to the area of direct legislation. Although in recent years the public relations people are frequently found in the coaching box during political campaigns, the basic question is really how to secure an enlightened public opinion in this age of mass communications.

Often voters *do* appear to discriminate between proposals on the same subject, as they did in 1988 when they approved one of five propositions dealing with automobile insurance on the same ballot. In 1996 two initiatives dealing with campaign finance reform were voted on; one lost while the other won handily. In 2002 one proposition diverting general fund monies for after-school programs won while another that would have rewarded contributors to its campaign with millions of dollars in projects lost.

In recent years voter cynicism concerning this procedure may have been given a booster shot by repeated court interventions into propositions approved by the electorate. Proposition 103 guaranteed a 20 percent reduction in auto insurance; the courts held insurance companies had a right to receive a fair return on their investment, nullifying the guarantee. In 1994 Californians overwhelmingly approved Proposition 187 denying a variety of services to illegal immigrants. Suits immediately tied that measure up in court for years with Governor Davis ultimately deciding to cease the fight to restore it. Two years later the voters saw three measures they passed, Proposition 208 on campaign finance reform, Proposition 209 limiting state affirmative action programs, and the aforementioned Proposition 215, challenged and effectively barred from implementation by court action. Those bringing suit noted, however, that no law, approved by no matter how large a majority, can be allowed to stand if in violation of basic constitutional principles. At issue in these instances was what were these principles and how are they to be interpreted?

## High Costs

Perhaps the most severe criticism of the initiative and referendum is that the expense of petition circulation and ballot proposition campaigns discourages all except highly organized special-interest groups from using them. With the state's continued growth, these requirements almost certainly will increase. With the big numbers involved these days a new industry has developed: Companies that specialize in circulating petitions to get propositions on the ballot. Paid by the signature (from 65 cents to as much as $6 each though usually around $1.50 apiece), they will work for any cause and may even carry petitions for opposing interests. They focus on malls, markets, racetracks, anywhere people move slowly, and usually have little understanding of the issues they are pushing. If it takes too long to explain, profits go down. The average cost of qualifying an initiative now runs in excess of $1,000,000.

In January 1999, the United States Supreme Court struck down rules that had governed those who are professional signature gatherers. In an earlier ruling the Court had held it was legal to pay such persons and in this case went further, asserting state laws requiring that those circulating petitions had to be registered voters in the state were unconstitutional. The immediate reaction of state officials was that this decision would act to "further commercialize" the procedure.

Then comes the campaign. Costs are enormous in a state as large—and as media conscious—as California. Television is crucial in many cases; radio and direct mail important in virtually all successful efforts (see Chapter 4). Millions are spent to convince or dissuade the voters by using 30-second television spots focused on imagery and slogans. Up until 1998 the height of prolific spending had taken place ten years earlier when there were five initiatives on the ballot dealing with auto insurance. One report showed the contending special interests, primarily insurance companies and trial lawyers, spent over $80 million on a losing campaign. (The winner, Proposition 103, was backed by Ralph Nader and that campaign cost less than $3 million.) The total spent on all 28 measures that year was $133.4 million. That amount paled in comparison with the flood of cash spent on the more controversial propositions at the 2005 special election. Public employee unions spent well over $80 million to defeat Governor Schwarzenegger's four "reform" initiatives and the pharmaceutical industry paid out $80 million to sell its positions on two propositions. In all some $230 million was spent, much to the delight of television stations and campaign consultants around the state.

Money does not always win elections, as shown by Proposition 103. However, one estimate from California Common Cause is that in the contests with a substantial difference in the amounts spent, in roughly 90 percent of such cases the side with the bigger checkbook has won. That usually means special interests have put a great deal of money into the electoral pot. Examples of campaigns that resulted in losses for the underfinanced side include an antismoking initiative in 1980 (Proposition 10), a gun-control measure in 1982 (Proposition 15), the school voucher initiative in the special election in 1993 (Proposition 174), and the afore-mentioned "third party" suits ban in 2000 (Propositions 30 and 31).

## Radical and Irresponsible Legislation

There is the possibility that an initiative or referendum measure will be hastily pre-pared with more emotion than reason in order to take advantage of a given situation. Sponsors representing narrow interests promote their own causes without regard for the general welfare of the public. With a well-organized and effective campaign a proposal could be approved by a majority of the voters, and once the legislation was passed, the sponsors would have no more responsibility for the political and social consequences of their proposal, for it would now become the duty of the legislature, the governor, and the courts to enforce and implement the initiative or referendum. Critics of direct legislation point out that under these conditions the very fabric of legislative processes and representative government is being threatened.

Supporters of the initiative and referendum respond by emphasizing that the purpose of direct legislation is to act as a check on the legislature, not to replace rep-resentative government. Public and special-interest groups employ the initiative and referendum to raise important issues after failing to receive satisfaction from the leg-islature. People go through this difficult process because they feel the legislature has not done its job.

As far as the criticism relating to radical and hastily drawn proposals is con-cerned, it can be shown that very few measures of this type have been successful. Proposals for the single tax, for instance, have been turned down six times by the voters. An initiative making radical changes and providing for unreasonably large pension payments, although originally approved under the McLain plan in 1948, was repealed by a subsequent initiative and voted down by the electorate. In fact, the voting record of the public stands up well. The California voters have approved only about one-third of the measures submitted through the petition process. Among those that have been accepted are some highly regarded public policies such as the merit system for government employees, a centralized executive budget, state finan-cial support of elementary and secondary schools, and coastline conservation. Were it left to the legislature, these reforms might never have come about.

## Proposals for Reform

Today Hiram Johnson would not recognize the system he proposed in 1911 as a means of breaking the special-interest influence on the state's legislative process. Largely because of the large amounts of money necessary to qualify and to secure a favorable vote for the initiative, the will of special interests has most frequently prevailed.

Scholars and representatives of public-interest groups such as Common Cause have suggested several reforms to restore the process to its original intent. Among the ideas are: limiting the number of initiatives on any one ballot, limiting the subjects that can be addressed, increasing the number of signatures required on petitions, and limiting those paid to circulate petitions. A state commission in 1994 proposed extending the period for circulating petitions from 150 to 180 days to give volunteer-based efforts (as opposed to paid efforts by professionals) a more level playing field. The commission also suggested listing in the ballot pamphlet and on the ballot the names of the five biggest contributors to a campaign to increase voter awareness.

One reform was undertaken by the California State Supreme Court in 1991. The justices invoked a constitutional requirement that holds initiatives must deal with one subject, not a variety of them. Proposition 105, known as the "truth in advertising" initiative, was approved by the voters in 1990 but the court ruled that while all its provisions dealt with informing the public (publishing the health and safety records of nursing homes, warnings on products that should not be poured down the drain, requiring companies to say whether they had investments in South Africa, etc.), the scope of the proposition was so broad virtually anything could be included, ". . . essentially obliterating the constitutional requirement." The state supreme court took the rare step of removing from the March 2000 ballot Proposition 24, a measure that would have lowered legislative salaries and changed the means of redrawing election district lines on the grounds the proposition violated the single subject rule.

One of the most prominent and controversial proposals as advanced by the League of Women Voters would allow initiatives to go straight to the legislature for vote instead of to the ballot. If the legislature approved, and upon being signed by the governor, the measure would become law, eliminating the need for a costly and time-consuming campaign. However, if the legislature added amendments that the backers did not like, or if the legislature refused to approve the initiative, it would be referred to the electorate for vote. This process, known as the "indirect initiative," was on California's books between 1912 and 1966.

## RECALL

By means of the recall, voters in California may remove from office any *elected* state official before the expiration of his or her term. A proposition approved by the voters in 1974 provided that all elected state and local officials are subject to recall at any time after their election. In contrast to an impeached official (for whom a misdemeanor is the required indictment for removal), the recalled official need not have violated any law.

## Signatures Required

To recall an official elected by the entire state, the petition must be signed by registered voters equal to at least 12 percent of the total vote cast in the last election for the office involved. The petition must also contain signatures of voters in at least five counties equal to not less than 1 percent of the vote cast for the office in each of these counties.

If the recall involves state officials elected by districts (members of the legislature, district courts of appeal judges, and members of the Board of Equalization), the petition must contain signatures of voters in the district equal to at least 20 percent of the vote cast for the office in the last election. Because of the large number of signatures required for a recall of state officials, this process is rarely used.

## Procedure

The procedure for circulating the recall petition and verifying the signatures is the same as that for referendum and initiative petitions, except that proponents have a 160-day time limit for filing signed petitions. The recall petition must contain a statement of grounds for removal, but because there is no requirement for specific charges, the petition may, in fact, say no more than "we don't like the way the official is performing." Upon certification of the petition by the secretary of state, the governor is required to call an election to take place within 180 days from the date of qualification.

Candidates who want to replace the official to be recalled are required to file a petition 25 days before the election, signed by at least 1 percent of the vote cast for that office at the last election.

If the recall fails, the state reimburses the incumbent for election expenses incurred, and another recall election of this individual may not be initiated until six months after the election.

## Extent Used

Only one recall of a statewide officer has actually been on the ballot, mainly because of the large number of signatures necessary to qualify the petition. Among those who have been subject to recall petitions are Governor Ronald Reagan (1967, 1968, 1972), Governor Jerry Brown (1979, 1980), Chief Justice Rose Bird (1981, 1982), and Governor Pete Wilson (1991, 1992). None of these petitions secured the necessary signatures to qualify for the ballot. Recall efforts brought against state legislators have proven almost as futile.

The most famous recall, in this or any other state, was the one that removed Governor Gray Davis from office in 2004 (see Chapter 3).

## Recall of Local Officials

As with direct legislation, local governments may set their own recall procedures under general requirements of the state legislature. Local governments are prohibited from requiring petition signatures equal to more than 25 percent of the vote cast in the previous election for the office involved. The number varies depending on whether the recall is for a county office, city council, or a school or special district office. If enough signatures are secured, an election is called and a ballot prepared asking, "Shall (name of official) be removed from the office of (title)?" A majority of "yes" votes removes the public official from office. Most local jurisdictions allow voters to select a successor by plurality vote from a list of persons who have qualified to run if the recall succeeds. A state law prohibits a recalled official from being a candidate to succeed himself. In addition, the state legislature has ruled that in city recall elections voters may not simultaneously choose a successor—either the city council appoints a successor or the voters choose one at a later election.

Local recall attempts have taken place frequently in California. They have focused on judges ("soft" on crime, enforcing school busing), city council members, county supervisors, and those serving on local school boards.

A well-publicized example was the effort in 1983 to recall the then-mayor of San Francisco, Dianne Feinstein. A white supremacist group, the White Panthers, started the petition drive, citing Feinstein's sponsorship of a city ordinance banning handgun ownership. Other groups joined in, including gay rights groups, which sought to oust her for her veto of "domestic partners" legislation that would have given official recognition to homosexual and other unmarried couples. The mayor's supporters pointed to her record on crime and a budget surplus and the recall failed by a 6–1 margin. Another well-publicized effort was directed against State Senator David Roberti in 1994, only months before term limits were to force him out of the senate in any event. Mounted by gun owners opposed to his long-running efforts on behalf of gun control (he was the author of the ban on semiautomatic weapons passed by the legislature in 1989), Roberti easily survived the recall attempt.

## Evaluation of Recall

The generally accepted purpose of the recall is to give the voters a chance to remove from office elected officials who have demonstrated incompetence and corruption but who are not necessarily guilty of criminal action. (When criminal action is involved, the impeachment process may be used.) A brief examination of the issues that have caused recall elections will reveal how well the purpose of the recall in California has been accomplished.

Most of the recall petitions cite causes that are related to corruption, misbehavior, or ineffective administration on the part of elected officials. Charges of bribery, graft, and improper personal conduct are common. Many recalls list unsatisfactory personnel relations as the reason for removing elected officials. For instance, the firing of a city manager or a police chief may cause enough unfavorable public reaction to bring about a recall of members of the city council.

However, some recall movements take place because of the alleged unresponsiveness of the official or officials involved. The charges may be the result of a dispute over a single major policy between the elected officials and some of their constituents. Those who sponsor the recall might even be those who had opposed the incumbent in the previous election. This particular type of recall raises some serious questions, because it may be true that the public good may require leaders who adopt unpopular policies—policies that may be beneficial in future months or even years. It may be argued that voters should employ regular elections, not the recall, to decide policy issues. If the time between elections is too long, the initiative or referendum is available. The threat of removal at any time may make elected public officials reluctant to alienate political factions or organized interests, and a sacrifice of the public good might be the result.

Despite the controversy over the proper use of the recall, there is every indication that it will continue to be popular, particularly with local governments in California.

## REVIEW QUESTIONS

1. When the Progressives initiated the direct democracy procedures described in this chapter, what was their primary goal? Looking at how they have been used in the past 20 to 25 years, do you believe that goal is still being met? Why or why not?
2. What are the problems cited concerning the kinds of issues that have been brought to the people through the direct initiative in recent years? How might reinstitution of the indirect initiative affect these problems? (pp. 96–99)
3. Other than the indirect initiative, what are some of the suggestions that have been made to improve the operation of direct democracy here? (p. 100)
4. Who are subject to recall? What reason was initially given for including this procedure in the package of reforms pushed by the Progressives? What has been the motivation behind recent recall efforts? (pp. 100–102)

## SELECTED WEB SITES

For updates on the status of statewide initiatives and referenda, the secretary of state's site www.ss.ca.gov is a prime source. It lists those in circulation, those pending qualification (the signatures are being processed), those that have qualified, and those that have been withdrawn or failed to qualify.

For a historical look at initiatives since 1944, see www.scu.edu/law/pubs/Props.htm.

For a discussion of how to create an initiative, an interesting description is found in The Initiative Cookbook at www.democracyctr.org/cookbook.htlm.

The speaker of the assembly maintains a web site, www.cainintiative.org, that provides information, reports and evaluations of the initiative process.

Cal Voter puts out a handy summary of propositions that have been before the voters the last eight years.

## SELECTED REFERENCES

Baldassarare, Mark, *California in the New Millennium*, Berkeley and Los Angeles: University of California Press, 2000, Chapters 1–3.

Broder, David, "Californocracy in Action," *Los Angeles Times*, August 13, 1997.

——, *Democracy Derailed*, New York: Harcourt, Inc., 2000.

Cain, Bruce, and Roger G. Noll, eds., *Constitutional Reform in California*, Berkeley: Institute of Governmental Studies Press, 1995.

California Commission on Campaign Financing, *Democracy by Initiative: Shaping California's Fourth Branch of Government*, Los Angeles: Center for Responsive Government, 1992.

Citizen's Commission on Ballot Initiatives, "Report and Recommendations on the Statewide Initiative Process," Sacramento: State of California, 1994.

Dubois, Philip L., and Floyd F. Feeny, *Improving the California Initiative Process: Options for Change,* Berkeley: University of California, 1992.

Ferejohn, John, "Reforming the Initiative Process," in *Constitutional Reform in California,* Berkeley: Institute of Governmental Studies Press, 1995.

Jeffe, Sherry Bebitch, "Risk Wary Voters Look for Security in a 'No' Vote," *Los Angeles Times,* November 7, 1993.

Naisbitt, John, *Megatrends,* New York: Warner Books, 1992.

Price, Charles, "Initiative Reform," *California Journal,* April 1994.

———, "Tracing the Money," *California Journal,* August 1998.

Price, Charles, and Robert Watson, "Initiatives: Too Much of a Good Thing?" in Thomas Hoeber and Larry Gertson, eds., Sacramento: *California Government and Politics Annual,* 1993.

Schrag, Peter, "March of the Plebesites," in *Paradise Lost,* New York: The New Press, 1998.

Scott, Steve, "Ballot Bulge," *California Journal,* July 1996.

Weintraub, Daniel, "The Initiative: Time to Reform the Reformers Tool," *Sacramento Bee,* February 15, 2001.

# Chapter

# 6

# The Legislature

The California legislature plays a vital role in the government and politics of the state. Its members, as lawmakers, represent local views at the state level and are constantly engaged in mediating conflicts and reconciling pressures from competing special-interest groups. It is important to understand how well these lawmakers represent and carry out the will of the citizens of California.

## COMPOSITION AND STRUCTURE

Similar to the Congress of the United States and to the legislatures of all states in the Union but one, California has a *bicameral* (two-house) legislature. At the 1849 convention the proposal for a two-house legislature was passed unanimously and without debate. The more numerous house was named the "assembly"; the less numerous house was named the "senate."

Before 1926 representation in both houses was based on population. In that year a constitutional amendment instituting the "federal plan" was approved by the voters. This plan retained population as the basis of representation in the assembly and provided for geographical-area representation in the senate. However, the "federal plan" was replaced in 1966 under the Reapportionment Act of 1965, which returned to population as the basis for representation by districts in both houses (see Figure 6.1 and Figure 6.2).

## Apportionment of Assembly Seats

The assembly has 80 members—somewhat fewer than the lower house in most state legislatures. According to the California constitution, assembly members are to be elected from districts "as nearly equal in population as may be." To paraphrase the old

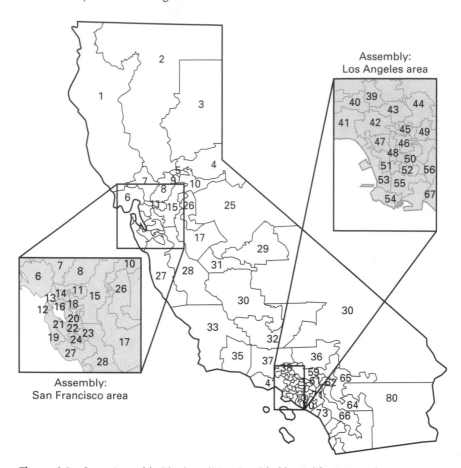

**Figure 6.1**     State Assembly Districts. (Map Provided by *California Journal*)

saying, all assembly districts are created equal, but some are more equal than others. Unequal districts come about naturally through population growth and shifts between the reapportionment the legislature makes after each ten-year census.

## Apportionment of Senate Seats

California's second constitution (1879) set the number of state senate seats at 40, and the size has not been changed since. The difficulty under the "federal plan" was how to divide 40 senators equally among the state's 58 counties. It was decided that county lines should be the basis of division and that no county could have more than one senatorial district. However, it was further provided that a senatorial district could cover as many as three sparsely populated counties. As a result of apportionment by the legislature in accord with this formula, the majority of counties had one senator each representing them in Sacramento, but some counties were represented by only one-third of a senator. While some counties, such as Mono and Alpine, were represented by one-third of a senator, those really shortchanged lived in the most populous counties. Some 60 percent of the people resided in four counties

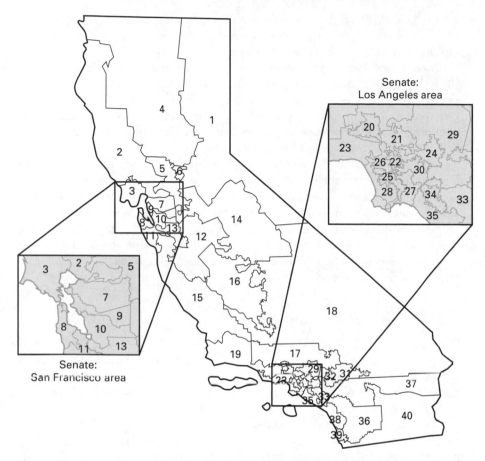

**Figure 6.2**   State Senate Districts. (Map Provided by *California Journal*)

(San Francisco, Alameda, Los Angeles, and San Diego) and were represented by just four senators. The rest of the counties with 40 percent of the population elected the other 36. The senator from Los Angeles County represented 6.5 million people; the senator from District 28 (Inyo, Mono, and Alpine counties) represented fewer than 15,000—a ratio of about 440 to 1! This imbalance had the dubious honor of being more severe than that of any upper house in the United States.

## REAPPORTIONMENT—CONTROVERSIES AND PLANS

### The U.S. Supreme Court and Reapportionment

The move for California senate reapportionment was given tremendous impetus by the U.S. Supreme Court in the decision of *Baker v. Carr* (1962), in which the court declared that state legislative reapportionment was within the purview of the federal courts.

On June 15, 1964, the U.S. Supreme Court, in a historic decision (*Reynolds v. Sims*) involving six different suits in six states, held that the districts in *both* houses of state legislatures must be "substantially equal" in population. The court said that there was no valid analogy between state legislatures and the federal Congress in which the Senate is based not on population but on two members for each state. The specific provision in the Constitution for the Senate, the court said, resulted from a compromise among the sovereign states that formed the Union. But counties and other subdivisions of the state have never been sovereign, and states are subject to the Constitution's overriding requirement of equality.

The decision cited the Fourteenth Amendment of the Constitution, which provided that "no state shall . . . deny to any person within its jurisdiction the equal protection of the laws." Chief Justice Earl Warren, a former governor of California, said "legislators represent people, not trees or acres. Legislators are elected by voters, not farms or cities or economic interests."[1] The chief justice specifically said that both houses of a bicameral legislature must be based on population. To apply the rule to only one house, he said, would permit a minority veto in the other and thus stalemate or frustrate the will of the majority.

## State Battles over Reapportionment

The reapportionment of 1966 dramatically changed politics in California. The balance between north and south was upset as at one stroke both houses of the legislature became dominated by Southern California. If the Supreme Court order was based on principle (one person, one vote), the result nonetheless was to have major political consequences.

There is a provision in the constitution of the state of Maryland that reads, in part, that "each legislative district shall consist of adjoining territory, be compact in form, of substantially equal population" and "due regard be given to natural boundaries of political subdivisions."

A student of California political redistricting would quickly realize that, other than the court mandated equal population and contiguity provisions, the other Maryland mandates are not present here. Election districts often appear to emulate drunken amoebas, stretching wriggling tendrils out in all directions and forming the weirdest of shapes. One district in the 1980s resembled an elephant's head with the bulk running from the Nevada border to the Pacific but with another section running, like an elephant's trunk, south across the Tehachipis to Magic Mountain. The purpose? To round up as many Republican voters as possible in a single district thus assuring several neighboring districts safe Democratic majorities. This is a process known as *compaction*.

Of course reapportionment itself is almost always political; it must be inasmuch as those drawing the lines are, in most cases, politicians. Controversy has surrounded every reapportionment effort in recent years, beginning with the deadlock that developed between a Democratic legislature and then-Governor Ronald Reagan

---

[1] *New York Times*, June 16, 1964.

following the 1970 census. The legislature refused to bend but was unable to over-turn Governor Reagan's vetoes of plans he believed unfair to Republicans. The impasse was broken only when the state supreme court appointed three retired judges as special "masters" to create the new legislative and congressional districts. Instead of making districts that were "safe" for this or that party or incumbent, the masters, employing computer technology, redistricted using criteria foreign to most partisan plans: compactness, community of interest, and of course population equal-ity. Two assembly seats were "nested" in each senate district. The result was districts that were more competitive, as shifts in party control of legislative seats over the next several elections showed. Reinforcing the 1966 change, the north-south balance now had the eight southern counties with 23 senate seats and 48 in the assembly.

New battles arose following the 1980 census. The legislature, still solidly in Democratic control, approved congressional and state legislative district lines that had in large measure been drafted by Congressman Philip Burton (D-San Fran-cisco). Though the Democrats held a slim 22–21 edge in California's congres-sional delegation following the 1980 election, Burton's plan was designed to ensure a 28–17 majority following the 1982 elections and through the remainder of the decade. Republicans found themselves gerrymandered out of their districts or, in several instances, lumped together in the same district, ensuring that one of them would not survive. The Burton plans (he termed them "my contribution to modern art" for the sometimes weird shapes the districts took) was signed into law by Governor Jerry Brown. The fight was not over, however. Republicans, using the referendum by petition procedure, got all three plans on the June 1982 ballot and all three were rejected by the voters.

A second plan, dubbed Burton II, was unveiled and found by most to be at least as biased as the Burton I plan had been. It was signed into law by Governor Brown on his last day in office. Republicans were once again "outraged" and sought to place another initiative before the voters, the so-called Sebastiani initiative, named for its principal author, Assemblyman Don Sebastiani. It secured over 700,000 signatures, considerably more than the number required to qualify it for the ballot. This effort was declared unconstitutional by the state supreme court, which held that reappor-tionment could take place only once every ten years, this despite the fact it already had taken place twice.

Undaunted, the Republicans drafted a new initiative to create a nonpartisan commission of retired superior court judges to undertake redistricting in the future. After a long and, on the side of the opponents, very costly campaign, the proposal was defeated by a ten-point margin. Television commercials urged a "no" vote saying the proposal would let politicians draw election lines, an interesting message since the proposal was to take that power *away* from the politicians in Sacramento.

Having lost at the polls, the Republicans decided to challenge the Democratic reapportionment in the courts. They were encouraged by a decision of the U.S. Supreme Court relating to an Indiana case in 1986 stating that a legal action against a political gerrymander existed where an electoral system had been arranged in a manner that degraded a voter's or a group of voters' influence on the political process as a whole. California Republicans maintained that in the outcome of three elections

(1982, 1984, and 1986) the proportion of 40 percent of congressional seats they had won was well below the 45–50 percent of the popular votes the GOP had received.

In 1987, however, a specially empaneled federal court decided (*Badham v. Eu*) by a 2–1 margin against the Republican challenge, maintaining that, inasmuch as the GOP had won the gubernatorial election, a U.S. Senate seat, and 40 percent of the House of Representatives seats, it had not been excluded from the political process. It was then clear that any new reapportionment plan would be determined by the state legislature elected in 1990—the time of the next census.

A replay of the 1970–1972 scenario took place when newly elected Republican Governor Pete Wilson vetoed redistricting plans forwarded to him by the Democrat-controlled legislature. (The main reason he received such strong support from the Republican right was to prevent the party from being "Burtonized" again.) Once again the Democrats could not override the governor's vetoes and the matter went to the state supreme court. Masters were appointed and in due course, districts that lacked any similarity to "modern art" emerged. The masters returned to the practice of "nesting" two assembly seats in each senate district, generally thought to be less confusing to voters. The most significant change from the Burton districts, however, lay in their relatively more competitive character.

A different pattern developed in the reapportionment that followed the 2000 census. Instead of the usual inter-party feuding, consensus reigned. Democrats seeking to avoid a court challenge threatened by the Republicans whose appointees dominated the state court, agreed to what became known as an "incumbent protection" plan. For example, Democrats held a 50 to 30 edge in the assembly and agreed to keep the ratio exactly the same in the new arrangement. "Nesting" was abandoned as was community of interest. As was pointed out by the *California Journal*, Anaheim, the state's tenth largest city is divided among no fewer than five assembly districts in Orange County and is not the largest population center in any of them. The lack of competitive districts is cited by some as one cause for declining vote turnout. Apparently voters were not too concerned by the lack of their ability to change representatives, which critics described as a death blow to democracy, turning down by a substantial margin Governor Schwarzenegger's proposition to reform the system in 2005.

## QUALIFICATIONS, TERMS, AND COMPENSATION

To be eligible for election to the state legislature an individual must be 18 years old, a U.S. citizen, a resident of the state for three years, and a resident of the district for one year previous to election.

Members of the assembly have terms of two years with a limitation of three terms, whereas state senators serve for four years with a limitation of two terms. A large proportion of the members are reelected but for no more than a second term for senators or a third for members of the assembly. Restrictions are established under voter-approved term limits. The longer term for senators has tended to make this office more attractive than that of a member of the assembly, who must conduct a campaign every two years.

Before 1966, when California had a part-time legislature, members' annual salaries were set at $6,000. When the constitution was revised in that year providing for a full-time legislature, the annual salary was raised to $16,000 and the legislature was allowed to set the amount of its own salaries with a limitation of no more than a 5 percent increase each year.

Legislative salaries are now set by an independent commission created following approval of Proposition 112 in 1990. Under the proposition the power to raise their own salaries was taken from the legislature (something they wanted, given the unpopularity of such raises with the public) and given to the California Citizens Compensation Commission. Its first meetings resulted in an increase in legislative salaries from $40,816 to $52,500. Another change, illustrated by the foregoing, was the lifting of a 5 percent cap on annual salary increases adopted years before. The Commission dramatically increased legislative salaries in 1994, arguing that with term limits the job had to be made more attractive to those who could take a mid-career sabbatical as lawmakers. The Commission settled on $72,000 as appropriate, a 37 percent increase. Before the end of the century, the Commission voted three more times to increase salaries. After the most recent change the salary was set at $110,000. In addition to their salaries, legislators receive a per diem (per day) tax-free allowance to cover living expenses while away from their homes ($135 a day in 2005 or an average of $28,000 a year). Other perquisites include the use of a state-owned car with a credit card for free gas and oil and maintenance of the leased car and a telephone credit card for official calls. One source of supplementing their incomes was taken away by Proposition 112.

("Every ten years." Dennis Renault, *Sacramento Bee*)

Previously, many legislators pocketed thousands of dollars in speaking fees known as *honoraria*. There were occasions when little was done for the $2,000 or $3,000 check and often there was at least the appearance of conflict interest. That practice was eliminated by the proposition.

## MEMBERS OF THE LEGISLATURE

Traditionally, there has been a preponderance of attorneys and businesspeople as members of the California legislature. These occupations lend themselves well to the legislative schedules and sessions, because they allow persons to take leave and to be absent from their offices or places of business for a period without any sacrifice; in fact, such governmental experience may enhance their regular positions and interests. Most state legislators have had previous experience in government by serving at the state, county, or city level before their election. A notable development in recent years has been the increase in the number of former staff members elected to the legislature. These former staffers run as "insiders," people knowledgeable about the politics of Sacramento. There has also been an increase in the number of women, blacks, and Hispanics elected, the last, especially, aided by redistricting.

Because of the change in annual sessions and the accompanying increase in salaries, the California legislature has now become more a "professional legislature," in which members serve on a full-time basis and look on their job as a profession in itself. This is in contrast with most state legislatures, "citizen legislatures," where members serve only part-time and have other full-time jobs.

### Legislative Officers

**In the Senate**   The lieutenant governor of the state is the president of the senate and presides over senate sessions but may not introduce a bill or vote on a measure except in the case of a tie vote. The senators elect a president pro tempore (or pro tem) from their membership to preside over the senate when the lieutenant governor is absent. The president pro tem is regarded as the most important official of the senate, serving as chairperson of the powerful rules committee. Under the constitution the president pro tem becomes the acting governor when both the governor and the lieutenant governor are out of the state. In 1968 when both Governor Reagan and Lieutenant Governor Robert Finch were in Florida attending the Republican convention, Senator Hugh Burns, president pro tem, successfully invoked this power and adjourned the legislature despite the opposition of Assembly Speaker Jesse Unruh. Nonmembers are elected by the senate to serve as secretary, sergeant-at-arms, chief clerk, and chaplain.

**In the Assembly**   A member of the assembly, the speaker, who functions as the presiding officer, is elected by the members of the house and retains all voting and debating rights. As the most powerful member of the state legislature, the speaker appoints all committee chairpersons and selects nearly all committee members (except those on the Rules Committee). The speaker also designates his or her choices for assembly majority party positions including the majority party leader, the caucus chairperson, the speaker pro tem, and party whips. In addition, the speaker has the power to make the bill referrals to committees and is also in charge of the assignment of legislative offices and the allocation of office staff for all members of the assembly. (This was not true during the period of turbulence in 1995 when Democrats and Republicans were either evenly split or where defections by one or two Republicans led to a temporary arrangement under which committee chairmanships were evenly divided between the parties and the speaker's powers were significantly reduced.)

In recent times the speaker came to be seen as second only to the governor in power, though the influence of term limits makes it unlikely any subsequent speaker will ever achieve the power of some past occupants of that office. As an elected office, the speakership is controlled by the majority party. A number of strong speakers have occupied the office over the years. Probably the most respected was Jesse Unruh, famous for his statement that "money is the mother's milk of politics." However, the most powerful may well have been Willie Brown, a master political tactician and fervent party man. Indeed, the longer his tenure in office the more partisan the temper of the assembly became. This was not entirely Brown's fault, as more conservative Republicans came to win elections and posed a blunt challenge to his role. Brown survived several rebellions, both by Republicans and by conservative Democrats such as the "Gang of Five," and served nearly 15 years as speaker until, facing term limits, he ran successfully for mayor of San Francisco.

## Other Officers

A speaker pro tempore, also elected from the assembly, presides in the absence of the speaker. Nonmember officers include the chief clerk, the sergeant-at-arms, the minutes clerk, and the chaplain.

## Serving Both Houses

Three major officers serve both houses of the legislature: the legislative analyst, the legislative counsel, and the state auditor (formerly auditor general). The legislative analyst, as the chief fiscal advisor to the legislature, provides an analysis of the annual governor's budget, as well as a review of any bill that has a fiscal implication. The detailed study of the budget becomes the basis for legislative hearings on the fiscal program of the state government. The legislative counsel is the legislature's legal specialist and expert on drafting bills. This official prepares or assists in preparing measures for legislators and also writes digests of bills for use by the legislature. The function of the state auditor is to keep close scrutiny over the financial management of state agencies and to keep the legislature advised of ways and means to secure more efficient and economic operation of the state government. All three officials are appointed by, and are responsible to, the legislature. Their services are very significant to the legislative process.

## The Committee System

The committee system in the California legislature is a vital part of the legislative process and organization. Each house maintains its own set of standing committees to handle bills dealing with basic and general subjects such as agriculture, education, finance, local government, and resources.[2] Senate and assembly subcommittees and select committees are created from time to time to consider special subjects as they arise and need attention. The California legislature also has established several joint committees made up of an equal number of members from each house to work on continuing matters such as audit, budget, and rules during the session, throughout recesses, and after adjournment. Generally, each senator serves on four committees, and the average member of the assembly is assigned to three committees.

Committees vary in size from 5 to 21 and are made up of both Democrats and Republicans in varying proportions. Assignments to committees are not made on the basis of seniority, as is true in the U.S. Congress, and it is even possible, though rare, to have a committee chaired by a member of the minority party.

## Party Organization in the Legislature

California's atmosphere of nonpartisanship (or *bipartisanship*, as state legislators prefer to call it) used to prevail at the state capitol. "The words 'Democrat' and 'Republican' are not often heard on the floor of the houses," reported the secretary of the senate in 1957, "and when they are heard it is frequently in some friendly or humorous connection."[3] Since the Democrats assumed control of the administration and the legislature in 1959, party alignments have become increasingly more marked.

There has been much more partisanship exhibited in the assembly than in the state senate. Cooperation between Democratic leaders and Republican leaders, especially during the tenures of David Roberti, the Democratic leader of the senate, and Republican leader Ken Maddy, was reasonably frequent. Compromises leading to bipartisan votes were not unusual. As already noted, however, the assembly has been far more partisan with party lines in general holding firm. The caucus system (meetings of all members of the party in the legislature to decide positions to be taken and strategies to be used) is used extensively by both parties.

## SESSIONS

Several state legislatures are in session for only short periods during the year, and generally the length of the session is limited by law. Some 15 states convene only once every two years for legislative sessions. (California had this arrangement from 1862 to 1946.) These practices are in contrast with the U.S. Congress, which convenes in early January and usually does not adjourn until late in the summer or early in the fall, when it deems it has finished its annual business. Until California

---

[2]There were 25 standing committees of the senate and 30 standing committees of the assembly in the 1998–1999 legislature.

[3]Joseph A. Beek, The California Legislature (Sacramento: State Printing Office, 1957), p. 152.

changed its plan for legislative sessions with constitutional revision in 1966, New York was the only state having annual year-long legislative sessions.

Today, sessions of the legislature begin on the first Monday in December of even-numbered years and must close no later than November 30 of the following even-numbered year. Thus sessions are not annual but biannual, that is, bills can be carried over from one even-numbered year through the next.

## Extraordinary (Special) Sessions

The legislature can be called into extraordinary session by the governor at *any* time between regular sessions or even concurrently with regular sessions. To call an extraordinary session, the governor issues a proclamation stating the purpose of the session and listing the subject to be considered. On such occasions the legislature has power to legislate only on subjects specified in the proclamation. The governor thus has a tighter control over legislation in extraordinary sessions than in regular sessions. The governor's power to call extraordinary sessions can also be used as a threat to encourage the legislature to act on certain measures deemed important by the governor.

The legislature has frequently been called into special session over the years. The record was set by Governor Culbert Olson, who called five such sessions in 1940. Some topics covered in the years since include medical malpractice, prisons, and earthquake relief.

## LEGISLATIVE REORGANIZATION

The state legislature became a full-time body in 1966 with voter approval of Proposition 1A. A second ballot measure, Proposition 4, was approved in 1972, changing the legislative calendar from one-year to two-year sessions.

Bills may be introduced in either the first or the second year, and bills introduced in the first year are automatically carried over to the second, except in the case of bills that have not been passed by their house of origin by January 30 of the second year. No bill may be passed by either house on or after September 1 of the even-numbered year, except statutes calling elections, providing tax levies, or appropriations; "urgency measures"; and bills passed over the governor's veto. The legislature may not present any bill to the governor after November 15 of the second year. Most newly enacted statutes go into effect after January 1 but only after 90 days have passed since enactment; otherwise they do not go into effect, in the absence of an urgency clause, until the next January 1.

In many respects, this plan resembles the system now used in the U.S. Congress.

## LEGISLATIVE ACTION

The legislature may take action in any of three basic ways: It may express an opinion; it may pass a law; or it may refer a measure to the voters for approval, which is required with bond issues and constitutional amendments.

Resolutions are used for expressions of opinion by one or both houses of the legislature. *House resolutions* are made by one house only and may pertain to any matter. *Joint resolutions* are expressions by both houses relating only to national government matters. They are usually expressions of approval or disapproval by the California legislature of legislation pending in Congress. *Concurrent resolutions* are used for all other matters on which both houses wish to express an opinion or must act jointly, as for adjournment or recess or to commend individuals for public service.

Constitutional amendments and bond issues are treated as regular bills but are submitted to the voters for final adoption or rejection at the following general election instead of being sent to the governor for signing.

## How a Bill Becomes a Law

1. **Introduction.** The act of introducing a bill consists of a legislator submitting a signed copy to the clerk of the house to which the legislator belongs. Although all bills must be formally introduced by members of the legislature, most of them originate in government agencies, the office of the governor, or with pressure groups. In fact, more often than not the legislator acts merely as an intermediary for other interested parties. After submission of the signed copy, the bill is numbered, given its "first reading," and assigned to an appropriate committee. (Committee assignment is the responsibility of the assembly speaker and the senate committee on rules.)

2. **Consideration by Committee.** The fate of most bills is determined by the committee to which they are assigned. Public hearings are scheduled for important legislation, and anyone wanting to testify is usually given an opportunity to appear. Committees have the authority to subpoena witnesses and documentary evidence related to their investigations. (Failure to honor a subpoena is grounds for legal prosecution.) A committee may dispose of a bill in any of the following ways: (a) table it, that is, postpone action indefinitely; (b) report it out (back to the whole house) without recommendation; or (c) report it out with the recommendation "do pass," either in its original form or as amended by the committee. Many bills (more than half in the assembly) are never reported out of committee—they are *pigeonholed,* to use the legislative vernacular. However, a bill can be forced out of committee by a majority vote of all members in the house concerned, but this process is rarely used. Usually, the house follows the committee's recommendations.

3. **Consideration on the Floor.** After the bill has been reported from committee it is given a "second reading," at which time committee amendments and amendments from the floor are adopted. It is then reprinted with the amendments for the "third reading," which opens floor debate. Debate may be closed and the question brought to a vote in each house by a majority vote, so there can be no minority "filibusters" in the California legislature. A bill may be passed with or without amendments, referred back to committee, or rejected. The final vote on passage of a bill is by roll call—the vote of each member placed in the record—in each house. The senate retains the traditional oral roll call, the clerk droning out

A State Assembly Committee Meeting. (Courtesy *Sirlin Studios*)

the name of every member. The assembly uses an instantaneous electric record-ing device that simultaneously flashes all votes on a scoreboard in view of every-one as members press the "yes" or "no" buttons at their desks. It takes 41 votes in the assembly to pass an ordinary bill and 21 in the senate (a majority of the total membership of each house). To pass a constitutional amendment, an urgency measure, or a budget bill, or to override a governor's veto, 54 assembly votes and 27 senate votes (a two-thirds majority of each house) are required. Once a bill is passed by either house, it is signed by the presiding officer and sent to the other house for consideration. Final passage by the legislature requires approval by both houses.

4. **Referral to Conference Committee.** If the second house to consider a bill passes it with amendments and the originating house refuses to concur in these amend-ments, a conference among selected members of both houses is called to iron out the differences. The conference committee is composed of three members of the assembly appointed by the speaker and three senators appointed by the commit-tee on rules. Two of the members from each house must be from the majority that voted to pass the bill and one from the minority. If the report of the confer-ence committee is not accepted by both houses, another conference committee is convened, but there can be no more than three such committees for one bill. The conference committee is extremely powerful and influential, because practically every major piece of legislation is referred to this committee. In turn, the report

of these six legislators is generally approved by the two houses and then becomes law. It is interesting to note that for many years conference committee meetings were closed; it was not until 1974 that they were ordered open to the public.

5. **For Approval by Governor.** After an agreed-upon version of a bill has been passed by both houses, it is technically referred to as a legislative act. If it is signed by the governor, it will go into effect the following January 1, providing 90 days have passed since signing.[4] If the governor fails to sign the bill within 12 days after receiving it and the legislature is still in session, the bill becomes a law without the governor's signature. A bill passed within the last 12 days of a general session will become law unless the governor vetoes it within 30 days after the end of the session.

6. **Overriding the Governor's Veto.** A bill returned to the legislature by the governor with his or her objections can be passed and become law over these objections only by a vote of two-thirds of the elected members of each house. If the legislature is unable to obtain such a vote against the governor's action, the bill fails to become a law. A special five-day veto session of the legislature, called for the purpose of considering and possibly overriding the governor's vetoes as established by the 1966 constitutional revision, was eliminated by Proposition 4 in 1972. No governor's veto was overridden by the legislature from 1946 until 1974, when a Reagan veto was overruled (for a full discussion of the veto power, refer to Chapter 7).

## Amount of Legislation

More than 4,000 bills are now introduced at each session of the legislature. The number any one legislator may introduce is now limited to 40 for a member of the assembly and 65 for a senator. About one-third of them are almost immediately abandoned and never receive serious consideration by the committees or on the floor of the legislature. Most of them have been introduced by legislators to satisfy their constituents, and the authors themselves have little enthusiasm or hope for passage. Another one-third of the measures introduced is killed either by the committee or on the floor of the assembly or the senate, or are vetoed by the governor. Thus in recent years about 1,100-1,400 bills have finally become law during each legislative session.

Unfortunately, a large number of bills do not reach the senate and assembly floors until the last moments of the closing session of the legislature. In spite of the reorganization, which placed the legislature on a full-time basis, lawmakers allow bills to proceed through committee earlier in the session but then fail to seek the required final votes on the floor until the last days of session, when the press of time might thwart organized opposition. The result is a huge backlog of bills that await action. In the 1987 session, for instance, there were about 400 measures still pending when the legislature began its last week of sessions. After the end-of-session frenzy, some 120 bills simply died on the senate and assembly floors. There was nothing necessarily wrong with them; lawmakers simply ran out of time.

---

[4]If an urgency clause has been attached to the bill and two-thirds of the members of each house have approved its passage, it becomes a law as soon as the governor signs it.

The State Senate in Session. (Courtesy *Sirlin Studios*)

## Media Coverage

Though news coverage of the legislature is not good (there is no television station from outside Sacramento with a crew permanently assigned to that "beat"), some television stations do carry CAL-SPAN, the state equivalent of the national network covering Congress, C-SPAN. It carries legislative debates and committee hearings to a potential audience of some two million in the state. In general, however, media coverage of what goes on in Sacramento tends to be very limited unless there are dramatic or scandalous developments. A survey by the Annenberg School of Communications at the University of Southern California in 1989 found local television and radio newscasts devoted approximately 2 percent of air time to Sacramento government and politics.

## EVALUATING THE CALIFORNIA LEGISLATURE

In the 1960s and 1970s the California legislature experienced many major reforms. During this period the time limits on sessions were removed, legislators were given more adequate compensation, more effective regulations on lobbyists and conflicts of interest were passed, and the principle of "one person-one vote" was applied in the reapportionment of the senate, which improved the pattern of representation. A strong system of standing committees was given well-defined jurisdiction, and the number of joint committees was increased, thus facilitating more cooperation between the two houses.

As a result of these changes, California's legislature has been considered one of the best in the nation. Historically, California's legislature has been in the forefront of such reforms as openness of meetings, regulation of lobbyists, disclosure of campaign contributions and spending, and conflict-of-interest laws. However, in recent years there has been increasing concern about special-interest influence and the inability of the legislature to act on major issues when faced with intense lobbying by major campaign contributors. Enter the initiative process.

When the legislature failed to act on a plan to safeguard the state's coastline, voters approved Proposition 20 in 1972, establishing the California Coastal Commission. When the legislature balked at campaign reform, the voters approved the Political Reform Act of 1974. Probably the best-known instance was passage of Proposition 13 in 1978 limiting property taxes, action taken by the voters when the legislature and governor seemed unable to act (see Chapter 10). In 1988, faced with inaction on escalating automobile insurance rates, they approved Proposition 103 in an attempt to roll back those rates. The message has been clear: If the legislature will not or cannot act, the people will.

## Current Criticisms

In recent years the great reputation of the legislature has suffered a number of blows. Increased partisanship, especially in the assembly, led to a phenomenon known as legislative gridlock. That gridlock was enhanced by increasingly powerful special interests that exercised an effective veto power over legislation they opposed. The aforementioned auto insurance crisis, which involved the insurance industry, the trial lawyers and the medical profession, each able to block the proposals of the others, is an example. A poll taken in 1988 during this crisis found 86 percent of Californians agreeing with the statement that "campaign contributions by special interests are corrupting the state legislature." In 1999 another poll found 70 percent of those interviewed believed legislators were more interested in the views of lobbyists than those of the public. Then there was the partisan struggle between the Democratically controlled legislature and successive Republican governors. All this led to impasse and alienated a public fed up with an apparently powerless government in Sacramento.

On top of everything else came the disclosures that some members of the legislature had been caught, on videotape in some instances, with their hands in the political cookie jar. Payoffs had been made by Federal Bureau of Investigation agents to legislators and their aides to gain approval of a bill giving a fictitious shrimp-packing company financial aid. The investigation, known popularly as "the F.B.I. 'sting' " operation, led to the conviction of three state senators, one member of the assembly, several staff members, and a prominent lobbyist, and indictment of several others who played the political game in Sacramento.

A recurring criticism involves the end-of-session rush to pass legislation with minimal consideration (short committee hearings or none at all). Literally hundreds of bills may be voted on in a day, most with the majority of those voting having little or no idea what is in them.

The problem is made all the worse by a growing practice of what is called GANDA. This stands for "gut and amend." A bill originally on one subject is in effect hijacked, its substance removed and new material totally unrelated to the original bill inserted. An example from the end-of-session rush in 2002 was a bill by a Republican legislator that was intended to help a few rural schools. It was taken over by a Democrat who "gutted" it of the school material and "amended" it to impose a requirement that private utilities obtain at least 20 percent of the electricity they sell from wind, solar, geothermal, or other renewable sources. That this can be misleading understates the chaos that occurs in the end-of-session rush.

These and other perceived shortcomings of the legislature are evident in more recent polls as well. Even though the public appeared to side with the legislature in defeating Governor Schwarzenegger's reform package in the 2005 special election, that did not translate into popular support for the legislature. A Public Policy Institute poll conducted following that election found approval of the legislature had fallen to just 20 percent with 66 percent of the public disapproving of its performance. While that might be expected among Republicans (76 percent disapproval), Democrats (58 percent), and independents agreed (68 percent) the legislators were doing a poor job. As Dan Walters of the *Sacramento Bee* wrote early in 2006, due to gerrymandered districts, ". . . few, if any, incumbent legislators need worry about reelection."

**Term Limits**    The impact of term limits, its advantages, and disadvantages, is the subject of considerable debate, at least among academics. The concept remains popular with the public, if perhaps not quite as fervently pushed as when they approved Proposition 140, which limited members of the assembly to three, two-year terms and state senators and statewide elected officials to two, four-year terms in office. Still, a Field Poll taken in October 2004 found 75 percent of Californians supported term limits.

Those favoring term limits pointed to the long tenure of a great number of elected officials, many protected by gerrymandered districts from which they could not be dislodged. They asserted an elitist attitude by those holding secure seats and a lack of responsiveness to voter concerns. There was no other way of "cleaning house," they said. And there were too many politicians with no experience in the "real world." As one wag put it, "[he] never held a job in a place without a dome." Term limits would ensure there would be open seats on a regular basis and that would mean more competitive elections.

Opponents argued you should not throw the baby out with the bathwater (all legislators, good and bad, would be removed) and that the voters could always remove a legislator at election time. They also expressed concern that, by mandating a revolving door of "citizen legislators," the voters would be ensuring inexperienced lawmakers who might well be overmatched by lobbyists and bureaucrats with much greater experience and expertise. Many agreed with the argument that the complexity of issues before the legislature meant that staff—with long experience unmatched by elected members—would become more important and more influential.

These arguments proved ineffective and Proposition 140 passed easily. Members of the legislature took their case all the way to the U.S. Supreme Court, but were told the states had the right to determine the conditions for state office. The impact was quickly felt. The decision left many legislators both bitter and casting about for ways of extending their lives in government. Some retired, but many opted to run for other offices. Members of the assembly looked to the state senate, Congress, or local government while state-elected officials in some cases sought to shift to other state offices. Bill Jones moved from the assembly to secretary of state in 1996, for example. Many termed-out politicians sought and received appointments to one of the many state boards and commissions. This has the virtue of keeping experienced public officials directly involved in government and is in part a response to the criticism of term limits that they remove from office those with the greatest expertise in government.

Among the changes brought by term limits were both the good and the not so good. There are more women and minorities, though these "new" members tend to be from backgrounds similar to their predecessors, coming from local government. On the negative side, according to research published by the Public Policy Institute of California, fiscal discipline has declined, fewer bills are screened in committee and legislative oversight over the executive branch has become less effective.

Observers say term limits, now that they have had an opportunity to settle into place for several years, have had a number of consequences. The power of the speaker, once rated the second greatest in state government, has been significantly degraded. With so little time to develop the kinds of ties Willie Brown and others used to elevate the speaker's position, that was to be expected. Today the most powerful member of the legislature is, most believe, the president pro tem of the senate from San Francisco. While most speakers hold that position for no more than two years, senate leaders can exercise their authority for four to six years, a major advantage in gaining and exercising power. Term limits have also resulted in more "open" seats (no incumbent is running) and these tend to be more competitive, though the competition is almost entirely in the primaries rather than in general elections as a result of gerrymandering.

## REVIEW QUESTIONS

1. What were the various battles over reapportionment that have taken place since 1970? What role has the state supreme court played? (pp. 108–110)
2. How are legislative salaries determined? What other financial rewards do members have? (pp. 111–112)
3. Compare and contrast the powers of the leaders of the two houses. (pp. 112–113)
4. What process is followed by which a bill becomes a law? What functions are performed in this process by the committees and the legislative analyst? (pp. 116–118)
5. What accounts for the relatively low esteem in which the legislature is held by the public? (pp. 119–121)
6. What are the arguments for and against term limits? What impacts have they had on the legislature? (pp. 121–122)

# SELECTED WEB SITES ――――――――――

There are several sites that provide information on the status of bills being considered by the legislature. Two that are quite useful are the legislative web sites themselves: www.assembly.ca.gov and www.senate.ca.gov. In each case you can discover the status of any pending legislation by entering the bill number and/or the author's name. These same sites will give you information on the various kinds of committees and their members.

In addition, there are several others that are helpful. The legislative analyst site (www.lao.ca.gov) provides analyses of upcoming ballot propositions as well as projections of economic growth in the state.

The legislative counsel's page (www.leginfo.ca.gov) will give access to the many state codes (laws) by category as well as information on the legislative process.

# SELECTED REFERENCES ――――――――――

Bell, Charles, and Charles Price, "20 Years of a Full-Time Legislature," *California Journal,* January 1987.

Block, A.G., "'Nesting' in the Assembly Does Not Refer to a Comfort Zone," *California Journal,* July 1993.

―――― , "Putting the Pieces Together," *California Journal,* March 2001.

Cain, Bruce, "Redistricting: Public Policy or Just Politics," in John J. Kirlin and Jeffrey I. Chapman, eds., *California Policy Choices,* Vol. 6, Los Angeles: University of Southern California School of Public Administration, 1990.

*California Journal,* January 2002 (This issue is devoted entirely to reapportionment.)

*California Political Almanac,* Sacramento: California Journal Press, annual.

Driscoll, James, *California Legislature,* Sacramento: State Printing Office, 1978.

Endicott, William, "Limit on Terms Makes its Mark," *Sacramento Bee,* July 17, 1993.

Gunnison, Robert B., "In Sacramento, Term Limits Have Handed Staff New Clout," *San Francisco Chronicle,* January 5, 1997.

Hyink, Bernard, "The California Legislature Looks at the State Constitution," *Western Political Quarterly,* March 1962.

Jeffe, Sherry Bebitch, "Have the Voters Created Their Own Dream Legislature?" *Los Angeles Times,* December 1, 1996.

Legislative Analyst, *California Legislative Interim Committee and Reports,* Sacramento: State Printing Office, biennial.

Price, Charles, and Helen Neves, "Term Limits: California's Gift (?) to the Nation," *California Journal,* December 1991.

Vanz, Max, "Assembly Profile Little Changed by Term Limits," *Los Angeles Times,* December 2, 1996.

―――― , "Liz Hill: Here Today, Here Tomorrow," *California Journal,* July 1999.

---

# The Executive and the Administration

The governor is the most visible political personality in California, and almost every resident knows the names Ronald Reagan, Jerry Brown, George Deukmejian, Peter Wilson, Gray Davis, and Arnold Schwarzenegger. Californians expect the governor to provide the same type of executive and administrative leadership for the state as the president of the United States provides for the nation. Yet unlike the federal government, but like most state governments, California's government has several elected executive officials. In addition to the governor, there are 11 state executives—lieutenant governor, attorney general, secretary of state, controller, treasurer, superintendent of public instruction, insurance commissioner, and four members of the Board of Equalization—all elected directly by the people (see Figure 7.1). The voters have, with some regularity, elected governors of one party and lieutenant governors or attorneys general of another. In 1990 Democrat Leo McCarthy was elected to a third term as lieutenant governor serving with his second Republican governor (Deukmejian and Wilson). Republican Mike Curb was elected to that same position along with Democratic Governor Jerry Brown. And in 1994 the voters chose Democrat Gray Davis to serve as second to Republican Pete Wilson, a pattern broken in 1998 when Democrats Davis and Cruz Bustamante were elected to the two top spots. As can be seen in Figure 7.2, the same pattern has been typical of the attorney general's position. Originated to prevent excessive concentration of power in the hands of one person, this arrangement has contributed to a divided administrative structure.

    This "plural executive" system contrasts with the national government, in which the president and vice-president are always of the same party and the president has the power to appoint and remove the major executive officers. Although the power

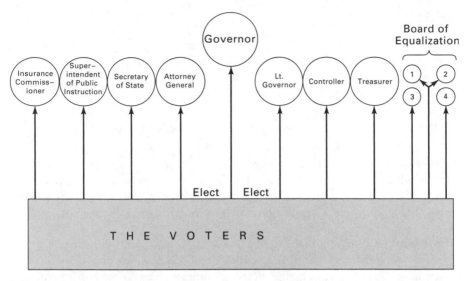

**Figure 7.1**  The Plural Executive.

**ELECTED STATE OFFICERS, 1959–2007**

| Term of Office | Governor | Lt. Governor | Attorney General | Secretary of State | Controller | Treasurer |
|---|---|---|---|---|---|---|
| 1959–67 | Edmund G. Brown | Glenn M. Anderson | Stanley Mosk (Thomas Lynch 1964)* | Frank M. Jordan | Alan Cranston | Bert A. Betts |
| 1967–71 | Ronald Reagan | Robert Finch (Ed Reinecke 1969–)* | Thomas Lynch | Frank M. Jordan | Houston Flournoy | Ivy Baker Priest |
| 1971–75 | Ronald Reagan | Ed Reinecke | Evelle Younger | Edmund G. Brown Jr. | Houston Flournoy | Ivy Baker Priest |
| 1976–79 | Edmund G. Brown Jr. | Mervyn Dymally | Evelle Younger | March Fong | Kenneth Cory | Jesse Unruh |
| 1979–83 | Edmund G. Brown Jr. | Mike Curb | George Deukmejian | March Fong Eu | Kenneth Cory | Jesse Unruh |
| 1983–87 | George Deukmejian | Leo McCarthy | John Van de Kamp | March Fong Eu | Kenneth Cory | Jesse Unruh |
| 1987–91 | George Deukmejian | Leo McCarthy | John Van de Kamp | March Fong Eu | Gray Davis | Jesse Unruh (1987) Thomas Hayes* |
| 1991–95 | Pete Wilson | Leo McCarthy | Dan Lungren | March Fong Eu | Gray Davis | Kathleen Brown |
| 1995–99 | Pete Wilson | Gray Davis | Dan Lungren | Bill Jones | Kathleen Connell | Matt Fong |
| 1999–2003 | Gray Davis | Cruz Bustamante | Bill Lockyer | Bill Jones | Kathleen Connell | Philip Angelides |
| 2003–2007 | Gray Davis  Arnold Schwarzenegger | Cruz Bustamante | Bill Lockyer | Kevin Shelly | Steve Westly | Philip Angelides |

☐ Republican
☐ Democratic

*Served out the unexpired term of the elected officer.

**Figure 7.2**  Elected State Officers, 1959–2007.

of the governor has been augmented by the establishment of the executive budget and the item veto, the dominant fact is that the 11 executive officers mentioned are not dependent on the governor for their jobs.

## THE GOVERNOR

As the state's chief executive, the governor has the responsibility of carrying out the laws enacted by the legislature and those initiated by the people. This broad executive power, plus other constitutionally delegated powers, makes the governor the most important public official in the state.

### Major Powers

A governor's ability to *direct* public policy depends on using the constants and variables attached to California governorship. The constants are the constitutional powers inherent in the position. The variables are the governor's administrative and political leadership in exercising these powers. These constant and variable powers, when used strategically or aggressively, can have a significant impact on public policy.

**The Executive Budget**    Probably the most important grant of authority to the governor is in the constitutional amendment of 1922, which placed the duty of originating the annual state budget in the governor's office. Whereas formerly each department and agency submitted its own request for funds to the legislature, under the present system all requests for appropriations must be channeled through the governor. The aim was to eliminate piecemeal and happenstance financial legislation and to diminish the interplay of politics among the legislature, individual departments, and pressure groups.

The governor has the final responsibility for preparing and submitting to the legislature an annual budget containing most of anticipated state income and expenditures. Under the constitution the revenues must be sufficient to support the proposed budget, and if they are not, the governor must recommend tax changes. The technical and detailed work of reviewing and making budget estimates for the various departments, holding hearings, and composing the budget documents is the task of the Department of Finance, which is directly responsible to the governor. After the governor has approved the budget document, the governor submits it to the legislature with a message outlining and defending the year's financial program. Until the budget has been passed, the legislature may not take up any other appropriation measures except those for operational expenses of the legislature itself, unless the governor specially requests an emergency bill.

The governor is in a strong position when dealing with the state's financial programs, though of course the legislature plays a major role. The two-thirds requirement for approval of the budget may force concessions from the governor or be used by the governor if his or her party is in the minority to gain concessions from the opposition.

**The Veto**    The governor can also influence legislation through the exercise of, or the threat of exercising, the veto. The governor has two classes of veto: the *general veto* for rejecting an entire bill and the *item veto* for rejecting only portions of bills.

1. **The General Veto.** The governor may disapprove a bill within 12 days after receiving it by sending it back to the legislature. The vetoed bill is usually

accompanied by a written statement from the governor indicating any objections. A vetoed bill can be passed over the governor's objections only by a two-thirds vote of the elected members of both houses.[1] If the governor neither signs nor formally rejects a bill within 12 days of receiving it, as long as the legislature has not yet adjourned, the bill becomes law without the governor's signature. Until Proposition 6 was passed in 1966, if the legislature adjourned before the 12-day period had expired, the governor was allowed 30 days after adjournment in which to sign the bill. If after the 30-day period the bill remained unsigned, it was considered a *pocket veto*, and there was no possibility for the legislature to override the veto.

An examination of the veto records of the last six governors shows they were not reluctant to use this power. Edmund "Pat" Brown vetoed 6 percent of legislative bills presented to him and Edmund "Jerry" Brown turned down 7 percent. Both were Democrats. The rate for Republican governors Ronald Reagan and George Deukmejian was about 12 percent. Such a differential can be explained by the fact that for most of the time involved the state legislature was under the control of the Democrats with whom these men more often disagreed. Pete Wilson entered office striking a conciliatory tone toward the Democratically controlled legislature, but soon found himself at loggerheads with its leadership. He vetoed 17 percent of the bills placed on his desk in his first term. In his first year in office Gray Davis vetoed even more legislation, 22 percent, than did Reagan or Wilson. Given that he was working with a Democratic legislature, that surprised many. This possibly can be explained by a determined centrist reacting to a liberal-dominated legislature that had high expectations for change after 16 years of Republican governors. In his first two years in office, Governor Schwarzenegger's veto rate was the second highest since World War II, reflecting his increasingly hostile relationship with the legislature.

2. **The Item Veto.** California's governor, like the chief executives of four-fifths of the states, may reject individual items in any appropriations bill.[2] California's governor may either *strike out* an item completely or *reduce* it but may make *no increases* in expenditures. The legislature has the same power to override an item veto as a general veto. However, it rarely uses this device, almost always allowing a bill that has received an item veto to take effect. The purpose of the item veto, instituted along with the executive budget in 1922, was to strengthen the governor's hand in the formulation of the state's fiscal program. Whereas previously the governor had either to accept a bill or to reject it *in toto*—thus encouraging legislators to add unrelated "riders" to the budget bill or other vital legislation—the governor may now reject only those provisions that are found to be objectionable, while retaining the basic measure.

---

[1]The California legislature rarely has been successful in overriding a governor's veto. For the first time since 1946, both houses in 1974 secured the necessary two-thirds vote to override Governor Reagan's veto of a bill relating to closure of state hospitals. Although Governor Jerry Brown was overridden eight times in 1979, all but one of the bills involved a conflict over employee salaries.

[2]A few states go even further and allow their governors to apply the item veto to all legislation.

Initially, the item veto was not used often by California governors. However, more recent governors, including Ronald Reagan, Jerry Brown, George Deukmejian, Pete Wilson, Gray Davis, and Arnold Schwarzenegger have frequently "blue penciled" certain items involving appropriations by decreasing the amount or eliminating the item entirely.

**Recommending Legislation**    Although the governor may not formally introduce a bill to the legislature, many proposals for legislative action emanate from the governor's office. The constitution requires the governor to send a message to the legislature at the beginning of every regular session describing the condition of the state and recommending action on specific matters. It matters not whether the State of the State message is long or short (Jerry Brown's state addresses lasted less than ten minutes); it receives a good deal of public attention and becomes the keystone of the governor's policy for the ensuing year. Like the State of the Union message of the president of the United States, it receives serious consideration by the legislature.

Every governor builds a legislative program around a series of specific proposals, which are drafted into measures for introduction into either the assembly or the senate. The governor's office makes an agreement with a legislator, who is generally a political ally and colleague of the governor, to introduce these bills. Such agreements are frequent and come as a result of the governor's political influence. Throughout the course of the legislative session the governor normally sends numerous informed messages on various matters encouraging the passage of legislation that he or she favors. In February 1979 Jerry Brown became the first governor ever to testify before a legislative committee when he appeared before the Assembly Ways and Means Committee in support of a proposal to convene a national constitutional convention to write an amendment requiring a balanced federal budget. The threat of the governor's veto and the ability to call extraordinary sessions give weight to the governor's recommendations, but their success or failure depends on his or her political influence with the members of the legislature and an ability to win their support.

**Calling Special Sessions**    The state constitution provides that "on extraordinary occasions the governor by proclamation may convene the legislature in special session. When so convened it has power to legislate only on subjects specified in the proclamation but may provide for expenses and other matters incidental to the session" (Article IV, section 3b). Governors have used this device frequently. They may, and often do, call these extraordinary sessions to meet at the same time the legislature is sitting in regular session, and on these occasions the results are sometimes truly extraordinary.[3] The effect of the governor's power to call sessions and to specify their business is readily seen: Senate and assembly leaders know they cannot ignore a governor's legislative program.

**Appointing State Officers**    Although the governor's power of appointment is limited by the plural executive system, which provides for the direct election of many

---

[3]See discussion of *extraordinary sessions* in Chapter 6, p. 115.

important officials, and by the large state civil service program, it is nonetheless a substantial power. California's governor appoints most of the top administrative officials, including the director of finance, the secretaries of the five major administrative agencies (business, transportation, and housing; health and welfare; resources; state and consumer services; youth and adult correctional), and most of the department heads. Two departments are headed by elective officials: the department of justice, which is directed by the state attorney general, and the department of education, whose head is the superintendent of public instruction.[4]

The governor also appoints members of nearly 300 boards and commissions with some 2,000 members, bodies such as the Public Utilities Commission, the Transportation Commission, the Agricultural Relations Board, the Post-Secondary Educational Commission, and the Fair Political Practices Commission, many of whom have terms overlapping the governor's four-year term; thus any one governor may not have the opportunity of making all board and commission appointments. These are important appointments. California has more licensed professions than any state in the Union, 39, covering a wide variety of professions, from barbers and beauticians, plumbers and carpenters to doctors and nurses, and lawyers. In addition, more visible bodies, members of which serve staggered terms, are appointed, include the Public Utilities Commission, Agricultural Labor Relations Board, the Fair Political Practices Commission, and Transportation Commission. Their terms often overlap those of the governors who may arrive only to face members hostile to his or her policies.

The governor's appointments to these high offices are subject to review and approval by the state senate, and the law requires the secretary of state to post notices of vacancies in appointed positions. The many interest groups are active in proposing candidates for the governor's approval and appointment.

The governor is given a free hand to appoint members of his or her cabinet. This group of 10 to 12 individuals comprises the governor's administration, a legislative secretary, and an appointments secretary, all of whom serve at the pleasure of the governor.

Another facet of the governor's appointment power is the responsibility for filling any unexpired terms (because of resignation, disability, death, or conviction of crime) of certain elected officials: U.S. senators, state executive officers, and judges of the state courts.[5] Filling vacancies on the court bench has become a frequently exercised and important duty.

When a judicial office becomes vacant or when the legislature establishes a new superior or municipal judgeship, the governor is authorized to make a new appointment. The governor's appointments to the state supreme court and the courts of

---

[4] A constitutional amendment to have the superintendent appointed by the state board of education (rather than elected) failed to pass in the November 1958 election. An attempt to change the method of selection, which would allow the legislature to determine how the superintendent should be chosen, was defeated in the 1968 proposal to revise Article IX of the state constitution.

[5] When vacancies occur in many other elective offices, as in the state senate and assembly, the governor issues writs for special elections. In any office in which there is no provision for filling a vacancy, the governor has general constitutional authority to make an appointment.

appeal are subject to review by the Commission on Judicial Appointments, consisting of the chief justice of the state supreme court, the state attorney general, and a judge of the state court of appeals. One of the most controversial appointments was that of Rose Bird to chief justice of the state supreme court by Governor Edmund "Jerry" Brown in 1977. The first woman to be appointed to this post, she had no previous experience as a judge, and this caused considerable opposition from the legal profession and the California State Bar Association (see Chapter 8 for further discussion of Rose Bird).

**Power as Political Leader**    Occupancy of the office itself brings to the governor, whether the person be a strong or a weak leader, a position of political prominence second to none in the state. The governor is looked on as the titular leader of his or her party, often becoming its favorite candidate at the presidential nominating convention; with the increased electoral weight of California, the governor is automatically regarded as a presidential possibility. Even Arnold Schwarzenegger, Austrian born and thus not eligible under the Constitution, briefly sparked interest in a constitutional amendment that would have allowed him to serve. The position's prestige and its resultant influence over public opinion may be used—if a governor is so inclined—as a whip to corral would-be mavericks in the party or in the state government. Such influence can be exerted through informal conferences, breakfasts, press conferences, and phone calls.

## Other Powers

The governorship carries with it many other responsibilities in addition to the major powers already discussed. Many of them are the traditional duties of any governmental chief executive in the United States, whether it be president, governor, or mayor.

**Commander in Chief of the State Militia**    Whenever police officers of the state, counties, or cities are unable to handle emergency situations such as fires, earthquakes, or floods, or to quell civil disturbances such as riots, insurrections, or strikes, the governor may call out the state militia. The militia—now integrated with California's National Guard units—is a standby military reserve composed primarily of men who have served in the nation's military forces. Although the governor may order the militia to act at his or her own discretion, the governor rarely ever calls on it except on request from a local law-enforcement official.[6] The actual administration of the militia is delegated to the adjutant general of the California National Guard, an appointee of the governor, subject to presidential approval.

**Executive Clemency**    Except in the case of impeachment, the governor has power to grant pardons, reprieves, and commutations of sentence to individuals convicted of any felony. The difficult nature of such decisions and the large number of requests

---

[6]Occasionally, the Guard may be called into national action; for example, in 1950 California's 40th Division was sent to Korea. The National Guard was also called to quell the Watts riot in 1965 and again for the Rodney King riots in 1992.

place a heavy strain on the chief executive. "I'd bleed from every pore each time I went over a case," recalled Goodwin Knight. As quoted in the *Sacramento Bee*, Goodwin said:

> You realize that all you have to do is scratch your name on a piece of paper—you do it as governor about 20 times a day anyhow—and a man can live. A flick of the wrist and I can let him breathe, I'd tell myself. And if you did not many people would know . . . Executive clemency appeals are strenuous and the toughest thing a governor has to face. The evening before the day of execution isn't pleasant.[7]

The burden is eased somewhat by two agencies—the Adult Authority and the Board of Trustees of the California Institution for Women—which act in an advisory capacity to the governor. Yet all final decisions are the governor's alone and not subject to overrule; however, the governor may not pardon a person twice convicted of felonies without the recommendation of the state supreme court.

**Ceremonial Functions** Representing the state at all sorts of public functions demands a great deal of time and effort. The governor must host visiting dignitaries, deliver dedicatory addresses, proclaim a multitude of special "days" and "weeks," cut ribbons at the opening of new freeways, ride in parades, drink the first glass of orange juice at the Orange Show, and sample the first date at the Indio Date Festival. Although some governors may find, and have found, such activities to be not unpleasant, these ceremonial functions all too often prevent a chief executive from attending to the pressing business awaiting her or him in Sacramento.

## Qualifications, Term, Succession, and Salary

To be elected governor of California a person must be a voter who has been both a U.S. citizen and a resident of California for five years preceding election. The governor is elected for a four-year term, beginning with the first Monday after January 1 following election.

Before 1967 the constitution contained a detailed list of succession to the office of governor in case the governor is unable to complete the four-year term. The 1966 constitutional revision provides that the lieutenant governor succeeds to the office, but further successors are to be designated by the legislature through statutes. Constitutional revision also authorized the California Supreme Court to determine when the governor is unable to carry out his or her duties and should be removed from office.

California paid its governor the same yearly salary, $49,100, for 20 years until 1987. The governors of 38 smaller states were paid more, and all ten of the state executive officers have received more—their annual salary level in 1983 was $63,628. The governor's salary now is set by the California Citizens Compensation

---

[7]June 11, 1959, Sec. A.

Commission, which raised it to $175,000 a year, effective the end of 2000 where it remains in 2006.[8] The person holding the office also enjoys a number of "perks," including the services of a limousine and driver, money to cover expenses for having to maintain two residences, and a liberal travel allowance. There is, in addition, an expense account for running the governor's office.

## Who Becomes Governor?

Most of California's governors have been about 50 years old at the time of inauguration and have brought with them previous experience in state government. With the exceptions of Hiram Johnson, a noted criminal lawyer from San Francisco, Ronald Reagan, a motion picture and television actor, and Arnold Schwarzenegger, another screen hero, all of California's chief executives had previously held important public offices in the state. The attorney general's office has become increasingly regarded as a steppingstone to the governorship (as it indeed served for Earl Warren, Edmund "Pat" Brown, and George Deukmejian). Lieutenant governors have succeeded to the office of governor in seven instances because of the death or resignation of the incumbent, the most recent being Goodwin Knight's assumption of the office upon the appointment of Earl Warren to the U.S. Supreme Court in 1953.

## Gray Davis: The Surprise Governor

Gray Davis can be described as a surprise in two senses. First, it was a surprise that he survived a hot primary and won by such a big margin in the general election. But the surprises did not stop with his victory over Dan Lungren in November 1998. His performance in office was not what many had expected either. His ties to the unpopular Jerry Brown, an avowed liberal (he was Brown's chief of staff), led to expectations he would govern from the left.

Instead he early on proved to be much more of a centrist than either his foes had feared or his fans had forecast. While ultimately dropping the state's appeal to reinstate Proposition 187's strictures on illegal immigrants, a step praised by civil rights advocates, they were dismayed when he vetoed a bill that would have required ethnicity records be kept by law enforcement agencies on arrests made for minor road violations. The bill was intended to discover the extent to which D.W.B. (driving while black) was being used by law enforcement personnel who were treating racial minorities as suspects simply because of the color of their skin. He likewise refused to approve legislation that would have allowed state agencies to recruit women and minorities, saying it contradicted Proposition 209, which ended affirmative action in hiring. And he said no to a bill that would have required employers to notify their employees if their e-mail and computers were being monitored, thought by activists to be an invasion of privacy.

In many areas Davis governed from the left, then the right, then the center. The environment, business regulation, welfare funding are all examples. In some

---

[8]The commission raised the salary again in 2000, this time to $175,000. However Governor Davis indicated at that time he would decline to accept the increase.

instances he was firmly liberal as in his support for gay rights, signing bills that banned harassment of gays in schools, and making it illegal to discriminate in rental housing based on sexual orientation. His stance on labor issues was likewise consistent. He signed legislation to restore the eight-hour day as the standard by which overtime is calculated after it had been changed to a 40-hour week under Wilson and created the state university system as an agency shop where nonunion faculty are required to pay a significant percentage of the standard union dues, though fewer than half of university faculty belong.

Some see his left, right, center decisions as a reflection of the "canoe theory" advocated by his old boss, Jerry Brown. Under that theory you paddle a little to the left, then paddle a little to the right, and keep on going right down the middle.

Perhaps one of governor Davis's most remarkable achievements in four years in office was his record breaking fund raising. No one in the history of any state raised as much. Columnist E. J. Dionne of the *Washington Post* syndicate wrote, "Davis is to fund raising what Barry Bonds is to homers."[9] He spent $10 million in the primary in 2002 to destroy a potential Republican challenger (see Chapter 3) and entered the general election campaign with an excess of $50 million. Republicans claimed he spent more time raising campaign cash than he did running the state. His defenders noted he *had* to do this because he was not, as were his challengers, rich. All this did him less good than might have been expected, he being less than well regarded by the public, especially after his handling of the energy crisis (see Chapter 11).

## Arnold Schwarzenegger: Action Hero as Governor

In his first two years in office, the man known as "the Terminator" acted both as the opposite of his film image and as its embodiment. In the first few months, Arnold, as he was known by those who could not spell his name, made significant efforts to court the Democratic leadership of the legislature that had so vigorously fought his election. An open hand (often holding a cigar) was extended and cooperation promised. Compromise was no longer a dirty word in Sacramento. The most notable product of this period was passage of a significant reform of what everyone agreed was a broken worker's compensation system.

Over the succeeding months, the governor grew increasingly frustrated by what he viewed as the unwillingness of the legislature to work with him to mend what he saw (and others as well) as a badly flawed, even dysfunctional, governing system. A major sticking point was, as shown in Chapter 10, a budgetary process that inevitably led to major deficits. The governor pledged not to approve any tax increase (and actually cut the car tax by two-thirds as his first act upon becoming governor, a move applauded by the public and frowned upon by those who saw the action as only making a bad budget situation worse). The decision by Arnold to assume again his Terminator personality was made with the intention of bludgeoning his opponents into submission. (He termed them "girlie men" for his belief they

---

[9]E. J. Dionne, *Washington Post*, August 13, 2002.

Governor Arnold Schwarzenegger.

could not stand up to special interests.) The implements chosen were the "reform" propositions detailed in Chapter 3. With voter rejection of these reforms the governor once again pledged to work with the legislature to advance the interest of the people of the state. In softening his image, he admitted to making mistakes (he declared, for example, he should have listened to his wife, Maria Schriver, who discouraged him in his plans for a special election) and adopted a number of policy initiatives designed to move him back toward the political center. An increase of a dollar in the minimum wage, freezing college tuition for a year and, most sweeping, a series of bond issues to address growing needs for school construction in anticipation of a major increase in the number of children to be educated in the future, levee repairs in the Sacramento area to prevent flooding rivaling the disaster following Hurricane Katrina in 2005, and a vast program to deal with highway construction needs. But with a Democratic leadership that was both emboldened by his defeats and intent on retaking the governorship in 2006, prospects for such cooperation were not viewed as good. Still the Terminator had succeeded in placing his agenda on the state's policy front burner and a stepped-down version of his bond proposals was placed on the November 2006 ballot by the legislature.

## THE LIEUTENANT GOVERNOR

The constitutional status of California's lieutenant governor is much like that of the U.S. vice-president—once described by Benjamin Franklin as "His Most Superfluous Majesty." This does not mean that any occupant of either post is doomed to obscurity and political impotency, but there is a built-in anonymity to the office that is difficult to overcome. The lieutenant governor serves as president of the senate but has only a casting vote (one needed to break a tie). He or she becomes acting governor upon any temporary disability of the governor or upon the governor's absence from the state; he or she becomes governor when a vacancy occurs in the office of governor.

The spotlight may fall on a lieutenant governor, however, if the person who is then governor has a flair for travel. The lieutenant governor is "acting governor" when the chief executive is out of the state or physically disabled. This provision was the cause of an interesting controversy involving Mike Curb, a Republican who had been elected lieutenant governor in 1978 at the same time Democrat Jerry Brown had been reelected governor. Later in 1979 when the governor was out of state,

(Rex Babin, *Sacramento Bee*)

Curb, as "acting governor," appointed a judge to the appellate court. Upon return to California, Brown withdrew the appointment and substituted his own. This conflict in action was appealed to the courts for decision. The state supreme court concluded that Curb had the authority to make the appointment, though Brown had the authority to withdraw this particular appointment as it had not yet been confirmed by the Commission on Judicial Appointments.

The California Constitutional Revision Commission suggested that, in order to avoid this kind of political maneuvering, an amendment to the state constitution be approved requiring the governor and lieutenant governor to run as a ticket, as do presidential and vice presidential candidates. The idea was soundly rejected by both the politicians and the public.

By virtue of the office, the lieutenant governor also serves as a member of the State Lands Commission, the University of California Regents, and the board of trustees of the California State Universities and Colleges.

## THE ATTORNEY GENERAL

The attorney general is the most important executive officer in the state after the governor. Article V, section 13, of the constitution specifies that among the responsibilities of the attorney general:

> ... It shall be the duty of the Attorney General to see that the laws of the State are uniformly and adequately enforced. He [or she] shall have direct supervision over such other law. ... Whenever in the opinion of the Attorney General any law of the State is not being adequately enforced in any county, it shall be the duty of the Attorney General to prosecute any violations of law of which the superior court shall have jurisdiction, and in such cases the Attorney General shall have all the powers of a district attorney. ...

Although the attorney general has the responsibility for the enforcement of state laws, local law enforcement is generally left to the cities and counties. The attorney general's responsibility for local law enforcement involves her or him directly with the state's difficult crime problems, including narcotics, illegal gambling, and juvenile delinquency. The attorney general heads the Department of Justice and is legal counsel for the state and most state agencies, rendering them legal advice and representing them in court. Another duty is to prepare the titles and summaries of all ballot propositions submitted to the voters in state elections.

Persons who serve in this office are often selected as candidates for governor, as in the case of Earl Warren in 1942, Pat Brown in 1958, Evelle Younger in 1978, and George Deukmejian in 1982.

## THE SECRETARY OF STATE

The secretary of state is California's chief clerk and as such has the responsibility of keeping the official record of the acts of the legislature and the executive departments. The secretary of state appoints a keeper of the archives, who maintains the central records depository in which are kept the enrolled copy of the constitution, all acts and resolutions passed by the legislature, the journals of the senate and the assembly, other official deeds, parchments, maps, papers, and the Great Seal of the state.[10]

An especially important function of the secretary of state is the supervision of elections. He or she certifies initiative, referendum, and recall petitions and assigns them places on the ballot (see Chapter 5); publishes official and sample ballots and the voters' preelection booklet; certifies and maintains the records of affidavits of candidacy and campaign finances; and certifies and publishes election results. In much of these elections administration responsibilities, the secretary of state works through and with county election officials.

The secretary of state also processes charters and collects fees for the incorporation of private businesses, counties, and cities.

This office used to attract little interest, and its occupants have exercised few discretionary powers. From 1911 to 1970, except for a brief three-and-a-half years, Frank C. and Frank M. Jordan (father and son) held this office, and most voters were not aware that these individuals were two different persons. However, when Jerry Brown assumed office in 1970, he actively led moves to reform campaign methods and ballot procedures, and this position became a steppingstone to the governor's office. It is interesting to note that Governor Reagan in his State of the State message proposed a constitutional amendment for making the office of secretary of state nonpartisan. He maintained that this officer should be free of conflict of interest in the conduct of elections and in reporting campaign contributions. In 1975 March Fong Eu succeeded Brown in this office and became the first Asian to hold a statewide office in California. And in 1994 Bill Jones of Fresno became the first candidate from the Central Valley to win statewide office. After Jones was "termed out," Kevin Shelly was elected to succeed him.

## THE CONTROLLER

The state's chief accounting and disbursing officer is the controller, who maintains accounts of all state and local government finances, authorizes withdrawals from the state treasury, and audits all financial claims against the state. This officer also has general responsibility for overseeing the collection of all state taxes, with specific responsibility for the collection of inheritance and gift taxes, the gasoline tax, and the motor-vehicle-transportation license tax, the insurance-company tax, and the petroleum gas tax (for an explanation of these and other state taxes see Chapter 10).

The controller is a member of several boards and commissions, including the state Board of Equalization, the Franchise Tax Board, the state Board of Control, the State Lands Commission, and the Water Resources Control Board. The criticism has been leveled that the controller is a member of too many unrelated boards and that his or her efforts are spread too thin.

The office of controller has become one of the most important in the state. The controller's staff includes about 100 tax appraisers who are appointed, thus affording considerable patronage. As the elective state fiscal officer, the controller is a key per-

---

[10]The Great Seal must be affixed to all documents signed by the governor.

son in state government. Both Thomas Kuchel and Alan Cranston served in this office before their election to the U.S. Senate in 1954 and 1968, respectively. Houston Flournoy, a candidate for governor in 1974, was state controller from 1966 to 1974. Ken Cory, a former state assembly member, was elected to a third term as controller in 1982. He decided not to run for a fourth term, and Gray Davis, an assembly member and former chief of staff for Governor Jerry Brown, was elected to the office in 1986, serving until 1994 when he successfully ran for lieutenant governor and was succeeded by fellow Democrat Kathleen Connell who was followed, in turn, by Steve Westly.

## THE TREASURER

It is the duty of the state treasurer to provide for the safekeeping of public funds, but this officer is a custodian only, having no authority to issue payment of monies except upon authorization of the controller. The treasurer is required to report periodically to the legislature on the condition of the state treasury.

Elected for four years, the treasurer is also the chief administrative officer for the sale and redemption of state bonds and the investment of surplus state funds under general authorization of the legislature.

Ivy Baker Priest, elected in 1966, became the first woman to occupy this post. She was formerly treasurer of the national government in the Eisenhower administration. Jesse Unruh, former speaker of the state assembly and a candidate for governor in 1970, became state treasurer in 1974. As state treasurer, he was reelected in 1978, 1982, and 1986—the last time without opposition in the primary and in the general election. Unruh expanded the role of the treasurer's office and increased the state's billions of dollars that he invested for it.

Governor George Deukmejian appointed Dan Lungren, a Republican U.S. congressional representative from Long Beach, to fill Unruh's position as state treasurer. This appointment was subject to confirmation by the state legislature and the assembly voted 43–32 to confirm the nomination, but the senate voted 21–19 to reject the nomination. After his nomination of Dan Lungren to replace Jesse Unruh failed in the senate, Deukmejian gained approval of state auditor Thomas Hayes, a far less partisan choice. The governor knew it would be hard for the legislature to refuse confirmation of their own auditor general whom they had appointed. He in turn was defeated in 1990 by Kathleen Brown, sister of Jerry and daughter of Pat. Another example of "family ties" followed when Matt Fong, son of March Fong Eu, was elected to this office in 1994. Phil Angelides followed in 1999.

## THE STATE BOARD OF EQUALIZATION

The State Board of Equalization, composed of four members (each elected from one of four districts) and the state controller who serves ex officio, is the state's major tax agency. The four members are all elected on a partisan basis in gubernatorial election years for terms of four years.

The board surveys average levels of property-tax assessment in the 58 counties with a view to equalizing assessments throughout the state, assesses the property of public utilities for purposes of local taxation, and assists local assessors in their duties.

State taxes administered by the board account for more than half of the state's revenue and include sales and use tax, cigarette tax, alcoholic-beverage tax, motor-vehicle-fuel license tax, insurance tax, and state-assessed property tax.

## THE SUPERINTENDENT OF PUBLIC INSTRUCTION

The position of the superintendent of public instruction in the state executive hierarchy is a peculiar one because the superintendent is the only state executive officer elected on a nonpartisan ballot. Although elected by the voters every four years, the superintendent is responsible in some respects to the ten-person state Board of Education appointed by the governor and serves as secretary and executive officer of the board. He or she is administrative head of the state Department of Education and in that capacity is expected to execute Board of Education policies.

This led to a major confrontation between a conservative board of education and the more liberal superintendent, Bill Honig. Elected in 1982, Honig campaigned for a return to "traditional" education and an increase in state funding for schools. That eventually brought him into a confrontation with Governor Deukmejian, a controversy that continued when Pete Wilson took over the governor's chair. Wilson's attempt (ultimately unsuccessful) to cut the education budget as a means of dealing with budgetary red ink in the early 1990s led to open warfare between the two.

The conflict with the Board of Education arose out of the belief of board members that Honig was usurping their power to make policy and their control over the Department of Education. Ultimately Honig lost when he was convicted (some felt unfairly) of criminal conflict of interest with respect to his wife's work with the Quality Education Project (QEP). She was president of this nonprofit foundation and a jury found him guilty of illegally approving $337,000 worth of contracts with QEP. The funds went to enhance parent involvement in the schools, a highly commendable objective, but the process by which the funds were received was deemed improper.

The superintendent has general responsibility for administering the state laws relating to public schools in California and appoints the boards and commissions within the Department of Education—two important ones being the curriculum commission and the credentials commission. In addition, the superintendent sits as an ex officio member on the Board of Regents of the University of California and the Board of Trustees of the State Universities and Colleges.

## THE INSURANCE COMMISSIONER

The state's voters chose to make the position of insurance commissioner an elective rather than appointive office when they approved Proposition 103 in 1988. Some previous holders of the position had come under fire as being too close to the insurance industry they were to regulate.

Though some provisions of Proposition 103 were modified by the courts, the responsibility of the insurance commissioner to review and approve insurance rate increases has been upheld (though subject to challenge in the courts if the existing rates do not permit a "fair and reasonable return" on the company's investment). The first elected commissioner, John Garamendi, proved an ardent advocate for consumer rights and pressed for rate reform during his four years in office. He chose to seek the Democratic nomination for governor in 1994 and was defeated by Kathleen Brown in the primary. A Republican, Chuck Quakenbush replaced him and was one of only two Republicans running for statewide office to survive the electoral debacle suffered by his party in 1998.

A move to return the commissioner's office to the ranks of the appointed was initiated in 2000. It resulted following allegations that the incumbent, Chuck Quakenbush, had mishandled, if not illegally, funds that were to be used to assist those who had suffered losses in the Northridge earthquake. Fines were assessed against several insurance companies for their actions dealing with claims from those insured. However, none of the money, amounting to over $11 million, had by May 2000 gone to any of the quake victims. Those backing the change pointed to the high cost of running for office and the opportunities for insurance companies regulated by the commissioner to contribute to a candidate for that office, raising questions of improper influence.

## THE ADMINISTRATIVE BRANCH

A good share of the work of state government is carried on by myriad state agencies, departments, boards, and commissions. Because of its size and scope of power, this collection of governmental units often is considered to be a fourth branch of government and is referred to as the administration or the bureaucracy. The function of this branch of government is to implement and enforce public policy and to perform public services as determined by the legislature and the people of California.

The governor is the manager of this large structure, and all departments are responsible to the governor except two: The Department of Justice reports to the elected attorney general, and the Department of Education is accountable to the elected superintendent of public instruction. The governor is the appointing power of most of the important officers of the administration and thus has some control over policy. However, an increasing number of commissions and boards, such as the Public Utilities Commission, the Fair Political Practices Commission, and the Agricultural Relations Board, have powers established by the legislature or by the direct initiative and thus are independent of the governor. Also, although the governor appoints the members of these governmental bodies, their terms overlap that of the governor, and they are beyond the reach of the appointing power. These independent boards and commissions cover a wide range of important areas of government activities and are involved in policymaking as well as administration.

The governor maintains several "staff" agencies that serve as advisors in different areas of administrative policy. The functions of staff organizations are to plan, advise, observe, and assist the chief executive officer—but not to command. The all-important Department of Finance supervises all financial operations of the administration and recommends fiscal policy to the governor. The other staff offices—the Office of Planning and Research, the Office of Emergency Services, the Department of Personnel Administration, and the Office of Criminal Justice Planning—all serve as advisors to the governor in other specific areas.

Most of the state administration consists of "line" agencies and departments. In contrast with "staff" organizations, "line" agencies have their own authority and power of command in the exercise of their functions. Most of the "line" departments that perform direct services to Californians are now organized into five superagencies: business, transportation, and housing; resources; health and welfare; youth and adult correctional; and state and consumer services. The various departments and offices are grouped on a functional basis with the aim of simplifying governmental procedures. Each superagency is headed by a governor-appointed secretary who is responsible for coordinating the activities of the departments assigned to the agency and for handling communications between the department and the governor's office. Selected directors of "staff" and "line" agencies including the chief of staff, the director of finance, and the secretaries of the superagencies serve as members of the governor's cabinet. This body acts in an advisory capacity to the governor and serves as a coordinating body to the state administration.

## REVIEW QUESTIONS ——————————

1. What are the advantages and disadvantages of the plural executive? (chapter theme, no specific page reference.)
2. Which of the governor's powers are the most important? Why? (pp. 126–131)
3. Identify the principal functions and powers of each of the statewide elected officials. (pp. 135–140)
4. Distinguish between "line" and "staff" agencies and departments. (pp. 114–142)

## SELECTED WEB SITES ——————————

The principal site for the governor, his home page, is www.ca.gov/s/governor. There you will find a listing of legislative priorities, key bills, and executive orders he has issued.

The attorney general's site, at www.caag.state.ca.us, contains information on criminal statistics, various kinds of consumer fraud, and a description of legal opinions rendered. The web pages of the remaining statewide elected officials may be accessed through www.ca.gov/s/govt/constoffs.html#controller, or treasurer, or insurance, etc.

All department and agencies, boards and commissions have web pages. These may be found at www.ca.gov/search/hello.html. Simply bring the desired one up by highlighting it with your cursor.

## SELECTED REFERENCES ——————————

Barabak, Mark Z., "Davis' Drive Has Been Unswerving," *Los Angeles Times*, October 11, 2002.
Block. A. G., "The Wilson Legacy," *California Journal*, November 1998.

*California Political Almanac,* Sacramento: California Journal Press, annual.

Cannon, Lou, *Ronnie to Jesse: A Political Odyssey of Two Political Champions,* Garden City, NY: Doubleday, 1969.

Fairbanks, Robert, "Unruh's Growing Power," *California Journal,* February 1983.

Melendy, H. Brett, and Benjamin F. Gilbert, *The Governors of California: Peter H. Burnett to Edmund G. Brown,* Georgetown, CA: Talisman Press, 1965.

Park, Robert, *Jerry Brown: The Philosopher Prince,* Briarcliff Manor, NY: Stein and Day, 1978.

Quinn, T. Anthony, and Ed Saltzman, *California Public Administration,* Sacramento: California Journal Press, 1982.

Saltzman, Ed, "Judging Jerry," *California Journal,* June 1982.

Skelton, George, "A Split Verdict on Deukmejian's Legacy," *Los Angeles Times,* December 30, 1990.

Zeigler, Richard, "Pete Wilson: Steering Through a Sea of Woes," *California Journal,* April 1992.

# Chapter

# 8

# The Judiciary

In the United States the judiciary differs from the other two branches of government, the legislative and the executive, in that the courts do not initiate action but only react when a request for action is brought to them. Before our courts issue a judgment someone from outside the judicial system must file a suit or enter a plea.

Our national courts tend to have more prestige than our state courts. However, some of the most controversial—even lurid—cases are found in state courts. In California in recent years screaming headlines have chronicled the progress and announced the verdicts in such cases as the McMartin school case (alleged child molestation), the Rodney King beating and the Reginald Denny assault cases (the verdict in the first case was the spark that gave rise to the LA riots and the other a result of the riots), the Menendez brothers (as their parents watched television the brothers shot them), and the most watched courtroom drama in history, the case of football great O. J. Simpson (accused of killing his former wife and her friend with a knife). The cases that are most likely to affect the average citizen are heard in state courts, from murder to fraud to traffic violations.

The states exercise police power, the power to protect the health, safety, and morals of their citizens. From murder to arson, from fraud to sanitation and traffic violations, the state's jurisdiction over criminal law is very extensive. The same can be said with respect to civil law, where suits for damages, and such matters as divorces, wills, and breach-of-contract suits are taken up in state courts. California's judicial system is the largest in the United States with 337 courts and some 1,610 judges. Nearly nine million cases are filed each year at a cost of approximately $2.5 billion a year.

## ORGANIZATION, JURISDICTION, AND PERSONNEL

California's court system is organized on four levels: (1) municipal courts (largely merged with superior courts since 1998) and sometimes called "inferior" courts; (2) superior courts; (3) district courts of appeal; and (4) the supreme court (see Figure 8.1).

### The Inferior Courts

There have been two major changes in recent years in the organization of the court system in California. Until 1995 justice courts served populations of less than 40,000 and municipal courts populations over 40,000. The voters passed Proposition 191 at the November 1994 general election, eliminating justice courts. The action was less

(Denis Renault, *Sacramento Bee*)

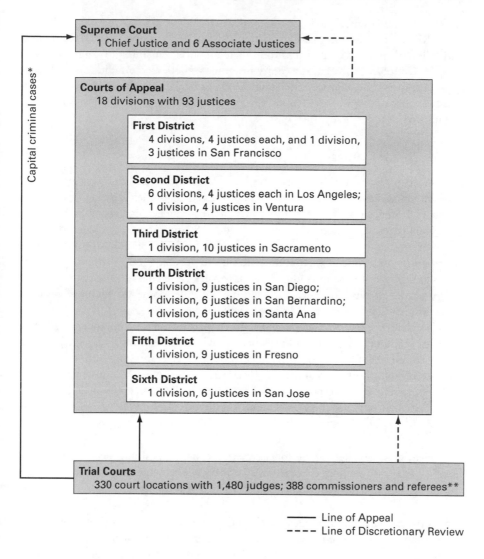

Capital criminal cases*

**Supreme Court**
1 Chief Justice and 6 Associate Justices

**Courts of Appeal**
18 divisions with 93 justices

**First District**
4 divisions, 4 justices each, and 1 division,
3 justices in San Francisco

**Second District**
6 divisions, 4 justices each in Los Angeles;
1 division, 4 justices in Ventura

**Third District**
1 division, 10 justices in Sacramento

**Fourth District**
1 division, 9 justices in San Diego;
1 division, 6 justices in San Bernardino;
1 division, 6 justices in Santa Ana

**Fifth District**
1 division, 9 justices in Fresno

**Sixth District**
1 division, 6 justices in San Jose

**Trial Courts**
330 court locations with 1,480 judges; 388 commissioners and referees**

——— Line of Appeal
- - - - Line of Discretionary Review

\* Death penalty cases are automatically appealed from the superior court directly to the Supreme Court.
\*\* As of June 30, 1998.

**Figure 8.1**    Organization of the California Court System.

drastic than it might seem. Revisions over the years had made the jurisdiction of justice courts, the qualifications of judges to serve on them, and the rules followed by
them identical with municipal courts. Proposition 191 transformed justice courts into
municipal courts and made justice court judges full-time municipal court judges. The
second change came in 1998 when voters approved a constitutional amendment permitting merger of municipal and superior courts.

Proposition 220 provided that, upon a vote of a majority of superior court
judges and a majority of municipal court judges in a county, that county's municipal

courts would be transformed into superior courts. Most did just that. By 2000 only Kern, Kings, and Monterey counties had failed to vote for unification. By 2002 these had followed suit and there were no municipal courts remaining in California. Los Angeles County was the latest to unify in January 2000, creating the world's largest trial court with general jurisdiction. Some 260 municipal court judges from 25 courts became superior court judges joining their colleagues for a grand total of 563 judges serving on the county's superior court.

## The Superior Courts

The superior courts are the general trial courts of the state. Each county has one superior court; however, a court may be authorized by the legislature to establish a number of judgeships. The superior court of Los Angeles, for example, has more than 550 judges, and Alameda has 68, Orange 108, and Fresno 35. Each judge conducts a set of trials in his or her own courtroom. In the larger counties the superior court judges select one of their number to be the presiding judge, who has the duty of assigning cases to the individual judges. In very large counties the tendency is to assign particular types of cases, for example, juvenile, domestic relations, probate, and criminal, to judges in specialized divisions of the court.

The distinctions between municipal and superior courts no longer apply. Before unification municipal courts had jurisdiction over civil cases involving suits for less than $25,000 and superior courts handled those over that amount. With the merger, all cases of first resort are handled by the superior court of each county. Preliminary hearings, heretofor the responsibility of the municipal courts, are now held in superior courts that retain such areas of responsibility as cases involving minors, annulments, divorce and, of course, felonies.

**Qualifications**   To be eligible for a superior court judgeship a person must have been a citizen of the United States for five years, a practicing attorney in California for ten years, and a resident of the county for two years.

**Election**   Superior-court judges are elected in nonpartisan primary elections in the same manner as municipal judges. Most superior court incumbent judges are reelected automatically, but occasionally, a judge will have a challenger or an incumbent will decide not to run for reelection. Challenges to incumbents in superior-court elections are rare. The low visibility of incumbents, the high cost of campaigning, and the slim chance of winning the election discourage individuals from competing for the office.

## The Courts of Appeal

The state courts of appeal are the intermediate layer of tribunals between the superior courts and the supreme court. Three such courts were created by constitutional amendment in 1904, and in 1928 another amendment gave the legislature authority to increase the number of appeals courts as it saw fit. The state is now divided into six districts with one appeals court in each.

California State Supreme Court (Courtesy California State Supreme Court)

The jurisdiction of the district courts is strictly appellate. They review cases already tried in the superior courts and are the review courts for appeals from decisions of quasi-judicial agencies, such as the state industrial accident commission. Some cases appealed from the superior courts go directly to the supreme court for review (see the next section), but many of them wind up on the dockets of a district court of appeal anyway, since the high court may delegate any cases it wishes to them. The supreme court also has the right, however, to assume jurisdiction over any case on a district court's calendar.

## The State Supreme Court

The supreme court is the top state court. Its decisions are final and cannot be appealed unless the U.S. Supreme Court finds that a decision has violated the federal Constitution.

There are six associate justices on the supreme court and one chief justice. The chief justice may convene the court at any time. Concurrence of four judges present at the argument is necessary for a judgment.

The jurisdiction of the supreme court is both appellate and original, but deciding appeals from the lower courts constitutes most of its work. Practically all of the cases reaching the court on appeal originate in a superior court, are then appealed to a district court of appeal, and from there are carried to the supreme court. Cases in which the death sentence is imposed may be appealed directly from the superior courts to the supreme court. The supreme court also can order certain unique cases transferred to it from the courts of appeal before hearing. Because the supreme court usually has discretionary jurisdiction, it hears only about 3 percent of the cases submitted to it. For the most part, the court considers only cases involving a public policy.

The supreme court has original jurisdiction to issue writs of mandamus (to compel a public corporation or officer to act in accord with legal obligations), prohibition (to prevent a lower court from exercising jurisdiction over a suit pending before it), and habeas corpus.

**Qualifications**     To be eligible for a supreme- or appeals-court judgeship a person must meet certain minimal requirements: The person must be a U.S. citizen, a California resident, and a practicing attorney in the state for ten years.

**Election**     The present method of electing judges to the state supreme court and the district courts of appeal was instituted by a constitutional amendment in 1934. It put an end to contested elections to all appellate courts in an effort to insulate the judiciary from political pressures. High court justices continue to stand for election after appointment by the governor, but they do not run against anyone.

Supreme- and appeals-court judges serve for staggered terms of 12 years. At the end of the 12-year term, these judges may run for reelection. In this case, only the name of the incumbent, without opponents, appears on the ballot for the judgeship. If the incumbent does not choose to seek another term, the governor appoints an individual who, as nominee, becomes the only person listed on the ballot. The governor also appoints persons to appellate judgeships in cases of the resignation or death of a judge prior to the completion of the term of office. In such cases the appointee (without opposition) would be subject to confirmation at the next general election and would also be on the ballot at the time of expiration of the particular 12-year term to which the replaced judge had been appointed.

In appointing judges the governor is subject to certain procedures. Before making a nomination, he or she must consult the Commission on Judicial Nominees—a 25-member commission appointed by the Board of Governors of the State Bar of California, a private association of lawyers in California. This commission has 90 days in which to make a recommendation that consists of rating a nominee on a four-point scale: "exceptionally well-qualified," "well-qualified," "qualified," and "not qualified." The governor is not bound by the commission's report, but the commission may make the report public if the governor appoints a candidate it has rated as unqualified. However, another commission—the Commission on Judicial Appointments (consisting of the chief justice of the supreme court, the presiding judge of a district court of appeal, and the state attorney general)—has the authority to approve or reject a governor's appointment to California's appellate or supreme court.

Because the ballot for judges of the appellate courts and supreme courts contains only one name, voters record a "yes" or "no" vote to the question of the reelection of a judge. If a justice seeking reelection receives more "no" votes than "yes" votes, the governor appoints someone else to serve on the court until the next election. Until 1986 all supreme- and appeals-court incumbents or nominees whose names appeared on the ballot had received a majority of "yes" votes. However, on a few occasions campaigns for "no" votes have been launched against certain judges in controversial cases. For example, in 1966 right-wing groups in the state sought to defeat for reelection three of the supreme court justices who had declared Proposition 14 of 1964 (allowing racial discrimination in housing) unconstitutional. By all odds, the most effective campaign was that against Chief Justice Rose Bird in 1986.

## THE CASE OF ROSE BIRD

Rose Bird, the first woman to become the chief justice of the California State Supreme Court, also became the first justice under the present form of selection of judges to be voted out of office. In the November election of 1986 she lost reelection to office by a 2–1 margin. At the same time two associate justices of the supreme court, Joseph R. Grodin and Cruz Reynoso—other members of the court's liberal majority—also failed to receive a majority of "yes" votes (though by smaller margins than that of the chief justice) and thus did not retain their positions.

Rose Bird's tenure on the court was marked by controversy. Her unwillingness to approve any of the more than 50 death sentences in capital cases angered many voters who felt she was substituting her judgment for the law of the state. In many instances the grounds for reversing a death sentence appeared to the public to be stretching credibility. In one notable instance a man shot and killed three persons kneeling before him, having to reload twice, yet Bird with three other justices held there was inadequate evidence of an intent to kill.

Bird was approved by the narrowest margin in history in her first public confirmation vote in 1978 (51.7 percent). There was concern over her youth and lack of legal experience (she had never sat on any bench). Once confirmed, Bird became a lightning rod for the public's belief that the courts had grown too concerned with the rights of the accused and too little with the harm done to victims. Had she been simply a justice, that might have proved less true, but her highly visible stance as chief justice focused the public's attention on her and her role in a series of controversial decisions.

Several separate campaign organizations that spent between $8 million and $10 million waged efforts against her reconfirmation in 1986, though it is doubtful they had much effect. Public opinion polls taken before these campaigns got under way indicated the public opposed reconfirmation of Bird by a 2–1 margin. When the votes were tallied election night, Bird was rejected by a 2–1 margin. Both Cruz Reynoso and Joseph Grodin, targeted by anti-Bird campaigns as well, were also voted off the court.

## THE LUCAS AND GEORGE COURTS

Following a series of resignations, only Justice Stanley Mosk, appointed by Governor Edmund G. "Pat" Brown, remained of the "liberal" court of Rose Bird. Contrary to the expressed fears of Bird supporters, there has not been a rash of attempts to oust other judges and the independence of the courts has not been jeopardized. In fact, the less colorful (some have termed it a "gray flannel court") and less controversial court has seen public attention to its decisions dwindle. For some who would prefer a more pioneering court, that is disappointing. There has been more of an inclination to go along with federal standards rather than raise new state criteria. Where the Bird court appeared to seek out minor mistakes in judicial proceedings as a means of overturning convictions, the Lucas court has adopted the federal standard of "harmless error" under which, if the error had no effect on the outcome, it is ignored. Though the Lucas court has not been a "hanging court," it has been far more willing to uphold lower court convictions than its predecessor. With respect to capital punishment cases, for example, the Bird court overturned 64 of 68 cases reviewed. The rate of convictions upheld by the court since 1997 is roughly 90 percent. Finally, it might be noted the Lucas court has not always been quite as predictable as some people anticipated. When Dan Lungren was nominated by Governor Deukmejian to be state treasurer, Deukmejian maintained approval was required from only one house of the legislature. Opponents held both houses had to approve. The court sided with the opponents (and, because the senate refused to give its approval, Lungren was blocked from office). Though favorable to business, the court declined businesses's plea to make the "deep pockets" initiative (which banned a process under which those with money paid for damages even if only slightly at fault when others more at fault could not) retroactive. On the other hand, the court sided with the insurance companies when they complained that Proposition 103's requirement that all automobile insurance premiums be cut a minimum of 20 percent denied them a reasonable profit. And, in a blow to conservatives, the Lucas court consistently held that the state does have to pay for abortions for the poor.

Much the same might be said of the court under the leadership of Ronald George. Though generally conservative, the court has outraged conservatives from time to time, most notably in a case that led to a serious effort to deny to two justices, George and Associate Justice Ming Chin, reconfirmation by the voters in 1998. The decision involved reversal of an earlier action which upheld a state law requiring minors to obtain parental consent prior to having an abortion. By a narrow 4–3 vote, the majority, including George and Chin, declared on rehearing the case that the law was unconstitutional. Opponents of abortion fought to have the two men thrown off the court. They failed with George securing 75 percent approval and Chin 69 percent. In general, however, the court has pleased conservatives. In general George is seen as cautious as is his court. It (and he) stayed out of the controversies surrounding the recall election that removed Gray Davis from office as well as the issues over imposition of "three strikes" penalties for minor third offenses. With respect to same sex marriages, a decision was handed down, but on narrow legal grounds over whether San Francisco mayor Gavin Newsome had exceeded his power by granting marriages licenses to same sex couples (ruling he did not), but not over the more basic question of the legality of banning such unions.

There has been concern that fewer cases are being heard in recent years. That is at least in part due to the flood of death penalty cases inundating the court, and some, most notably former Chief Justice Lucas, have argued that such cases, instead of being automatically sent to the supreme court from superior courts, should first be reviewed at the appellate court level.

A major contributor to the court's workload has been multiple appeals (using the writ of habeas corpus, which asks for immediate investigation by the courts as to the propriety of the prisoner being held) that have stretched over many years. Many pointed to the case of Robert Alton Harris, who was given the death penalty for killing two teenage boys outside a fast food restaurant (after which he calmly ate their hamburgers). He spent 13 years on death row before his execution. His lawyers forwarded appeal after appeal, each on different grounds (he was the victim of child abuse, he was afflicted with fetal alcohol syndrome, the use of the gas chamber was cruel and unusual punishment, to mention just three), a practice called "piecemeal litigation" that delayed his execution and added to the court's case load.

In 1993, in the case of *In re Clark* (5 Cal. 4th, 750), the court in a 5–2 decision held that virtually all prisoners on death row would be allowed just one petition for a writ of habeas corpus. Additional applications will be rejected unless it can be shown that denying the writ would result in a "substantial miscarriage of justice." Critics stated the ruling created too rigid a standard and would hurt those accused who could not afford experienced trial lawyers. That it apparently has had little impact can be seen in the case of Stanley Tookie Williams, founder of the notorious Crips street gang. He was executed in December 2005 after spending nearly a quarter of a century on death row having been convicted of four brutal murders. Here, too, there were multiple appeals, from witness tampering to an allegedly botched ballistic test. All grounds used were ultimately rejected by every court that heard them.

Chief Justice Lucas resigned in May 1996 and Associate Justice Ronald George succeeded him as chief justice. Diversity appeared the watchword for the new court with three women, two Asians, and a black constituting the new George court. That became even more diverse with the death in 2001 of long serving (37 years) Stanley Mosk who was succeeded by first generation Mexican-American Carlos Moreno. With the departure of Janice Rogers Brown to the federal appeals bench in 2005, many expected Governor Schwarzenegger to appoint another black to the vacancy. It came as a surprise to some when he appointed San Francisco appeals court judge Carol Corrigan, a white woman. However, the nominee fit another profile the governor sought, in that she had a record as a centrist or moderate.

## The Judicial Council

California is among the three-fourths of the states that have established a judicial council to oversee the entire state court system. Although not a court, the Judicial Council is an integral part of the state's judicial organization and has some authority to make rulings on judicial procedure that have the force of law.

There are 21 members of the council, 15 of whom are drawn from the various levels of the court system. In addition, there are four members of the state bar and one appointee from each house of the legislature.

The chief justice is the presiding officer and, in that capacity, may temporarily reassign judges from courts with low demand to others with high workloads or where there is a vacancy.

The main business of the Judicial Council is to carry on a continuous study of the work of the courts. It publishes biennial reports showing the numbers and kinds of cases handled by the various levels. It recommends and sometimes decrees procedural improvements to the courts. It holds seminars that orient newly appointed judges and that keep them up-to-date on the law. The Judicial Council recommends constitutional and statutory changes to the legislature that would improve the administration of justice. The council appoints an administrative director to implement its decisions.

## Compensation of Judges

The salaries for the judges of all state courts are set by the legislature, the judges in each level of court receiving the same salary throughout the state. The justices of the state supreme court and the courts of appeal are paid from the state treasury; the wages of superior court judges are paid partly by the state and partly by the county; and the salaries of municipal-court judges are paid entirely by the county.

The pay of the chief justice in 2005 was $190,930 while that for associate justices was $182,071. Appellate-court judges were paid $170,694, and superior-court judges $149,160. The relative generosity of the legislature in this respect may be due to a belief that at some time in the future lawyer members might have occasion to appear before the court. Or it may simply be a fear of the court's political clout.

## Removal of Judges

There are several ways that judges may be removed from office, although they are seldom invoked. First, judges may be recalled by the voters. Second, they may be impeached by the assembly and convicted by a two-thirds vote of the senate. Third, if a court finds them guilty of a felony or any crime involving moral turpitude and if the conviction is upheld by a higher court, the supreme court must dismiss them from office. Finally, on the recommendation of the Commission on Judicial Performance[1] the state supreme court has the power to retire a judge for a disability that interferes with his or her ability to perform and is likely to continue or for willful misconduct (e.g., swearing, sexual harassment, ethnic bias).

The Commission acts to police judicial actions and may impose penalties less than removal from the bench. In several instances judges have been "admonished" for falling asleep during a trial. In another case a judge received the same penalty for improperly disclosing to a friend confidential information from the Department of Motor Vehicles. A more serious penalty, also less than removal, is a censure. A judge

---

[1]Composition of the Commission on Judicial Performance was changed by the voters when they approved Proposition 190 in November 1994. Responding to complaints the Commission was "stacked" in favor of judges, they enlarged the membership from nine to eleven and provided for six public members who are joined by three judges appointed by the supreme court and two members of the state Bar, who are appointed by the governor.

in Central California was censured for discussing pending cases with the media in violation of the code of judicial ethics.

A special procedure was created in 1976 by the voters when they amended the state constitution to deal with the supreme court. Upon recommendation of the Commission on Judicial Performance involving censure, removal or forced retirement of a justice shall be determined by a panel of seven chosen by lot from the ranks of the appellate-court judges.

In 1979, the Commission on Judicial Performance made an investigation into the conduct of the state supreme court—the first investigation of its kind in the nation. This action was taken following newspaper allegations that politically sensitive cases had been held up by the court until after the November 1978 general election, in which Chief Justice Bird and three associate justices were candidates for retention. The commission held hearings for nearly five weeks, and detailed accounts of how the state's top judges went about their business became available to the public.

Evidence gathered did not prove the justices guilty of wrongdoing or of intentionally delaying action on politically sensitive cases. However, exposing the many squabbles between the judges did considerable damage to the court's public image.

## THE ADMINISTRATION OF JUSTICE

The law enforceable in the state courts is found in the California constitution and in the state's body of statutory law that the legislature has incorporated into a series of codes, such as the *Civil Code,* the *Government Code,* the *Penal Code,* and the *Elections Code.* However, no written law can anticipate every variety of case that may arise. Judges must often rely on English common-law precedent to render a decision; sometimes they have no guide but their own sense of justice. Because of the complexity of the law, its interpretation, and its application to individual cases, detailed rules of procedure are established to protect citizens against arbitrary handling by the state's legal authorities and to ensure all citizens equitable treatment in court.

### Criminal Procedure

A criminal offense is a crime against society. There are three general categories of criminal offense: *felonies,* which are the most serious crimes, such as murder, armed robbery, rape, forgery, and perjury; *misdemeanors,* which are lesser offenses, such as selling liquor to a minor; and *infractions,* which are the least serious violations, such as illegal parking and operating an automobile without proper equipment. Upon conviction of a felony the judge may impose upon the defendant the sentence of one year or more in state prison or a heavy fine, or both. In the case of a misdemeanor the penalty may be a term of not more than one year in the county jail or a fine of not more than $1,000, or both. Those guilty of an infraction suffer only a fine.

The general rights of the accused in criminal cases are outlined in Article I of the state constitution. The defendant is guaranteed a preliminary hearing before a magistrate (if accused of a felony), the right to legal counsel, the right to know the charges against him or her, the right of trial by jury, the right to confront witnesses, and the right to summon witnesses on his or her own behalf. These provisions have been elaborated by the courts and the legislature to provide for the following procedures.

**In Cases of Felony**   (1) At the time of arrest, the accused is "booked" at the police station or the sheriff's office, and the section of the law that allegedly has been violated is listed against this name. (2) The accused is taken before a court for a preliminary hearing, whereupon the judge informs the accused of his or her rights under law. If the accused pleads guilty he or she is sentenced by the superior court; if the accused pleads not guilty, but the judge believes the evidence is strong enough, he or she is committed to the superior court for trial. Pending further action the accused is held in jail or released on bail. (3) An *information* (accusation) is signed against the accused, usually by the district attorney of the county, or the county's grand jury votes an *indictment*. (4) As just noted, when the accused appears in superior court he or she pleads either guilty or not guilty. If the plea is the former, the accused is sentenced; if the plea is the latter, a trial is held. The accused may waive jury trial, in which case the judge determines guilt or innocence. If the accused does not waive trial by jury, a panel of potential jury members is called up. Prosecuting and defense attorneys may question the prospective jurors and disqualify those whose impartiality is doubted. Ultimately, a jury of 12, satisfactory to both sides, is sworn in. (5) After hearing witnesses and arguments of attorneys, the jury strives for a unanimous verdict of guilty or not guilty. Death penalty cases require unanimity to convict; others may entail a super majority. If a decision cannot be reached within a reasonable time, the jury is dismissed, and a new trial is ordered. (6) A verdict of not guilty releases the defendant. If the verdict is guilty, the defendant is sentenced by the judge after an interval of a few days to allow for a probation report. During this period the defendant's attorney may make a motion for a new trial or file notice of appeal.

**In Cases of Misdemeanors**   The procedure usually is simpler for misdemeanors, a less serious type of crime. The accused (or attorney) is required to appear in a court in the county where the offense allegedly occurred. Frequently, those arrested plead guilty. But a defendant may plead not guilty and demand a jury trial or may waive this privilege in favor of a trial by the judge alone. If found guilty, the defendant may be fined or sentenced to the county jail, or both.

**In Cases of Infractions**   The 1968 legislature made provision for a type of criminal offense less serious than a misdemeanor, namely, the infraction. At first, very few offenses other than illegal parking were so classified. In the decade following, however, the list of infractions expanded enormously, so that today 80 percent of the violations defined in the California Vehicle Code are characterized as infractions. The list includes all speeding violations, for example. Typically, a person who is cited for an infraction does not appear before a judge; instead the person goes to the clerk of a nearby justice or municipal court and pays the ticket. (Technically, the defendant is not paying a fine, only posting bail and then automatically pleading guilty, which forfeits the bail.) However, if the prosecutor or the defendant requests a formal court trial, there is no jury, and the judge makes the decision as to innocence or guilt. In such a case free legal counsel is not guaranteed to the defendant, although he or she may hire a lawyer. If found guilty, the defendant may be fined but not sentenced to jail, unless he or she refuses to pay the fine. In certain counties, traffic violations are heard by special commissioners rather than by a judge.

**Plea Bargaining**    Important in actual law enforcement is the practice of *plea bargaining*. This occurs when a person is arrested and charged with a relatively serious criminal offense. However, before the case comes to trial the defendant (usually through the defendant's attorney) enters into an agreement with the prosecutor whereby the prosecutor reduces the charge, that is, accuses the defendant of a less serious crime, in return for which the defendant pleads guilty to the lesser offense. Thus a formal trial is avoided with its cost in time and money. Frequently, a felony is reduced to a misdemeanor. For example, if a person is caught throwing clods of dirt at passing automobiles, this individual could be booked on the felony charge of "throwing a missile with intent to do serious bodily harm," but the prosecutor may in return for a guilty plea reduce the charge to the misdemeanor of "throwing a substance at a vehicle." Rigorous advocates of law and order denounce plea bargaining as "coddling the criminals," but law-enforcement agents defend it as the only practical course in view of the crowded dockets of California's courts.

Proposition 8, approved by the voters in 1982, prohibited plea bargaining in any case in which the indictment or information charges any serious felony or any offense of driving while under the influence of alcohol, drugs, narcotics, or any other intoxicating substance, unless there is insufficient evidence to prove the case.

**The Grand Jury**    Every county in the state has a grand jury whose members are volunteers and serve for one year. Judges provide many nominees to the grand jury pools, though advertisements in the mass media result in others. The requirements to serve are simple: one must be a citizen, live in the county, and possess a sufficient grasp of the English language to be able to participate. Grand juries typically spend much of their time investigating the ways in which county government operates, making suggestions for improvement. In Fresno County, for example, a system under which pay for police and fire personnel was linked to the average salaries of comparable employees in eight other cities was recommended for elimination. (And it was later, by public vote.)

Much more dramatic are instances in which a grand jury indicts someone for a criminal offense. This power was enhanced in 1990 with voter approval of Proposition 115. Now indictments no longer need to be followed by another preliminary hearing. Instead they go directly to trial. That increased the frequency of using grand juries for indictments, up from 20 in 1989 to 540 in 1992. But, placed in perspective, the vast majority of indictments are not through grand juries. In Los Angeles County in 1992 there were 50 grand jury indictments out of 70,000 felony complaints.

One issue that has recently arisen involves this increased use and the composition of grand juries. Because they are volunteers and the work can be long and hard for very little money ($25 a day), those serving tend to be non-Hispanic whites. Many Hispanics cannot afford to serve or have been disqualified as noncitizens or by their statement that they are not fully comfortable with English. However, that results in grand juries that are not reflective of the county population in most cases. Several counties have developed second grand juries, which require service for a few weeks to three months and are drawn from regular jury lists. That is, of course, more expensive.

## Civil Procedures

California civil law, like all law based on English jurisprudence, is divided into two broad categories—cases at law and cases in equity. Cases *at law* generally include all suits brought by one party to collect money from another party for debts owed or for damages already done. Cases *in equity* are usually to prevent harm, especially irreparable damage. Equity also involves annulments and divorces (where often the harm already has been done), the administration of trusts, cancellation of fraudulent contracts, and various judicial writs and most injunctions.[2] A voter who feels that he or she has been deprived of his or her rights, for example, files an equity suit against the appropriate elections official.

**In Cases at Law**     The procedure for cases at law (provided they are for more than $5,000 in damages) is briefly as follows. (1) The plaintiff (or attorney) files suit against the defendant, stating the amount of money that is expected to be collected and the reasons for the claim. (2) The defendant, after having been notified of the suit, has any one of three options: not to contest the suit and allow the plaintiff to win by default; to settle the dispute with the plaintiff out of court; or to contest the matter, in which case the defendant's attorney files a formal answer to the charges and sometimes a countersuit. (3) Both parties appear in court and decide whether or not to waive a jury trial. If either party wants a jury trial, members are selected and sworn in (12 jurors unless both parties agree to fewer). (4) After witnesses are heard and arguments are given, the jury deliberates. The jury must decide whether the defendant is liable as charged and also to what amount the defendant is liable. (If a jury has been waived, the judge makes these decisions.) Three-fourths of the jurors must agree in order to deliver a verdict.

Another case at law is what is known as a small claims case. Under state law a claim against some person or other private entity may be filed for hearing in small claims court. The maximum amount of a claim for any one suit is $2,500, though two may be filed in any one year for a maximum of $5,000. A commissioner with the power of a judge presides. No attorneys are present. Arguments are presented by the contending parties and a decision rendered by the commissioner. If the decision is for the plaintiff, the defendant has the right to appeal. If it is against the plaintiff, no

---

[2]A well-known example of an *injunction* (in equity) is a court's order to a labor union to prevent a strike.

further recourse is available under state law and the decision stands. The popular syndicated television programs *The People's Court* and *Judge Judy* are examples of a small claims court in action.

**In Cases in Equity**    There are no jury trials in cases in equity. All issues of law and fact are determined by the judge. These are handled by superior-court judges. When a case involves a highly important matter, for example, in the attempt of one local government to compel another local government to fulfill a contract, the state supreme court may assume original jurisdiction.

The basic steps in equity procedure are as follows. (1) The plaintiff or attorney files a petition to the court requesting a specific action in equity, such as an injunction for a divorce. (2) The defendant is notified of the charges in the petition and is asked to appear in court to show good reason why the petition should not be granted. The defendant or attorney thereupon files a formal answer. (3) In open court before the judge, both sides present their arguments. (4) The judge renders a decision, which may be appealed by either party to a higher court.

## IMPROVING THE ADMINISTRATION OF JUSTICE

### Eliminating Unnecessary Delays

"Justice delayed is justice denied" is a long-held belief. In California's courts the denial has been prevalent. Civil cases in particular have seen delays of as much as seven years and typically of three to four years. In recognition of this sorry state of affairs, the state legislature in 1990 passed the Trial Court Delay Reduction Act. Under the old procedures different aspects of a complex case were heard before different judges. Now the same judge hears all aspects of civil cases from the filing of the complaint through pretrial motions to the trial itself. Judges have set strict deadlines and have the power to impose sanctions on lawyers who attempt delaying tactics. The impact has been impressive, at least in many courts. The new rules have encouraged more out-of-court settlements, relieving court congestion. For example, approximately 5 percent of cases filed in 1992 in Orange County actually went to trial. And the waiting period dropped from three to five years before the act to an average of 17 months in 1993.

Other proposals have been put forth to relieve court congestion. Some have urged that minor traffic violations be handled by the Department of Motor Vehicles. Others have suggested increased use of mediation and arbitration procedures as a means of cutting court caseloads. Another recommendation was turned down by the voters in 1988 when they rejected a (possibly flawed) no-fault auto insurance system that would have radically reduced the number of civil lawsuits in the courts. Medical malpractice cases might be handled by a special commission rather than the courts, a means of reducing court overload and at the same time cutting medical costs. Proposition 115, passed in 1990, allows judges—rather than lawyers—to question prospective jurors as a means of expediting the selection process. In view of the fact that a large volume of cases in the criminal courts deal with narcotics and

# Caucus

by Hügo

(Courtesy, *World West Features*)

alcohol addicts, it has been said these are, in many cases, medical problems and should be dealt with by special tribunals.

## Selecting Well-Qualified Judges

Although for the most part California citizens have been satisfied with the quality of the state judicial personnel, there has been some criticism of selecting judges on the basis of their political appeal. Some go so far as to criticize the whole system of popular election of judges. It has been suggested that judges be appointed by the governor with the consent of the state senate (similar to the national pattern). Others have proposed that the state supreme court (whether elected by the people or appointed by the governor) should appoint all lower-court judges. The Judicial Council has proposed a "merit plan" of selecting judges; that is, when the governor appoints a judge to fill any vacancy the governor selects a name from a list submitted by a nominating commission that consists of an equal number of judges, lawyers, and laypersons.

Others maintain that the method of selecting judges is adequate but that some of our most qualified lawyers do not seek judgeships because the salaries are lower than the income they receive from private practice. More security of tenure has also been advocated as a means of attracting better judges, the possibility of the recall being cited as a major deterrent (see discussion of the recall in Chapter 5).

## Reforming the Jury System

There is no significant movement to do away with the jury system, because it is generally regarded as a deeply rooted and valuable heritage of American jurisprudence. Yet thoughtful observers are aware of its imperfections. A person's peers are not always the best judges and often not the most objective. Jurors frequently confuse questions of moral right or wrong (which they are not expected to answer) with questions of legal fact, and when penalties are severe they will at times hesitate to convict in the face of overwhelming evidence.

Most suggestions are for improving the system rather than for tearing it down. Higher compensation and fewer exemptions from serving for professional persons would increase quality. One proposal would reduce the size of juries. In the case of *Williams v. Florida* (1971) the federal Supreme Court held that the U.S. Constitution permitted a state to decrease the number of jurors to six. California, so far, has retained the 12-member jury in criminal cases, although the state constitution does permit fewer jurors in a trial for a misdemeanor, provided both parties agree. It has been proposed that less than a unanimous vote, such as three-fourths, be required for conviction in any criminal case, except when the death penalty is involved. The state constitution also allows a jury of fewer than 12 persons in civil suits (subject to agreement by the plaintiff and the defendant), and furthermore only a three-fourths majority is necessary for a civil verdict. A committee of the Bar Association has suggested that an eight-member jury be made standard for all civil trials, with six votes being required for a verdict.[3]

## Reducing the High Cost of Justice

The right to a fair trial in court is one of our most treasured civil liberties, but it can be a very expensive privilege. Lawyers' fees are not low, nor is the cost of printing the record for an appeal to a higher court. Consequently, many persons do not have the money to avail themselves of their constitutional rights. Various attempts are being made to correct this inequity. In criminal proceedings, for example, indigents are furnished the services of a public defender or of a private attorney assigned by the court. In civil matters, county legal-aid societies and the California Rural Legal Assistance agency, financed by the national government, offer assistance to people with low incomes. It has been pointed out that these efforts still are not sufficient; public defenders are often overworked, and the private attorney appointed by the court to represent the indigent often is not as experienced as the high-priced lawyer a rich opponent has hired. There is pressure to increase the appropriations for the public defenders' offices.

---

[3]Pat B. Anderson, "Bar Suggests Ways to Cut Court Costs," *Los Angeles Times*, July 2, 1978.

## GETTING TOUGH ON CRIME

The voters have long favored a "get tough" approach to crime and criminals. In 1982 they adopted the Victim's Bill of Rights (Proposition 8), which includes restitution for the victim or victim's family by the felon and secures the right of that family to appear and testify at parole hearings, limits plea bargaining in serious felony and drunk driving cases, and lengthens a variety of sentences. In their approval in 1990 of Proposition 115, voters once again acted to toughen the criminal-justice system. This multifaceted initiative put into the state constitution the following, among other things, in addition to the aspects already referred to earlier: an expanded list of "special circumstances" (allowing imposition of the death penalty) to include killing a witness; a provision allowing minors 16 and 17 years old to be tried as adults and, if convicted of first degree murder with special circumstances, to be punished by life in prison without possibility of parole; permitting the introduction of hearsay evidence at preliminary hearings if given by trained and experienced officers; and establishing the crime of torture, which carries with it life imprisonment without possibility of parole. The move toward a three strikes and you're out initiative in 1994 simply continued this "get tough" policy of California's citizens (see Chapter 12). And in March 2000, voters approved Proposition 21, which tightened criminal procedures further, including a lowering of the age at which a juvenile can be tried in adult court to 14.

## REVIEW QUESTIONS

1. What are the levels of courts in California and how do their functions differ? What organizational changes have taken place in recent years? (pp. 144–198)
2. What are the principal differences in the court decisions handed down by the Bird and Lucas-George courts? How might each be judged on a conservative vs. liberal standard? (pp. 149–151)
3. What functions are performed by the Commission on Judicial Performance and the Commission on Judicial Appointments? (pp. 152–153)
4. What are the three types of crime prosecuted in California? How do cases at law differ from cases in equity? (pp. 154–155)
5. What changes have been implemented or proposed to improve the operation of the judicial system? (pp. 157–159)

## SELECTED WEB SITES

The Judicial Council maintains an extensive web site (www.courtinfo.ca.gov) covering a wide variety of topics associated with the administration of justice in California. Included are questions and answers involving "how to" issues (how to file a claim in small claims court; how to complain about the conduct of an attorney; how new judgeships are created). Texts of opinions of the supreme court and appellate courts over the previous 100 days are provided. Another site, www.leginfo.ca.gov/calaw.html, gives access to the texts of all 29 state codes, including civil, business, education, elections, and health and safety codes.

# SELECTED REFERENCES ───────────────

Adams, G. Dennis, Thomas A. Ault, and Alden J. Fulkerson, "Proposition 10: Court Unification Arguments," *Los Angeles Daily Law Journal,* October 25, 1982.

Barbieri, Richard, "Law-and-Order Court Shows No Sign of Softening," *The Recorder,* December 29, 1993.

Blume, William W., "California Courts in Historical Perspective," *Hastings Law Journal,* November 1970.

Chiang, Harriet, "Freed of Politics, State High Court is Showing its Independence," *San Francisco Chronicle,* September 6, 1999.

Cochran, Dena, "A Victim's Bill of Rights or a Lawyer's Employment Act?" *California Journal,* April 1982.

Egelko, Robert, "The Supreme Court's Revolving Door," in Thomas R. Hoeber and Charles M. Price, eds., *California Government and Politics Annual, 1993–94,* Sacramento: California Journal Press, 1993.

_____, "A Low Profile Court," *California Journal,* June 1994.

_____, "End of the Lucas Era," *California Journal,* July 1996.

Judicial Council of California, *Annual Reports,* Sacramento: State Printing Office, annual.

Maharaj, Davan, "Civil Justice Is Speedier in Courts These Days," *Los Angeles Times,* October 26, 1993.

McMillan, Penelope, "Grand Juries' Racial Makeup Under Challenge," *Los Angeles Times,* October 12, 1993.

Schreiber, Harry N., and Charles Ruhlin, "An Effective California Judicial System for the 21st Century" in Bruce E. Cain and Roger G. Noll, eds., *Constitutional Reform in California,* Berkeley: Institute of Governmental Studies Press, 1995.

Chapter

# 9

# Local Government in California

The men who met in Philadelphia in 1787 were among the wisest of all men. They were well-grounded in history and politics and created a governing structure for the country that has endured longer than any other in today's world. In one respect, however, they proved wildly off the mark. They expected that government closest to the people would be most responsive to and controlled by the people. Survey after survey indicates the public knows much more about what is going on in Washington, D.C., than they do about what state and, especially, local government officials are doing. Most know who the president is but the governor is less well known and for many the members of the local city council or board of supervisors are invisible.

Yet the Founding Fathers were right in one proposition, that the government that would prove to have the greatest impact on the lives of the citizenry would be local in nature. A quick look at some of the functions performed by city and county governments confirms the correctness of their vision. Among the many functions performed by counties in California are: law enforcement (sheriffs, the court system), building and maintaining roads, keeping records (births, deaths, divorces, property transfers), offering medical care to the poor, providing public transportation, administering welfare programs, and setting the rules for proper use of different parts of the county (land use rules). Counties also provide services to cities in such areas as law enforcement (cities have accused criminals tried in county courts and held in county jails), libraries, and indigent health care to cite just three.

When a city or county acts or does not act may well have a significant impact on the lives of those living in them. Pot holes in major roadways filled or not, trash collected or left to rot, parks with broken swings or shards of glass from discarded bottles, not to mention a promptly answered 911 call seeking help in putting a house fire out or dealing with an intruder—all are examples of functions performed by local governments, and that does not include school and special districts that provide everything from water to protection against proliferation of mosquitoes. Yes, the men at Philadelphia *were* right: local government *is* important to the quality of our daily lives. Nearly 8,000 of them that operate in California are essential to the well being of those living in the state.

## RELATION OF THE LOCAL UNITS TO THE STATE GOVERNMENT

All local governments in California, although they possess varying degrees of autonomy, are creatures and agents of the state. Their functions, powers, and structure are determined by the state constitution and by statutes of the state legislature, and they have no authority other than that granted by the state.

### Constitutional Provisions

The inherent right of the state legislature to create local governments, define their powers, and prescribe their structure is recognized in Article XI of the state constitution. However, the legislature does not have a free hand in the discharge of these functions. The constitution permits counties and cities to frame their own charters and outlines in detail of what provisions these charters must contain. Important financial relations between local governments and the state are also immune from legislative tampering—the most important being the distribution of motor vehicle tax funds and the constitution-set floor for funding per student of state money to local school districts. The direct relation between local law-enforcement officers and the attorney general also would require constitutional amendment to be altered.

### State-Local Relationships

Some administrative departments of the state government have established close relations with local government units, not so much because of a provision in the state constitution as because of the mutual advantages to be gained through practical, day-to-day cooperation. Local sheriffs' offices and police departments, for example, file copies of fingerprints and reports of crimes with the Bureau of Criminal Identification in the state Department of Justice, and the bureau in turn makes available to the local agencies a fund of information and expert analysis possible only in a centralized criminal information agency. The area of social welfare provides another illustration of coordinated effort between levels of government. The state director of social welfare and staff makes rules for the administration and distribution of public assistance monies. However, individuals desiring aid must apply at their county welfare department, and it is the local agency that gives them that check.

## THE COUNTY

The county is the local subdivision through which the state performs many of its most important functions: maintenance of public health programs, public relief administration, law enforcement, administration of justice, upkeep of roads, administration of elections, and the maintenance of vital statistics and property records.

In 1850, the California State Legislature created 27 counties, and by 1907 they had been subdivided to make up the present 58. From that time when Imperial County split from Riverside County no new county has been formed. Organizers for a proposed new county must present a petition containing signatures of a sufficient number of the county's registered voters to divide the county. This proposal is reviewed by the state to determine the economic viability of the proposed new county and at the same time to decide whether the division would drastically hurt the remaining county. If approved by the state, final approval requires concurrent voter majorities in both the proposed new county and the remaining territory. In the past 12 years, six of the attempts to form new counties have reached the election stage. In 1978 three areas in Los Angeles County attempted to break away: the Newhall-Saugus area, the Palos Verdes peninsula, and the South Bay area. Other attempts were made in 1982 in Eastern Fresno County, the Lake Tahoe region of eastern El Dorado County in 1984, and most recently, in 1988, the northern area of San Bernardino County. All were turned down by the voters.

California's counties vary widely in size, population, and economy. San Bernardino County with 20,164 square miles is larger than any county in the nation, and San Francisco with 46 square miles is among the smallest. Los Angeles County is the most populous—more than 9.8 million people—and Alpine with about 1,200 inhabitants is one of the least populated. Alameda County is one of the most highly industrialized counties in the United States, and Sierra County is one big forest area.

## Types of Counties

**The General-Law County**  Forty-seven of California's counties are organized under general laws enacted by the state legislature. The constitution provides (in Article XI, section 1b) that:

> The Legislature shall provide for county powers, an elected county sheriff and an elected governing body in each county . . . each governing body shall prescribe by ordinance the compensation of its members, but the ordinance prescribing such compensation shall be subject to referendum. The Legislature or the governing body may provide for other officers whose compensation shall be prescribed by the governing body. The governing body shall provide for the number, compensation, tenure, and appointment of employees.

Successive acts of the legislature have established the present statewide pattern in which the voters in each county elect a board of supervisors, sheriff, district attorney, coroner, assessor, tax collector, treasurer, auditor, county clerk, recorder, public administrator, superintendent of public schools, and judges of the superior municipal court. The voters clearly do not receive a short ballot in county elections. The legislature also requires that the board of supervisors appoint a long list of lesser officers, including a sealer of weights and measures, health officer, civil service commissioner, airport manager, and pound master.

The board of supervisors is the chief legislative and administrative body of the county. It adopts the county budget, enacts special taxes such as the 1 percent sales tax, and in some counties sits as a board of equalization to hear complaints against the property valuations set by the county assessor. (A constitutional amendment adopted in 1966 permits a county board of supervisors to create tax-assessment appeals boards to perform this function.) The board also has the power to enact criminal ordinances, such as prohibitions on gambling, to apply to residents of *un*incorporated areas (not part of cities) within its jurisdiction. It hires and fires county civil service personnel, approves all purchases made by the county, manages all county property, and markets bonds floated by the county and school districts. In election years the board serves as elections commission. Other ex officio roles of the supervisors are to act as board of directors for the county smog control, flood control, and road districts.

Probably the best known of all elected county officers is the sheriff, whose major responsibility is the apprehension of all alleged offenders against the criminal laws of the state and county within the unincorporated areas of the county. Other important officers concerned with law enforcement are the district attorney, who is the county's prosecuting officer in some criminal cases and represents the county in civil cases to which the county is a party, and the coroner, who is responsible for investigating the causes of deaths not attended by a physician, especially those that indicate violence, foul play, or poison.

The most important county officers concerned with finance are the assessor, the tax collector, the auditor, and the treasurer. The assessor, aided by a large staff of deputies, determines the taxable value of real and personal property in the county. The tax collector has a thankless job—mailing out tax bills to each property owner, deeding to the state property on which tax payments are delinquent, and collecting the various business and license fees. The auditor's (in some counties the controller's) duties are comparable to those of the state controller: authorizing all payments of county funds as provided for in the budget. The treasurer is the custodian of the county funds, depositing them in banks and making payments only when presented with warrants signed by the auditor.

Another officer with substantial responsibilities is the county clerk, who is the clerk of the superior court and in most counties the ex officio clerk for the board of supervisors. In many counties the clerk has the weighty duty of managing the official election machinery for state and county elections, which includes handling the filing of candidates' and direct legislation petitions, preparing the ballot, securing the necessary election supplies, and overseeing vote tabulations. (In a few of the larger counties these electoral functions are performed by a separate registrar of voters.) In addition, the county clerk issues marriage licenses to prospective couples.

Virtually all of the counties have in addition to the district attorney, whose jurisdiction is the criminal law, a county counsel whose field of operation is the civil law. The county counsel gives legal advice to the supervisors, other county officers, and to the various special districts within the county and also represents the county or a special district in the courts in a civil suit.

The county superintendent of schools approves the budgets and payrolls, maintains full records, and processes teacher certification for school districts within the county. It is this official's responsibility to see that the state laws on public education are observed by these districts.

These important county officers are elected directly by the people on a nonpartisan ballot and thus are neither subject to central lines of responsibility within the county government nor answerable to political parties. This independence in large part explains why many county officers and agencies seem to the citizen to have an existence of their own, unattached, and almost sovereign in their particular fields of activity.

**The Charter County**    A state constitutional amendment, adopted in 1911 and revised in 1970, permits a county to frame and adopt its own charter. The charter may be drafted by either the county board of supervisors or by a special charter commission of citizens elected by the voters of the county. After the document is completed it is submitted to the voters in a special election. If a majority votes approval, the new charter is then filed with the California secretary of state and goes into effect.

Large-scale revisions of existing county charters may be drafted either by the board of supervisors or by a charter commission. Individual amendments (or even outright repeal of the whole charter) may be proposed by either the board of supervisors or an initiative petition. All such changes must be ratified by the voters of the county at the polls.

A general-law county that has changed over to charter status is not completely exempt from all state laws governing the structure and operation of counties. For example, all charters must provide for an elected board of supervisors and for an elected sheriff.

Flexibility is allowed the charter county in determining the *number* of supervisors (the constitution specifies only that there shall be at least five), in deciding whether to make the lesser county officers appointive rather than elective, in setting the salary of its own officials, in providing, if it wishes, for a county-manager system of centralized administration, and in consolidating county offices.

Los Angeles in 1912 was the first county to adopt its own charter. Since then ten other counties have successfully completed all the required steps: San Bernardino, Butte, Tehama, Alameda, Fresno, Placer, Sacramento, San Diego, San Mateo, and Santa Clara. (San Francisco is a chartered city-county.)

The tendency is for the more populous, urban counties of California to use charters and for the rural counties to operate under the general law. However, Orange County, the third most populous county in the state, has never adopted its own charter, and the same is true of Contra Costa, Kern, Monterey, Riverside, San Joaquin, Santa Barbara, Sonoma, and Ventura counties, each of which has more than 250,000 inhabitants. On the other hand, Tehama County, with about 45,000 people, has its own charter.

## The Problem of Divided Responsibility

One of the greatest shortcomings of county government is its lack of integrated authority and responsibility. Unlike the national government, the typical county does not have one single elected official who has major administrative responsibility. Although the state government in California is headed by a plural executive, consisting of 12 elected officers, at least the responsibility for general executive policy is centered in one person—the governor. The county not only elects many of its subordinate administrative officers but divides its top executive authority among a five-member board of supervisors. If the voters are dissatisfied with the administration of their county, they do not know whom they should hold responsible.

Some charter counties in California, taking advantage of the structural flexibility the constitution allows, have made progress toward centering administrative responsibility. In Los Angeles County, for example, all officers except judges, the sheriff, the district attorney, and the assessor are appointive and are directly under the authority of the board of supervisors.

The legislature has tried consolidating county offices in some of the general-law counties. In five counties the positions of clerk and auditor have been merged; several counties have combined the duties of the sheriff and coroner into one office. Such consolidations, however, are usually possible only in counties of small population.

## The County Administrative Officer

The most effective and widely used means to bring greater integration to county government has been the establishment of some kind of appointive chief administrative officer. More than half of California's counties have created such a position. This officer is appointed by and responsible to the elected board of supervisors. Charter counties may legally establish the position of *county manager*, an official with considerable administrative authority—even the power to appoint and remove the heads of some county departments.[1] Charter and general-law counties may establish the position of chief administrative officer—essentially an agent of the board of supervisors. The principal functions of this officer are to implement the decisions of the board and include the preparation of the county budget. Although there is a legal difference between the *county manager* and the *chief administrative officer*, people generally refer to this official as the "county manager."

Although county administration has been somewhat more effectively coordinated by the county administrative officer, as far as the citizens are concerned the county is still an amorphous body speaking with many voices and, therefore, able to avoid specific responsibility for its actions. The feeling of many residents was voiced in one of the "Letters to the Times" in the summer of 1978:

> Would you buy stock in a $4.6 billion corporation that was directed by five presidents, each with the authority to act independently of each other and

---

[1] Only San Mateo County uses the title of county manager.

who rarely communicate with each other? Common sense tells us that we would not—yet this is the power structure of our largest local corporation—Los Angeles County![2]

## THE CITY

The California city or municipality is like the county in some respects. Both are creatures and administrative agents of the state, performing certain basic governmental functions, such as law enforcement, fire control, and sanitation. But the city is less of an arm of the state and more of a unit of local self-government than the county. Cities are incorporated areas within the larger territory of a county, voluntarily activated by residents within a local community to perform mutually desired services for which coordination and cooperation are necessary. Presumably, cities are agencies rendering needed services that neither private industry nor state and county are capable or desirous of providing.

Communities may decide to incorporate and become a city for many reasons, including the following: to obtain more control over money (after incorporation the city receives a portion of the sales tax and the motor vehicle fees generated within the city boundaries that formerly went to the county to spend anywhere within the county); to reject county plans for land use (most frequently residents of the unincorporated areas have felt that the county allowed too much development or the wrong type of development in their area); to secure a better identity (strong homeowners associations and chambers of commerce and ambitious politicians wish to exercise more leadership than was possible under county organization); and to prevent annexation (many unincorporated areas have been threatened by annexation and merger with neighboring cities).

California has become one of the most highly urbanized states in the nation and now contains more than 470 incorporated cities ranging in population from the 95 persons living in Vernon to the 3.8 million residents in nearby Los Angeles. In true California fashion the founders of some municipalities have adopted unorthodox and exotic names such as the City of Industry, the City of Commerce, the City of Hawaiian Gardens, and Paradise.

Proposition 13 has been the cause of an upsurge in the formation of new cities, and since 1978 over 70 new cities have received their charters. This initiative measure removed the financial argument against incorporation because it limited the level of taxes levied against a parcel of property. Prior to the act, cities would add their property tax average to that of the county, thus creating heavier tax burdens for city residents.

In order to meet the present conditions and to provide for the growth and orderly development of cities in the state, the legislature passed the Knox-Nesbit Act in 1962. Although final authority for local boundary change rests with the legislature, the law delegated powers to local agency formation commissions

---

[2]Jerry B. Epstein, in the *Los Angeles Times,* August 22, 1978.

(LAFCO), one in each county to deal with boundary changes. Each LAFCO has five members—two county supervisors, two representatives of the incorporated cities in the county, and a fifth member representing the public, selected by the other commissioners. This body serves as a planning and regulatory agency and ultimately establishes physical boundaries and service areas for every governmental agency in the county—the county, the cities, and the special districts. Among the factors that the commission takes into account when making decisions are natural boundaries, population density, the likelihood of significant growth in the area, the need for governmental services, and the cost and adequacy of service in the area.

With this legislation, when residents of a community wish to incorporate and become a city, they must follow the procedure as shown in the accompanying chart (see Figure 9.1).

## Annexation

Those communities that desire to be annexed must first negotiate with the given city to determine the fiscal feasibility and willingness of the city to add this area to its responsibility. If the city approves, a formal request with a plan of providing government services to the people is submitted to LAFCO. If LAFCO approves, the city holds a public hearing at which time residents of the area to be annexed may be heard. (Should LAFCO disapprove, annexation may not take place, and any new plan must wait at least one year before resubmission to LAFCO.) If 25 percent of the registered voters and property owners of the city sign a petition protesting the annexation, an election must be held at which time a majority of those voting is necessary to authorize the annexation. If less than 25 percent protest, the annexation takes place without an election.

## Fragmentation or De-annexation

The reverse of annexation takes place when an area seeks to split off from an existing city. That can take place when the people in a portion of a city develop a sense that their interests are not being well served. That, in turn, may be the result of a governing unit that has grown too large—a kind of refutation of the adage that bigger is better.

As the twenty-first century opened there was a strong movement to secede from two aspects of Los Angeles governance, the city government and the Los Angeles Unified School District. Some residents of San Pedro and Wilmington actively lobbied for funds from the state to study the feasibility of separating themselves from Los Angeles and residents of Hollywood sought to take their 160,000 citizens away from control by LA City Hall as well, but by far the most ambitious effort was led by an organization calling itself Valley VOTE (Voters Organized Toward Empowerment), which sought to incorporate the San Fernando Valley as what would be the sixth largest city in the state.

Two of the three secessionist movements received the go ahead from LAFCO. The San Pedro/Wilmington plan was deemed not economically viable, but the other two, Hollywood and San Fernando Valley made it to the November 2002 ballot. Just

**STEP 1:**
Residents of an unincorporated area decide to explore the possibility of creating their own city.

**STEP 2:**
A financial feasibility study is prepared by the residents or by a hired consultant.

**STEP 3:**
Incorporation advocates obtain signatures from at least 25% of the community's registered voters. Or, they convince the county or a community board, such as a water district, to pass a resolution supporting cityhood.

**STEP 4:**
An application is filed with the Local Agency Formation Commission.

**STEP 5:**
The LAFCO staff sets a hearing date, recommending in favor of or against the incorporation plan.

**STEP 6:***
LAFCO holds its hearing.

**STEP 7:**
The county Board of Supervisors holds a hearing to measure the extent of opposition to the plan. If 50% of the registered voters in the area sign petitions opposing cityhood, the plan dies.

**STEP 8:**
The incorporation measure goes before local voters, normally at the next general election. A simple majority is required for it to pass. The city's first council (usually five members) is also elected.

**STEP 9:**
The election results are certified by the Board of Supervisors and forwarded to LAFCO, which decides when the community becomes incorporated.

**STEP 10:**
The new city council is sworn in. It is required by law to adopt all county ordinances previously in effect, which may be amended at any time. This assures that the new city does not exist for a moment without laws.

**STEP 11:**
The city must adopt a general plan - the blueprint laying out future zoning, traffic and housing patterns - within 30 months.

*This is where the three incorporation drives in southern Orange County now sit. Dana Point has a second LAFCO hearing on May 5. Mission Viejo will be heard for the first time, and Laguna Niguel for the second time, at LAFCO's May 6 meeting.

Source: The Orange County Administrative Office

Nancy Ward/The Register

**Figure 9.1** Steps to Cityhood. (Courtesy Nancy Ward, *Orange County Register*)

how seriously this was viewed is indicated by the millions of dollars spent, especially by those opposed to the change. The stakes were, after all, high. With 160,000 living in Hollywood and 1.35 million in the Valley, these areas combined to make up some 40 percent of the population of Los Angeles.

Proponents argued Los Angeles was simply too large and access to government too difficult. Smaller government also promised greater local control. Opponents held there were cost savings that were achieved through "economies of scale" (the more of something you produce the lower the cost of one unit of it). An interesting side issue arose with respect to Hollywood and the famous Hollywood sign. It seems the famous landmark sign does not actually reside *in* Hollywood. But Los Angeles had no interest in giving it up. Perhaps a more serious issue was the amount of compensation Los Angeles was entitled to get should the Valley leave. LAFCO estimated that, to keep services at the same level would require $128 million a year. Los Angeles claimed the cost would be $288 million a year. In the November 2002 election both "independence" movements failed by overwhelming margins: 78–21 no for Hollywood and 66–33 no for the Valley.

## Types of Cities

**The General-Law City**    The vast majority of California municipalities (475 at the start of 2000) are incorporated under uniform state law provisions. The constitution of 1879 specified that the legislature could not enact a *special* law that granted a charter to a particular city; rather, the legislature had to pass *general* laws that set the procedure whereby the people of any locality that met the requirements could incorporate themselves into a municipality.

**The Charter City**    Once having become a general-law city, a municipality may, like a county, frame a charter of its own and thereby become somewhat more independent of the state legislature. In 2000 there were 102 charter cities in California, the majority of which were in densely populated areas. Almost all cities with more than 100,000 inhabitants are charter cities, Fremont, Fullerton, and Garden Grove being exceptions, and only a few charter cities have fewer than 10,000 inhabitants. Thus, although fewer than one-fifth of the total number of cities are chartered, they contain more than one-half of the state's population.

A city may gain charter status through procedures similar to those available to a county. The document may be drafted either by the city council or a charter commission elected for the purpose. The charter is submitted to the voters of the city, and if it is approved by them it becomes the organic law of the city.

The primary advantage a charter city has over a general-law city is greater *flexibility*—in determining structure, such as the number of council members, and in determining functions. The charter city has considerable power in municipal affairs. Occasionally, however, there have been conflicts with the legislature over the definition of a "municipal" matter. The California courts have grappled with this problem for more than 70 years and have yet to arrive at a satisfactory answer. Their practice has been to decide each case on its own merits. The salary of a San Francisco police officer, for example, is a "municipal" matter, whereas the license fee set for local

SAN FERNANDO VALLEY SECESSION MOVEMENT

(Rex Babin, *The Sacramento Bee*)

liquor dealers is within the jurisdiction of state agencies. Furthermore, the California Supreme Court in 1962 declared unconstitutional a Los Angeles ordinance against prostitution on the grounds that it went beyond the provisions of a preexisting state law. Similar problems arose when local authorities sought to prevent card-game gambling.

In spite of the advantages of operating under their own home-rule charters, most California cities, even those that have more than 50,000 inhabitants, have chosen to remain under the general law of the state. One reason is the cost, time, and political wrangling often involved in drawing up a charter. Another is that they have found that the general law itself often allows a city sufficient flexibility to meet the needs of its citizens. For example, a general-law city may elect its council members either at large or by districts; it may set up a city-manager system; it may provide either for the election or appointment of city officials such as city clerk or treasurer; and it may provide for the mayor to be elected separately from the city council.

Members of the city councils of most cities in this category are elected at large, that is, by citywide vote, and serve a four-year term. However, in a 1988 decision by the ninth Circuit Court of Appeals the court held that the City of Watsonville was perpetuating discrimination against its Latino residents by continuing to hold at-large elections for its city council. Latinos, it said, would have a better chance of electing one of their own if the city were divided into electoral districts for council elections. The Watsonville case could bring about a change in the method of electing members of the city council in many cities in California where there is a high proportion of Latino residents.

## Forms of City Government

California cities illustrate various types of two main forms of city government: (1) the mayor-council and (2) the council-manager (see Figure 9.2). Either plan may be selected by general-law and charter cities, but charter cities have a greater range of choice in that more variations of the mayor-council plan are open to them.

**The Mayor-Council Form**     The traditional form of American city government has been one in which a legislative body (the council) and the chief executive officer (the mayor) are elected separately by the voters of the city. Most municipalities in California do not follow this pattern today. In fact, only one-eighth of the California cities should be called mayor-council cities, and each of them varies widely in

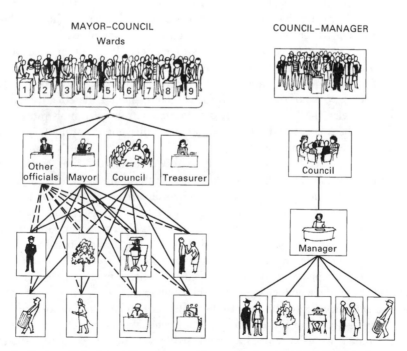

**Figure 9.2**   Forms of Municipal Government. (*Source:* National Municipal League)

structure. The main differentiation in this group is between strong-mayor and weak-mayor cities—terms that have nothing to do with the personality of the mayor but rather with the amount of power granted the mayor by the city's charter or by the state law.

In a *strong-mayor city* the mayor is the principal administrative officer, having the authority to appoint many of the city's officials and, under specified circumstances, to remove them. Typically, a strong mayor has a veto power over the ordinances passed by the council. The relationship between the mayor and the council in strong-mayor cities is similar to the relationship between the governor and the state legislature. Los Angeles and San Francisco are among the few cities in California that are considered to have the strong-mayor form of government. However, it is probably more correct to say that these two municipalities *approach* the strong-mayor system; in neither city does the mayor have the authority that other mayors have in some Eastern cities, such as New York and Chicago. (What local official in California has ever had the power in local, state, and national affairs that was exercised by the late Mayor Richard Daley of Chicago?) In Los Angeles the 15 members of the city council are elected by districts for staggered terms of four years each. The mayor, elected at large also for a four-year term, has the power to veto council ordinances, and the budget is prepared under the mayor's authority with the assistance of an appointed chief administrative officer. The appointive power of the Los Angeles mayor is somewhat limited, however. Some of the administrative departments of the city are run by general managers appointed by and directly responsible to the mayor, but 12 of the most important departments, including police, fire, water and power, recreation and parks, harbor, airport, and public works, are operated by boards of commissioners. Each board consists of five members appointed by the mayor with the consent of the city council. Commissioners serve longer terms than the mayor, and no board member may be removed by the mayor without the consent of the council. Mayors of Los Angeles for more than 60 years have complained that although the voters of the city hold them accountable for the effective government of Los Angeles, they do not have real power to control the administration, the basic decisions about police and fire protection, and other important matters being made by the semiautonomous commissions.

Most of the mayor-council cities in California fall into the *weak-mayor* (or *strong-council*) *city* category. Under this plan the council has substantial administrative as well as legislative power. The mayor is primarily a ceremonial figurehead, possessing little if any administrative authority. Usually, this person is a member of the council, selected by fellow members to serve as chairperson and mayor for a one-year term. The mayor presides over council sessions, digs the first shovelful of dirt for new public buildings, and presents visiting celebrities with keys to the city but has no veto or appointive powers. The city's administrative jobs are filled either by election or through council appointments. The mayor, solely as agent of the council and acting under its orders, may undertake to coordinate the day-to-day operations of the municipality, or this task may be undertaken by the city clerk or the city engineer. Some general-law cities have provided by vote of the people that the mayor is to be elected independently of the council and at large; however, they have not substantially increased the mayor's powers.

**The Council-Manager Form**   The most prevalent type of city government in California is one in which a city manager is appointed by the elected council. California leads all other states in the number of municipalities organized in this manner. More than three-fourths of the state's incorporated cities have delegated most administrative functions to a central office, thus bringing about a more complete integration of municipal activities. A city may choose this plan by a vote of the people or through council ordinance. The typical city manager supervises the administration of ordinances passed by the council and has the power to appoint and remove most of the heads of the city's administrative departments. The manager is selected for an indefinite term and holds office as long as he or she enjoys the confidence of the majority of the council, whether it be for 20 days or 20 years. This system is similar to that of a private corporation—the voters being the stockholders; the council, the board of directors' and the city manager, the general manager. The mayor in such a city presides over the council and has ceremonial duties.

About 120 California cities have adopted a modified form of council-manager government in which the council appoints an administrative officer somewhat more restricted in functions than a city manager. Such an officer does not have appointment or removal power over all administrative officials and is subject to greater control by the council. This type of arrangement is often a step toward the adoption of a true council-manager form of government.

Most authorities in the field of public administration agree that the manager form of government does much to integrate authority and responsibility in government, thereby improving the services of the city to its people. A professionally trained administrator not required to face periodic public elections is better qualified to execute the policies of the city council and to manage the technical and complex business of modern city government.

## THE CITY AND COUNTY OF SAN FRANCISCO

San Francisco is one of the very few city-county governments in the United States.[3] Rather than maintaining two sets of officers performing overlapping functions in the same metropolitan area, the city and county of San Francisco has one board of supervisors (its ordinance-passing body), one police force, and one set of financial officers. Unlike the citizens of metropolitan Los Angeles who, if involved in an auto accident, might have to determine the side of the street they were on before deciding to call the chief of police or the sheriff, San Franciscans know who is responsible for them and to whom they are responsible.[4]

San Francisco's Board of Supervisors consists of 11 members elected at large for four-year terms, six and five members, respectively, coming up for election every

[3]Denver is also a city-county, but certain cities like Philadelphia, although they have consolidated most city and county functions, still operate with some elected county officials independent of the government.

[4]There are fine divisions of authority among some San Francisco officials, but they are based on function rather than geography. The sheriff thus acts in civil matters and the police chief in criminal matters. A similar division exists between the city attorney and the district attorney.

two years. The mayor is elected at large every four years and is the city's chief admin-istrative and ceremonial officer. He or she is considered a stronger mayor than the mayor in Los Angeles, since, in addition to having the veto power and authority over the budget, the mayor of San Francisco also has full appointment power over the police commission, the planning commission, and the civil service commission. However, there is one factor that seriously limits the authority of the San Francisco mayor; namely, the city employs a chief administrative officer (appointed by the mayor upon approval by the board but removable only by a two-thirds vote of the supervisors or by popular recall) who has direct supervision of nine other city depart-ments, including finance, purchasing, public works, and public health. Thus the city by the Golden Gate has really two top executives largely independent of each other.

## THE CASE OF LOS ANGELES

In 1985 Edmund Edelman, chairman of the Los Angeles Board of Supervisors, maintained "that the merger of the city of Los Angeles and the county would pro-vide the advantages of both forms of government and save taxpayers' money." This would be accomplished by the consolidation of the two separate offices or services (one in the city and one in the county) such as the crime labs, library systems, fire departments, and animal control departments. In 1978 this type of merger was approved by the voters in an advisory referendum, but was never implemented.

Both Mayor Richard Riordan and the City Council of Los Angeles in 1996 attempted to form panels to consider rewriting the 71-year-old governing charter that appears to be too antiquated to meet the problems of Los Angeles. The reform movement was encouraged by the several attempts of San Fernando Valley residents to secede from the city of Los Angeles.

A more modest change was undertaken in 1996 when the board of supervisors voted to designate its chairman mayor of the county. Though no new powers were given the position, it was deemed to be a better reflection of what the person holding it does than the term "chairman."

Two other modest proposals were rejected by the voters. One would have added four members to the five member County Board of Supervisors. With a population approaching ten million, it was thought making the size of the constituencies some-what smaller would enhance representative government. That was rejected by the voters in 1992. A second proposal, using the same rationale, was to expand the city council from 15 members to 21. That, too, was turned down by the voters in 1999.

## SPECIAL DISTRICTS

The most varied and least known of all units of government in the state are the special districts. They deal with matters such as water supply, irrigation, air pollu-tion, public education, and flood control—problems that extend beyond city and county boundaries. After all, flood waters originate high in the mountains and in their flow to the river or sea cross areas occupied by many cities and sometimes sev-eral counties. This was dramatically indicated by the torrential rains that led to massive flooding in Northern California and the Central Valley at the end of 1996.

Damage to cities and on farms across one-third of the state was estimated at close to $2 billion. Forming a third category of local government, special districts are created from time to time as the demand arises and as an alternative to city or county administration.

## Number and Types of Special Districts

California has more than 6,000 special districts whose total annual financial transactions amount to more than those of all cities and counties of the state. Then-Assembly Speaker Curt Pringle introduced a bill in June 1995 to shrink local governments in Orange County by more than 30 water and sewer districts into a single entity by 1998. Opponents representing special districts' employees questioned the proposal on the basis this would jeopardize the bond security of the districts and many district employees would lose their jobs. The proposal failed in the Senate.

California's special districts can best be classified according to the function they perform, ranging from public education to cemetery maintenance and mosquito abatement. The most widespread group of special districts is the school districts; so important are they, in fact, that the state controller in financial reports handles them as an entirely separate category from the other special districts. School districts account for more than one-fifth of the total number of special districts in the state, and they spend more money than any other form of local government.

Every square foot of the State of California is included in a public school district of some type. The approximately 1,100 districts in California are classified as elementary, high school, unified (covering both elementary and high school grades), and community college. Sometimes a high school district will include several elementary districts and is, therefore, known as a union high school district. When a district includes territory in more than one county it is called a joint district. Each district has its own governing board, usually consisting of five members; in practically every case they are elected by the voters of the district in a nonpartisan election for a four-year term. (A chartered city may provide for the appointment of its board of education.) Each board hires a superintendent, a professional educator who is responsible for administering the policies adopted by the board. Upon the recommendation of the superintendent the board hires the principals, the teachers, and all other employees of the district. It also adopts the annual budget and establishes the curriculum or course of study. However, the board is governed in almost every detail by state law and is accountable first to the county superintendent of schools but more importantly to one of two statewide boards for the performance of its legal obligations. The state Board of Education, consisting of ten members appointed by the governor, oversees the public schools from kindergarten through the twelfth grade (K–12). Its administrative agent is the state superintendent of public instruction, who is responsible for granting state credentials to teachers and for distributing state funds to the various school districts according to the formula adopted by the legislature. Somewhat lesser control is exercised over the 70 community college districts of the state by the state Board of Governors of the California Community Colleges, also appointed by the governor.

School board elections generally have a low voter turnout. Citizens frequently excuse themselves for not having gone to the polls on the grounds that there was no real contest or significant issue. However, in various localities in California there have been spirited election campaigns for the school board. Sometimes the issues are ideological. Recall elections that have focused on highly contentious issues over curriculum (peace studies, sex education, religion) can and have led to larger voter turnout, but those have tended to be infrequent.

**Other Special Districts**    California's nonschool special districts, totaling more than 5,000, present an amazing variety. There are currently on the statute books more than 200 enabling acts of the legislature that authorize the formation of the various districts. The state controller lists 57 different *types* of special districts that perform 30 basic activities or functions. (Usually, a special district will perform just one function, but some will conduct several activities simultaneously.) Second only to school districts in number are those focused on water, water delivery, water quality, farm irrigation, and the like.


## REGIONAL GOVERNMENT

Local government in California's metropolitan areas is a crazy quilt of counties, cities, and special districts, each with its own taxing authority, administration, and rules. This arrangement creates much confusion for the citizens. For example, it may be legal to park a pick-up truck on the east side of Citrus Avenue but not on the west side, since Citrus Avenue is the dividing line between two municipalities, the westerly one being very opposed to such plebeian vehicles vulgarizing its patrician curbs. However, the water one drinks, the air one breathes, and the highways one travels cross county, city, and special district lines, and the problems of pollution, traffic, and law enforcement must be handled on the basis of an entire metropolitan region.

Urban atomization is most marked in the two largest metropolitan areas of the state. The San Francisco Bay Area includes about 50 incorporated cities, nine counties, and a host of special districts. Most of the Los Angeles metropolitan area is included within Los Angeles County, but that county contains close to 90 municipalities, the largest being the city of Los Angeles itself. Some of the other cities, such as San Fernando, are enclaves completely surrounded by the "City of the Angels." A lesser degree of governmental fragmentation is to be found in some of the other cities, such as San Diego and Sacramento.

Many efforts have been made to bring order out of this urban chaos. One result has been the creation of the large regional special districts, such as the Bay Area Rapid Transit District, which furnishes public transportation for the people of several counties, but this expedient does not really solve the problem. The San Francisco Bay region not only has BART but also has several other regional special districts, for example, the Golden Gate Bridge and Highway District and the San Francisco Bay Air Pollution District. Each serves a single purpose, each has its own board of directors, each its own source of revenue, each its own bureaucracy, and each guards its own authority jealously. None can make and enforce a general plan of development that will make the Bay Area the beautiful and livable place it can be.

BART Train with San Francisco Skyline and Mt. Sutro in the Background. (Courtesy BART)

## Planning Commissions

Various measures short of regional government have been adopted to solve the metropolitan problems. In the past 35 years tens of thousands of acres of California's open space, fields, vineyards, and orchards have been gobbled up by housing tracts, shopping centers, and parking lots. This urban sprawl has given birth to a swarm of "slurbs"—"sloppy, sleazy, slovenly, slip-shod semicities" around the metropolitan centers.[5] Therefore, a strong demand has risen for careful planning for the future growth of metropolitan areas to preserve California's traditional beauty while accommodating its population increases. Consequently, a state law of 1953 authorized area planning commissions, one of the first of which was set up in a six-county area around Sacramento. The commission is appointed by the county supervisors and city councils of the region, and it merely makes recommendations to its constituent cities and counties on matters such as land use and zoning. Since that time other measures have been passed by the state legislature that favor regional planning. The U.S. Congress in 1966 added its support by offering national funds

---

[5]Samuel E. Wood and Alfred E. Heller, *California Going, Going* . . . (Sacramento: California Tomorrow, 1962), p. 10.

for urban-renewal projects, provided there was systematic metropolitan-wide planning for such projects. The result is that most areas of California today are under the jurisdiction of regional planning commissions. This is particularly true of the coastal areas following the passage of the California Coastal Zone Conservation Act of 1972, which created regional commissions with genuine authority to control development within their areas.

## Cooperative Efforts

The need for cooperation in a host of areas has led to councils of government that act as voluntary advisory bodies to their members. Mayors of cities meet periodically to address common problems such as air pollution, traffic congestion, and energy and water policy. Examples include the Association of Bay Area Governments (ABAG), which addresses concerns of San Francisco Bay Area cities and counties, the Southern California Association of Governments (SCAG), and the Sacramento Area Council of Governments (SACG). While helpful, these bodies can only *recommend* actions that then have to be ratified by the city council or county board of supervisors.

Another form of cooperation involves cities contracting with counties to furnish city residents with services. A number of these services may be said to be routinely provided, such as the running of elections, library services, tax assessments and collections, and enforcement of state health regulations. In tough economic times some cities have abolished their police forces and contracted with the county sheriff to deal with crime.

## CITIZEN PARTICIPATION

Observers of the American political scene have decried the apathy of the average voters toward their local governments. *This* is most unfortunate, because many of the decisions that affect our daily lives are made not in Washington or Sacramento but in our city halls, county courthouses, and boards of education headquarters. Furthermore, if citizens would stir themselves, their impact on the local officials would be more direct and persuasive than on state and national authorities. A delegation of irate homemakers may not be able to affect the course of a bill in Sacramento, but can derail efforts of real estate developers to railroad through the city planning commission a change of zoning that would erect a superfluous shopping center in the middle of a residential neighborhood. (For information concerning the financing of local governments in California, please refer to the discussion in Chapter 10.)

## REVIEW QUESTIONS

1. Identify the two major categories of counties. Which ones are most used by larger counties? Smaller ones? Why? (pp. 164–166)
2. What are the principal forms of city government? Which form is most often used? (p. 168)

3. What are the steps that have to be taken for an area to become a city? What specific function is played by LAFCO in this process? (p. 169)
4. What arguments were made in support of San Fernando Valley secession? Against? (p. 169–170)
5. What kinds of problems are best addressed by regional governments? (pp. 178–179)

## SELECTED WEB SITES

Specific cities have their own web sites such as www.losangeles.com and links are provided through the site maintained by the California League of Cities at www.cacities.org/. The same is true of county web sites that may be accessed through links with the California State Association of Counties at www.csac.counties.org/. The county Association of Counties site has, in addition, information on each county and discussions of issues of interest to county government. The League of Cities site has a listing of pending legislation of interest to the municipalities in the state.

## SELECTED REFERENCES

California Department of Education, *Fact Book,* Sacramento: State Printing Office, annually.

Dryden, Gail, ed., "The Road to Reforming Government in California," *California Voter,* League of Woman Voters of California, Spring 1998.

Feinbaum, Robert, "Climate Right for Creating New Cities," *California Journal,* October 1987.

Hanley, Craig, and A.G. Block, "Regional Government: Everybody Wants to Land on Boardwalk," in Thomas Hoeber and Larry Gertsen, *California Government and Politics Annual, 1992–93,* Sacramento, California Journal Press, 1992.

Post, A. Alan, *Report of Commission on Government Reform,* Sacramento: State Printing Office, 1979.

Reeves, Scott, "State Mandates Defy Logic," *Fresno Bee,* August 7, 1988.

Ross, Robert, *Perspectives on Local Government in California,* Belmont, CA: Star Publishing, 1987.

Starkey, Danielle, "Counties in Revolt," *California Journal,* August 1993.

State Controller, *Annual Report of Financial Transactions Concerning Cities of California,* Sacramento: State Printing Office, annually.

————, *Annual Report of Financial Transactions Concerning California Counties,* Sacramento: State Printing Office, annually.

————, *Annual Report of Financial Transactions Concerning School Districts of California,* Sacramento: State Printing Office, annually.

————, *Annual Report of Financial Transactions Concerning Special Districts of California,* Sacramento: State Printing Office, annually.

Chapter

# 10

---

# Financing California Government

The state of California, long seen as a land of opportunity and boundless wealth, hit hard times in the early 2000s. The collapse of the booming economies linked to, first, the Cold War with its massive defense contracts and, later, hit hard by the collapse of the Silicon Valley boom in high tech, was made all the harder to absorb by the impasse over spending cuts favored by Republicans and higher taxes offered as the solution to declining revenues by the Democrats. At the height of the boom times Governor Davis initially declined to support "on-going commitments," legislation encumbering large sums of money for annual expenditures over many years, opting instead for one-time costs for such items as bridges and irrigation upgrades. Ultimately, the governor backed down and massive new and on-going spending was built into the budget. With the eventual and major decrease of tax revenues in the early 2000s, deficits mounted to unprecedented levels. Borrowing to meet committed expenses became the order of the day. The times ahead looked dark indeed as larger and larger percentages of the budget had to be devoted to paying off loans and long term bonds.

What had been a budgetary nightmare brightened considerably in 2005. Legislative analyst Elizabeth Hill announced in November that a strengthening economy, combined with various budget reductions, had turned what had been expected to be more red ink for the fiscal year into a modest surplus. She warned, however, that the long-term prospects were not as positive, that unless spending was further curbed or taxes raised, a return to large scale deficits was likely. Even in good years, spending goes up an average of between 10 and 13 percent while revenues have gone up, again on average, about 7 percent. It was this phenomenon voters had sought to address when they passed the Gann spending limit (see below). Nevertheless, deficits persisted in the early 2000s with critics complaining the cuts made were too small to correct long-term problems that required major surgery, not Band-aids. This problem of what is termed a structural imbalance loomed as 2005 began, but the good times began to roll as the year progressed, so much so that the governor's budget for the 2006–2007 fiscal year contained no new taxes and a host of enhanced expenditures. Perhaps the most striking was an additional $4.2 billion for schools, bringing the total spending to $11,000 per child, a record. Overall the proposal raised the state's budget by 8 percent over the previous year to a total of $125.6 billion. There was at least muted pleasure in many quarters, especially in light of previous budgets from this governor that had requested almost across the board reductions. Still, some Republicans sought larger cuts to eliminate the deficit entirely while Democrats focused on the failure to include cost of living adjustments for many disabled and to help with child care for women on welfare. All of this did not include the most dramatic fiscal proposal made by the governor, a series of bond measures over two decades to address the infrastructure needs of the state as well as population growth and its impact on, for example, schools.

The continuing structural deficit problem led Governor Schwarzenegger to have Proposition 76 placed before the voters in November 2005. It sought to give the governor the ability to cut budget items in mid-year should revenues fail to match expenditures. Those going to the polls apparently felt the solution was worse than the problem, accepted the opponents' description of the proposal as a "power grab" and turned it down by a really decisive margin, 32–68. One explanation (other

## CALEEFORNEEYA

(Rex Babin, *The Sacramento Bee*)

than disenchantment with the governor) was that the idea of across the board cuts was opposed by teachers, firefighters, correctional officers, nurses, and others less explicitly targeted who felt threatened by the cuts.

The conflict between Republicans who refused to raise taxes under any circumstances and Democrats seeking more and more government services was summarized by columnist Dan Walters in the *Sacramento Bee.*

> We might want to know why . . . with a chronic state budget deficit, voters threw out a governor in 2003 because he couldn't deal with it, overwhelmingly rejected a ballot measure designed to make it easier to raise taxes in 2004 and then overwhelmingly rejected another measure this year to make it easier to cut state spending.

Or, as some wag said years ago, we Californians want a Cadillac of services on the VW budget.

The pessimism shown in Figure 10.1 on projected deficits moderated considerably in May 2006 with the release of new government estimates of revenue. With gasoline prices well over $3 a gallon funding for roads and freeways went up around a billion dollars while general fund revenues increased by a whopping $7.5 billion. Additional funds for education brought per pupil expenditures to $11,268, a new record, and largely balanced the books with the state's educational establishment. Significant increases were also given health and welfare programs and $500 for levee repair. Still, some cautioned against over-optimism, given the volatile nature of the revenue flow.

## STATE REVENUE: WHERE THE MONEY COMES FROM

Until 1950 in California nearly all of the state revenue was derived from the general property tax and a poll tax. However, with the coming of industry and the increase in population, additional funds became imperative.

As may be seen in Figure 10.1, California presently secures its revenue from several sources, nearly all of which are taxes of some sort. Only about 16 percent of total receipts is not from taxes and comes from such sources as royalties from oil and gas production on state-owned land, motor vehicle fees, horse racing fees, medical and board charges from state hospitals, traffic penalties, investment of state funds, fees and tuition at state universities and colleges, and regulatory charges and special fees for businesses and the professions. The remaining 84 percent of state revenue comes from various types of taxes.

### The Personal Income Tax

The leading source of revenue is currently the personal income tax. Not as high as the national income tax, it is similar in that the rates vary according to the size of the individual's income. Persons whose annual adjusted gross incomes are below $6,000

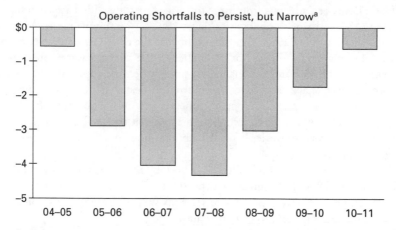

ᵃAnnual revenues minus expenditures excluding use of deficit-financing bonds.

**Figure 10.1**    Projected Deficits.

(or $12,000 for couples filing jointly) are not required to file tax returns. The system is highly progressive in that most of the revenue comes from those in higher income brackets with those making over $100,000 a year contributing over 50 percent of the funds received. The total amount received by this tax for 2006–2007 was projected to be $48.7 billion compared with $37.6 billion received four years earlier.

Since 1972, California has had a system of withholding for state personal income taxes similar to that used by the federal government. Withholding has prevented some tax dodging, and it provides monthly revenues that help the cash flow of state finances. In 1979 a tax indexing system was passed that uses brackets that are adjusted upward when necessary to compensate for inflation. This measure, as amended by the Jarvis-sponsored initiative of 1982, protects taxpayers from being placed in a higher tax bracket due to higher earnings that provide no greater purchasing power because of inflation.

Because of the growth of California's economy in the 1980s, coupled with a high rate of inflation, revenue realized through the state income tax grew by leaps and bounds. Slowed by the recession of the early 1990s, the personal income tax remains the leading source of revenue for the state, estimated to surpass the amount received through the sales tax in fiscal 2006 by 53.2 percent to 30.9 percent.

## The Sales Tax

First used in the days of the Great Depression, when other sources of revenue had dried up, the retail sales tax has become a major source of income. A tax of 7.25 percent on the sales price of all tangible goods, except food for home consumption, prescription drugs, electricity, gas and water, ambulatory aids, custom computer programs, and other minor items such as newspapers and magazines is collected by retail merchants from purchasers.

There have been add-ons from time to time. The state added a special half-cent sales tax in the midst of the budget crisis in 1991, a tax the people voted to make permanent in November 1993 with the intent that the added revenues be devoted to public safety programs. As a part of this increase, the sales tax was applied to snack foods, candy, magazines, and newspapers. It quickly became apparent that the line to be drawn between snacks and food was blurred at best. For example, popped popcorn was taxable as a snack; unpopped popcorn was not. The voters resolved this knotty question by approving an initiative in 1992 that repealed the snack tax.

A "use-tax" provision levies a similar tax on goods purchased outside the state for use in California.

With practically no cost of collection borne by the state, the retail sales tax has yielded between 28 and 38 percent of the total state revenue since it has been in effect. For 2006–2007 revenue from the sales tax was estimated to be approximately $28.3 billion or 30.9 percent of state revenues.

The principal objection to the sales tax has been that it is a *regressive* tax; that is, it is not based on a person's ability to pay. It is argued that the tax places an undue burden on large families with low incomes. An initiative measure to reduce the sales tax by 1 percent and to increase business and personal income taxes was placed on the 1958 ballot but was defeated.

## Taxes on Motorists

It is expensive to provide adequate facilities for California's highly mobile population. The costs to the state of constructing, maintaining, and policing an extensive network of highways generally exceed $2 billion a year. Californians, as a result, cannot escape paying plenty if they want to drive to work or take a holiday trip. The variety of special taxes and fees levied on motorists has caused the per capita car cost to zoom to the highest in the nation.

**Highway Users Taxes**    Income from this source goes to a special fund and is generated by the motor vehicle fuel tax (gasoline and diesel). It provides the major amount of money for maintaining, replacing, and constructing state highway and transportation facilities. Close to one-half of these revenues is apportioned to local jurisdictions for streets and highway use.

The current tax rate for motor vehicle fuel is 18 cents per gallon; aircraft fuel is taxed at two cents a gallon; and local transit systems and certain common carriers pay one cent per gallon.

**Motor Vehicle Taxes and Fees**    Motor vehicle fees consist of vehicle licenses, registration, weight and driver's license fees, and various other charges related to vehicle operation. Vehicle license fees are based on the "market value," which is the cost of the vehicle to the purchaser exclusive of sales tax adjusted by a depreciation schedule and is levied each year. This fee is imposed in lieu of a local personal property tax on automobiles. All of the revenue from this tax, other than administrative costs and fees on trailer coaches and mobile homes, are constitutionally dedicated to local governments.

Registration fees are based on a flat rate of $29 on all motor vehicles. Motor vehicle taxes and fees are collected and administered by the Department of Motor Vehicles.

## Bank and Corporation Taxes

Revenue from bank and corporation taxes for 2006–2007 was projected at about $10 billion, accounting for 10.9 percent of the state's total revenue for that year. A franchise tax and a corporate income tax are levied at 4.3 percent on profits. The franchise tax is imposed on corporations that do business in California, while the corporate income tax is imposed on corporations that do not do business in the state but derive income from California sources. Banks and other financial corporations pay an additional "bank tax" of approximately 1.5 percent on their net income.

## Insurance Tax

A tax rate of 2.35 percent is levied on gross premiums of the majority of insurance written in California. Certain pension and profit-sharing plans are exempt from this tax. Revenue from this source has been increasing gradually and currently accounts for roughly 2.6 percent of state revenues or $2.3 billion.

## Liquor Taxes

Taxes are levied on the manufacturers of all alcoholic beverages. Excise rates vary from $0.20 per gallon on beer and wine to $3.30 on distilled spirits per gallon. Revenue for 2006–2007 is expected to be about $300 million.

## Horse-Racing Fees

The state government is always a "winner" at the paramutual horse races. Revenues from horse racing are derived mainly from a fee on the amount wagered, "breakage" (odd cents on each dollar wagered), unclaimed winning tickets, and license fees, fines, and penalties). The total revenues from horse racing have increased during the last few years and now amount to approximately $60 million. About one-eighth of horse-racing revenues is earmarked for distribution to fairs and expositions, for wildlife restoration, and for research and improvement in animal husbandry and agriculture conducted primarily by the University of California and some of the state universities. The rest is returned to the general fund.

## Tobacco Tax

An excise tax imposed on distributors selling cigarettes in California has been 35 cents a pack since January 1989 as a result of Proposition 99. At the same time an excise tax was implemented at a rate "equivalent" to cigarettes upon cigars, chewing tobacco, snuff, and pipe tobacco. Effective January 1, 1994, with the passage of the Breast Cancer Act, the cigarette tax was increased an additional two cents a pack. Twenty-five cents of the total tax is allocated to a variety of antismoking programs and other objectives deemed socially desirable under the terms of Proposition 99.

Voters narrowly approved Proposition 10 in November 1998, imposing an additional tax of 50 cents a pack to be used in support of a variety of early childhood development programs. The new tax brought the total tax on a pack of cigarettes to 87 cents. Estimated revenue in 2006–2007: $1 billion, declining slightly as fewer people smoke.

## State Lottery

Included with other miscellaneous smaller sources of revenue is the income from the well-publicized California state lottery. A constitutional amendment initiative approved in November 1984 established the lottery. Lottery proposals to raise revenue for the state had been before the state legislature for the previous ten years but had never mustered the necessary two-thirds vote in both houses for passage; and California voters had once before, in 1964, rejected the plan for a lottery. However, in 1983 the California Poll indicated widespread support for a government-run lottery to raise revenue, and Proposition 37 passed with a 16-point margin.

As enacted, Proposition 37 created a state-run lottery with a state commission of five persons appointed by the governor to run it. Revenue from tickets costing a minimum of $1 and sold by retail businesses would be divided as follows: 50 percent for prizes, 16 percent for administration, and 34 percent for public education. Money appropriated for education was to be spent for educating students rather than for construction, buying property, or research. Distributed quarterly, lottery revenues are distributed to public education systems as follows: kindergarten through twelfth grade—81 percent; community colleges—12 percent; California state universities—4.5 percent; and the University of California—2.5 percent.

It is claimed that the lottery is a regressive tax because its burden falls primarily on those who can least afford to pay. Low-income players spend a proportionately larger share of their income on tickets with money they should be spending for food and other necessities. Yet demographic studies of seven states with lotteries indicate that 70–75 percent of lottery players are from households with $15,000 annual income or more.[1]

## STATE EXPENDITURES: WHERE THE MONEY GOES

### Types of Expenditures

The California state budget contains three general types of expenditures, which are referred to as state operations, local assistance, and capital outlay. Funds spent for state operations include those functions that are under direct state control; funds spent for local assistance are funds allocated to counties, cities, and special districts to cover services provided by local governments. Capital outlay designates those expenditures spent for state buildings and facilities. In recent years approximately

---

[1]Congressional Research Service, "Overview of State Lottery Operations," Library of Congress #85–52, 1986, p. 25.

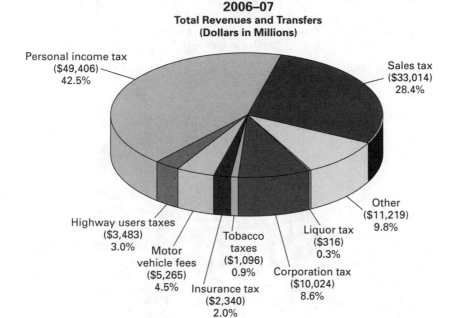

**Figure 10.2** Governor's Budget Summary, 2006-2007 (Total Revenues and Transfers).

60 percent of the money collected by the state has been allocated to local governments for designated services (local assistance) such as welfare and education (K–14). Funds spent for state operations themselves, such as the expenses of the legislature, the governor's office, various state agencies, and the state universities and colleges, amount to $1.9 billion.

**State Expenses** Figure 10.2 shows where the money goes and lists the various major functional areas under state government support. The appropriate percentage of the total budget for each category is also noted.

**Health and Welfare** The state expense for 2006–2007 projected at about $28.5 billion for health and welfare amounted to 29.1 percent of the state budget. The state has funded only about 35 percent of the total welfare cost for California residents, since the federal government paid about 50 percent of the welfare bill and the counties have contributed the other 15 percent.[2] Welfare benefits include family assistance; aid to the aged, blind, and disabled; general relief; food stamps; Medi-Cal assistance; and various other social services. The largest state expenditure ($26.8 billion) is for the immense Medi-Cal program, which funds medical services for more

---

[2]The figures cited here are for the 1996–1997 fiscal year. The welfare reform package passed by Congress, signed into law by President Clinton in 1996 and implemented in 1997, had a significant impact on both the percentages and the total amounts shown here as reductions are made in some areas and a share of the total burden shifts from the federal government to state and local authorities.

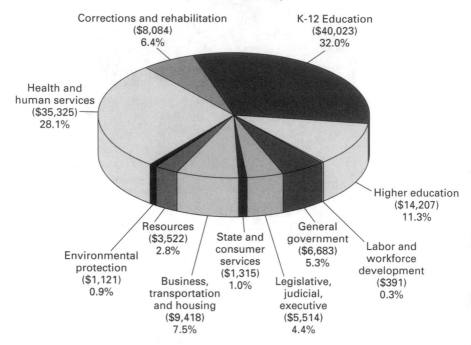

**2006–07**
**Total Expenditures**
**(Including Selected Bond Funds)**
**(Dollars in Millions)**

Corrections and rehabilitation
($8,084)
6.4%

K-12 Education
($40,023)
32.0%

Health and
human services
($35,325)
28.1%

Higher education
($14,207)
11.3%

Resources
($3,522)
2.8%

Environmental
protection
($1,121)
0.9%

State and
consumer
services
($1,315)
1.0%

Business,
transportation
and housing
($9,418)
7.5%

General
government
($6,683)
5.3%

Legislative,
judicial,
executive
($5,514)
4.4%

Labor and
workforce
development
($391)
0.3%

**Figure 10.3**    Governor's Budget Summary, 2006–2007 (Total Expenditures).

than 10 percent of California's population. The state also contributes large amounts to the total fund for aid to the aged, blind, and disabled and to the total fund for aid to families with dependent children. The state does not provide money for the food stamp program, which is wholly supported by the federal government.

**Education—Elementary and Secondary (K–12)**    Over 6.2 million of California's school-aged children are enrolled in the public elementary and secondary school system.

The 1999–2000 budget, in line with Governor Davis's program to upgrade the state's educational system, provided funds designed to hold high schools accountable for their performance and to reward schools demonstrating high level results and improvement. The state Department of Education is to develop standards that high schools will be required to meet in their students' achievement in reading, writing, and mathematics. And those students will be required to pass competency tests in these areas as a condition of graduation beginning in 2006. Proposition 98 mandates that some 40 percent of the general fund budget be devoted to kindergarten through grade 12. In recent budgets the actual amount has been somewhat higher than originally proposed because revenues were greater than expected. Additional spending on schools had, as noted, by 2006 raised per pupil spending nearly $11,000, a record.

**Higher Education**    High technology, biotechnology, and other scientific advances in business and industry today demand a pool of well-trained personnel. If California is to remain a leader in these fields, it must invest adequate funding to educate its citizens in the rapid changes in these fields. The 2006–2007 budget allocated 11.5 percent of general fund expenditures to the state's institutions of higher education. There are approximately 200,000 full time equivalent students enrolled in the campuses of the University of California, another 400,000 in the California State University (CSU) system, and approximately 1.7 million full-time equivalent attend one of the 107 community colleges in the state.[3]

In recent years, state policy has dictated that a substantial amount of money should go to subsidize students who are academically qualified to enter state institutions of higher education, but lack the financial resources. Approximately one-third of any increase in revenues from student fees is devoted to financial aid.

**Business, Transportation, and Housing**    About $2.7 billion (or about 2.8 percent of 2006–2007 expenditures) is spent by the various departments within the Business, Transportation, and Housing Agency. These funds are used for the general purposes of providing for efficient and safe movement of people and goods within the state, and for promoting a sound financial and business community while protecting the public from economic loss and illegal business practices.

With the large population of the state and the large number of immigrants adding to that population each year there is a serious challenge to state leaders to provide an adequate system of transportation. As noted in Chapter 11, the primary answer to the transportation needs of the state has been the automobile. Though enormous amounts of money have been allocated to the Department of Transportation (Caltrans) over the years, many believe the roads are in need of even more massive help. More and more people driving more and more cars and with limited rail and almost no subway (other than the Bay Area's BART) mean increased pressure on the state's roadways (see Chapter 12).

The California Highway Patrol is responsible for safe, lawful, rapid, and economical use of the state highway system. The Department of Motor Vehicles is in charge of the registration and collection of fees for California's more than 26 million vehicles and the processing of drivers' licenses. The remainder of the business and transportation expenditures is spent by the various departments involved in business areas, including the State Department of Banking, the Department of Commerce, the Department of Insurance, the Department of Real Estate, the Department of Savings and Loans, the Department of Housing and Community Development, and the Department of Alcoholic Beverage Control.

---

[3]A full time equivalent student is one carrying a 15 unit load. The actual number of bodies in these systems is therefore considerably higher.

Businesses that serve the state get funds through the budget. Examples are those that support research into foreign trade that benefits the state and American companies that have established offices in such places as Singapore, India, and Buenos Aires. Funds are also used for the California Film Commission that assists producers in finding suitable film making sites in California.

**Resources**     The cost of conserving California's natural resources and improving California's living environment is currently about $1.5 billion a year. The programs funded range from those designed to attain and maintain desirable standards of air and water purity to fighting forest fires, forest management, flood control, water development, oil drilling regulation, and the creation of recreational opportunities. Many boards, commissions, and departments are involved in implementing these programs. The largest share of the resources expenditures is for the Department of Forestry. The planning, developing, and operation of the state park system consisting of 287 parks, beaches, campgrounds, and historical sites costs approximately $290 million. The large state water program administered by the Department of Water Resources is financed by revenue from services and through revenue bonds.

**State and Consumer Services**     Most of the $500 million expended for state and consumer services is spent by the various staff and service agencies, including the Department of General Services, the Franchise Tax Board, the Office of the State Architect, the Personnel Board, the Public Employees Retirement System, and the State Teachers Retirement System. These state agencies that perform direct services to the public, such as the Department of Consumer Affairs, the Museum of Science and Industry, the state Fire Marshal, and the Department of Veterans Affairs, expend the remaining one-fourth in this budget category.

**Other Expenditures**     The funds expended in this category go to support the general government, which includes the legislature, the governor's office, the state courts, and certain other units, including the Fair Political Practices Commission, the Public Employment Relations Board, the Department of Food and Agriculture, the Department of Industrial Relations, and the Public Utilities Commission.

## THE BUDGET PROCESS

California's state budget contains a line-item listing of anticipated revenues and expenditures for a fiscal year beginning July 1 and ending June 30. The formulation of the budget by the governor and the legislature involves a rather lengthy process consisting of seven steps as follows: (1) The introduction of the governor's proposal is required by January 10 of each year according to the state constitution. The proposed budget is introduced separately in the senate and the assembly. (2) Review and analysis prepared by the state legislative analyst is made available to the Senate Finance Committee and the Assembly Ways and Means Committee. (3) In March and April budget subcommittees in each house conduct independent hearings on spending proposals for areas of government expenditures such as health, welfare, education, and other government services. (4) In May the State Department of Finance submits its final estimates of revenues for the coming fiscal year to the budget subcommittees. (5) The Senate Finance Committee and the Assembly Ways and Means Committee collect subcommittee reports for incorporation and adoption for each house. (6) The budget is adopted by both houses with two-thirds majorities. Differences are worked out by a two-house conference committee. Adoption by the legislature of a final spending plan has a deadline of June 15, which is missed more often than met. (7) The legislature sends the budget to the governor who has 12 days to sign it. Under the power of item veto, the governor can delete or decrease any individual line appropriations added by the legislature, although the state's chief executive cannot restore any proposals that the legislature deleted. The governor's veto can be overridden by a two-thirds majority vote in both houses of the legislature. (For further discussion of the item veto, refer to Chapter 7.)

Overshadowing the deliberations of the legislators and the governor in the budget process is the Gann Amendment to the state constitution limiting state spending.

## THE GANN SPENDING LIMITATION

Paul Gann, the co-author with Howard Jarvis of Proposition 13, organized the campaign for an initiative to limit government spending in California. With the support of many Democrats it qualified for the ballot in a special election in November 1979. Known as Proposition 4, it passed with a large 74 percent majority of the voters.

This proposition placed in the state constitution a provision limiting the amount of tax revenues that state and local governments can spend in any given year to the amount spent in 1978, adjusted annually for population growth and inflation. Thus, if inflation was 4 percent and population growth was 1 percent for a given year, all government spending—including that on education, prisons, and welfare— could grow no more than 5 percent over the base period of 1978. Tax revenues received in excess of the legal spending limit had to be returned to taxpayers.

Two propositions that would have loosened limits on government spending as provided by the Gann initiative were on the ballot in June 1988, but both were turned down by the voters. The voters changed the basis for operation of the Gann initiative in the June 1990 election when, instead of population growth and inflation (which hardly can account for new problems such as the AIDS epidemic or the greatly expanded need for bilingual teachers), the new reference point became changes in personal income.

## FINANCING LOCAL GOVERNMENT

Proposition 13 hurled the problem of financing California's local governments into the public limelight. The state's counties, cities, and special districts (including school districts) spend about twice as many tax dollars as the state government. The finances of counties, cities, school districts, and other special districts for the fiscal

**TABLE 10.1    Property Tax as Percentage of Total General Revenue**

|  | 1977–1978— Before Proposition 13 | 1978–1979— After Proposition 13 |
|---|---|---|
| Special districts—nonenterprise | 73.5% | 44.9% |
| School districts | 57.8 | 25.8 |
| Community college districts | 52.2 | 24.2 |
| Counties | 37.0 | 17.3 |
| Cities | 22.8 | 10.8 |
| Special districts—enterprise | 14.7 | 8.8 |

*Source:* California, Department of Finance, Program Evaluation Unit, January 1979.

year immediately preceding the passage of the Jarvis-Gann initiative are summarized in Table 10.1.

In the years before Proposition 13 the heaviest expenditures of California's counties had been for social welfare and amounted to about 40 percent of the typical California county budget. Other large disbursements had been for public protection (services of the sheriff, district attorney, and the courts) and for health programs. The largest expenditures of California's cities were for police and fire protection and street maintenance. School districts, by definition, spent almost all of their $8 billion budget for public education. The other special districts, having been created for a vast variety of purposes, spent their dollars on many different kinds of activities, ranging from laying sewer pipes to operating airports.

Before Proposition 13 the local governments received a significant share of their revenues from the general property tax. In 1976–1977 the counties received about 40 percent of their income from this source, the cities approximately 27 percent, the school districts more than 50 percent, and the other special districts more than 40 percent (some special districts, such as flood control and mosquito abatement, received almost 100 percent support from property taxes).

## THE TAX REVOLT: PROPOSITION 13

To those who voted for it (and to this day praise the names of Howard Jarvis and Paul Gann, the men who led the fight for it), Proposition 13 is a landmark victory for California tax payers, a victory that reigned in big government and preserved hundreds of thousands of home owners in their homes. To those who opposed it, virtually every fiscal evil that has confronted the state in the years since its passage can be traced to it. The high fees for running a red light or illegally parking in a handicapped space, the big bucks charged to obtain a simple copy of a police report, the dearth of new books in your local library, even the preference of local government in favor of development of strip malls instead of housing tracts all this and much more may be laid to Proposition 13. In other words, the voters, they say, blew it.

Of course the most immediate and obvious result of passing Proposition 13 was and is today putting a lid on what had been rapidly escalating property taxes. In the mid–1970s these were growing at an incredible rate with reassessments in 1978 running as much as 250 percent to 400 percent above previous valuations. Many of those on fixed incomes such as the retired faced the very real possibility of losing their homes, unable to pay the vastly increased taxes. Despite the opposition of many political leaders, including Governor Jerry Brown, Proposition 13 or the Jarvis-Gann initiative passed easily. It rolled back property taxes to 1 percent of assessed valuation in 1975–1976 and limited increases to just 2 percent a year. Furthermore, it prohibited local governments from imposing new taxes without approval of two-thirds of local voters since it also prevented the state from raising new taxes without a two-thirds vote of the legislature. This new amendment chopped $7 billion from the local property tax, the biggest source of revenue for cities, counties, school districts, and other special districts. At the time Proposition 13 was passed, property taxes provided between 55 and 65 percent of the total revenue of California cities and counties and an even larger share of the income for state schools and special districts.

What about the impact of Proposition 13 on California as it moves into the twenty-first century? There are several obvious ones.

- The size and number of fees imposed by local governments has increased enormously. With its principal source of income slashed, local government turned to increasing fees for virtually everything and adding fees for services that had been free. Water and sewer fees rose dramatically, document charges were imposed. Fees levied on builders for building and tourists for staying (in hotels and motels), for using formerly free horse trails in public parks all are examples.

- Public services have been reduced in many cases. Trash collections, at one time twice a week, now typically take place once, spending on books and periodicals in public and school libraries and their hours open have been cut as have the times museums are open.

- Decision-making has shifted to Sacramento. Those who fought for Proposition 13 were often conservatives dedicated to local control, yet an unintended consequence of its enactment has been to take decisions out of the hands of local government and move them to the state capital.

- Local government has tended to see new commercial development with its prospect for enhanced sales tax revenues as preferable to new home construction, which generates far less new money.

As noted in a perceptive article by Stephanie Simon in the *Los Angeles Times*,[4] all sorts of ailments have been attributed to Proposition 13 over the years. Kids overweight? It isn't too much television but schools dropping after hours sports programs. The acquittal of O.J. Simpson? That was not due to the eloquence of Johnnie Cochran but because the county had too little money to put on its best case. And so it goes.

---

[4]Stephanie Simon, "20 Years Later, Prop. 13 Still Marks California Life," *Los Angeles Times*, May 26, 1998.

Other taxes have gone up, most notably the sales tax. In one study, the total tax burden in 1998 was found to be just about the same as it was in 1978. Not that the public is in any mood to change things. A *Los Angeles Times* poll in April 1998 asked what people felt about Proposition 13. By a margin of 66 to 20 they expressed approval. As to its impact on public services, 29 percent said it had improved them, 32 percent said they had gotten worse, and 39 percent either said there had been no impact or had no idea what impact it might have had.

## LOSERS AND WINNERS IN THE "PROPOSITION 13 GAME"

As noted previously, local governments—counties, cities, school districts, and special districts—were losers as a result of Proposition 13. They lost a major source of revenue since the income from property taxes was drastically reduced. They were forced to cut expenditures and to seek new sources of revenue and at the same time to balance their budgets. To reduce expenditures it became necessary to make savings by decreasing personnel and holding the line on the rate of salaries and wages. In addition, some services—for example, library services and recreation privileges—were curtailed. At the same time cities, counties, and special districts raised fees for essential services such as rubbish collection and sewer services and increased rates of licenses and permits.

An excellent study showing who the winners from Proposition 13 were was made by Paul Richter, using the period 1978–1983 as a base for his research.

During this five-year period homeowners were the top winners because they received about one-third of the total savings of the first five "Jarvis years." Those who remained in homes they owned in 1978 did better than more recent buyers, because homes are reassessed to market value when they are bought or substantially improved. Owners of commercial and industrial property got 27 percent of the tax savings from Proposition 13, which amounted to nearly $2 billion in the first year. Landlords were also big winners, receiving about 17 percent of the property-tax savings, but only a small portion of these benefits was passed on to tenants because average rents continued to grow from 1978 to 1983. Agriculture received 13 percent of the savings owing to decreased property taxes on agricultural land. However, the Richter study revealed that the gross savings to each of these taxpaying groups was reduced by increases in their state and federal tax liabilities. These liabilities grew because lower property taxes reduced itemized income-tax deductions and increased taxable income. As a result, the federal government became a "winner," claiming about 15–25 percent of gross savings. Ironically, the state gained some 3–11 percent of the tax savings for the same reason.[5]

The tax system created by Proposition 13 was challenged in the courts in the early 1990s on the grounds that two pieces of essentially identical property could be

---

[5]Paul Richter, "Big Winners from California's Tax Cuts," *Los Angeles Times*, June 5, 1983.

Same schools; same police and fire protection; same libraries and parks; same water system and refuse collection...

(Dennis Renault, *Sacramento Bee*)

(and were) taxed at wildly different levels simply because one had changed hands (and thus been reappraised) and the other had not, reappraisal being undertaken only when a property changed ownership. This "dual roll" system was felt by many to be in violation of the equal protection clause of the U.S. Constitution. Opponents maintained no one should pay five or ten times the taxes to receive the same level of services. In June 1992 the Supreme Court ruled otherwise. The Court held the state had a "legitimate interest in local neighborhood preservation" (an issue not raised by the parties in their arguments) and that those buying homes know in advance they will be paying higher taxes and choose to make the purchase voluntarily. To overturn Proposition 13 would result in higher property taxes across the board and might well force many people from their homes, precisely what Proposition 13 was intended to prevent. Proposals to create a "two tier" system for private homes not reappraised until ownership changed and another for commercial enterprises (Macy's, Best Buy, etc.) have gotten nowhere.

## The County—A Big Loser

Decreased revenues for California's counties resulting from Proposition 13 forced a reexamination of the fiscal relationship between state and county governments. For many years the state legislature has required that the state's 58 counties provide and administer statewide programs at the local level without providing enough money to pay all costs. Such state-mandated programs include health and welfare services to the poor; maintenance of rural roads in agricultural areas; and services for city and county residents in the courts, and jail, and juvenile hall; as well as probation, district attorney, public defender, coroner, environmental health, weights and measures, and clerk-recorder services. The county also collects taxes for schools, special districts, and cities.

State and federal governments presently provide about 56 percent of the revenue for California counties, but the cost of these services has been growing faster than the increase in support. In most counties the state-mandated programs now consume as much as 90 percent of the county funds with financial support for local needs such as law enforcement, libraries, and parks continuing to shrink. These mandates, together with the loss of tax revenue from Proposition 13, have meant what one Sacramento lobbyist called "death by attrition" for local governments. Some programs were eliminated, as was the case with Butte County's libraries. Others have been cut drastically, as in Lassen County where an area the size of Connecticut was patrolled by just 13 sheriff's deputies. Cancer-screening clinics and dental clinics were shut down at South Lake Tahoe and Placerville. Nor has it been just in rural counties that cuts have been made. Los Angeles's museums were closed on a rotating basis and hours reduced for all.

## REVIEW QUESTIONS

1. What is the "structural deficit"? How has it been addressed? (pp. 183–184)
2. What are the principal sources of state income? (pp. 184–188)
3. Much controversy has surrounded the state lottery. Why is it considered a regressive tax? (p. 188)
4. What are the three largest areas on which the state spends its money? How does Proposition 98 affect this priority list? (pp. 190–191)
5. List the steps involved in the budget process. (pp. 192–193)
6. What is the Gann spending limit and how has it been altered? (p. 193)
7. What have been the effects of Proposition 13? Who have been the "winners" and "losers" since its passage? (pp. 194–198)

# SELECTED WEB SITES

There are several sites that provide information on budgetary matters. The Legislative Analyst's site, www. lao.ca.gov, is generally regarded as excellent. The office is essentially nonpartisan and advises the legislature on budget issues. The Department of Finance site, www.dof.ca.gov, has a wealth of information on the governor's budget broken down by departments and agencies as well as forecasts of economic growth. The California Taxpayers Association, www.caltax.org/, is a watchdog organization dedicated to protecting citizens from what they believe to be "excessive taxation."

# SELECTED REFERENCES

Barber, Mary Beth, "Local Government Hits the Wall," *California Journal,* August 1993.

Bowman, David, John W. Ellwood, Frank Neuhauser, and Eugene P. Smolensky, "Structural Deficit and the Long Term Fiscal Condition of the State," in John J. Kirlin and Jeffrey I. Chapman, eds., *California Policy Choices,* Vol. 9, Los Angeles: University of Southern California School of Public Administration, 1994.

California, Governor's Office, *Governor's Budget,* Sacramento: State Printing Office, annually.

California, Legislative Analyst, *Analysis of the Budget Bill,* Sacramento: State Printing Office, annually.

_____, *Perspectives and Issues,* Sacramento: State Printing Office, 1997, annually.

Chapman, Jeffrey I., "The Fiscal Context," in John J. Kirlin and Donald R. Winkler, eds., *California Policy Choices,* Vol. 7, University of Southern California School of Public Administration, Los Angeles, 1991.

Goldberg, Lenny, "Spending Limits: Straightjacket for California," *Los Angeles Times,* August 27, 1996.

Leary, Mary Ellen, "The Politics of Tax Repeal and Tax Reform in California," *California Journal,* September 1987.

Mundell, Ed, "Good News: Budget Good for Education," *San Diego Tribune,* July 16, 1996.

Quinn, Michelle, "Have Californians Soured on Their Games of Chance?" *California Journal,* December 1991.

Stall, Bill, and Ralph Frammolino, "Myths vs. Facts of Tax Burdens for Californians," *Los Angeles Times,* October 17, 1993.

# 11

---

# Economic Growth and the Quality of Life

John Q. Commuter sits alone in his car, stopped atop a freeway interchange while traffic on the freeway below him inches forward. His gaze shifts toward the horizon, which is obscured by a gray-brown layer of smog, and then to an orchard struggling to survive against the twin threats of air pollution and the spread of housing tracts in this suburban area. In cars stopped on both sides he sees Hispanics and Asians caught in the same traffic trap. As he waits he glances down at headlines in the morning newspaper carefully folded on the seat beside him. One reports on a new study of energy shortages; another proclaims a crisis in the water supply due to the twin threats of a prolonged drought and contamination. His car radio is tuned to an all-news station whose stories range from the latest gang killings to the impact of illegal aliens in the state and a new study showing California school children lagging in reading and writing skills. Suddenly his car lurches, not because traffic is moving again, but instead—he realizes with alarm—another earthquake has struck the Golden State.

This scenario may be a bit overdrawn (most commuters listen to music stations and have their newspapers turned to the sports or entertainment sections), but it highlights a number of the problems and issues facing California as it heads into the twenty-first century: traffic congestion, air pollution, urban sprawl, immigration, crime, water, and the ever-present danger of what scientists call the "Big One," a catastrophic earthquake they believe will strike the state within the next 20 years. To that list might be added a number of issues with which government must deal: the plight of the homeless, the rights of minorities (ethnics, gays, women), energy, providing quality education to an increasingly diverse population.

The challenges posed by these and other issues lie not just in their obvious complexity but in the need to deal with them for a population that has been growing between 400,000 and 700,000 a year. That is the equivalent of adding a Fresno, three Anaheims, or six Berkeleys every 12 months. These new residents must be served, protected, and in a whole host of ways dealt with, along with the over 37 million already in the state and another 8 million in the not-too-distant future. The burden this places on schools, police and fire departments, sewage disposal, street maintenance, welfare programs, and the like is noted almost daily in the media. California is a great and growing state, but its greatness is threatened by that very growth. This and the following chapter focus on some of the most difficult of these issues and problems and some of the attempts being made to deal with them.

As noted earlier in Chapter 1, the condition of the state's economy in recent years might, on a graph, look like a giant roller coaster. The recession of the early 1990s was followed by a rebound that made the economic situation look extremely rosy by mid-decade. The revenues flowing into the state government from income taxes, sales taxes, capital gains, and the like threatened to overflow state coffers as legislators, especially liberal Democrats, sought to find ways to spend them. Governor Davis warned that the good times might not last and urged one-time expenditures rather than new programs with ongoing commitments of tax dollars. Nonetheless, a number of new programs were instituted only to find Davis had been right: the boom times ended abruptly. A major factor was the collapse of the so-called dot coms, high-tech industries associated with Silicon Valley whose rapid growth had led to major capital gains and the taxes that went with them.

This does not mean that California is weak. Both by the measure of the state's budget and the personal income of its citizens, the state ranks with the major nations of the world. In international trade, California as a nation would be in the top ten. In agriculture fish, mineral wealth, and heavy manufacturing, California ranks at or near the top among the states.

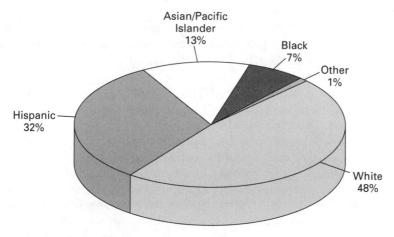

**Figure 11.1**    Population Shares by Race/Ethnicity.

The state has faced a variety of issues over the years: air pollution, transportation, earthquakes, and the like. Two of these, one old and one new, became the focus of attention early in the twenty-first century, the need for more water and the crisis in energy supply.

## THE ENERGY CRISIS

Into the softening economy of 2001 came an energy crisis. This case is highly complex and may only be summarized here. The issues are in some ways easily understood and in other ways very difficult to comprehend.

The origins of the crisis go back to 1996 when, in an action endorsed by both political parties (the votes were unanimous in both houses of the legislature and Governor Wilson signed the resulting bill) the power industry was partially deregulated. The argument that proved so persuasive was that, by removing government regulations on the purchase of power, competition would occur and, as everyone knows, competition leads to lower prices, right? What no one seemed to contemplate was the possibility that major suppliers might attempt to manipulate the power market. This never occurred to the state's leaders. Then in 2001 there was a sudden surge in the price of electricity being charged San Diego Gas and Electric. Politicians for the most part seemed content to let things develop in hopes the crisis would disappear. It did not. When the inadequacy of electricity supplies spread to the rest of the state and rolling blackouts occurred—and were predicted to become more frequent—finger pointing predominated. As several people have said, however, there was plenty of blame to go around.

Who was responsible for what happened? Just about everyone. Democrats, Republicans (that unanimous vote in the legislature), the Public Utilities Commission, Governor Wilson, lobbyists for the utilities, the list is long indeed. As far back as 1995 the state's utilities helped kill a plan to develop more power plants. Outside providers, typically in Texas, decided not to add transmission capacity for natural gas into the state about the same time. (Later revelations of market manipulation to increase prices by these providers including Enron with strategies code named "death star" and "get shorty" implicated these players as well.) Evidence surfaced in late 2002 that some power plants may have been deliberately shut down to create shortages. Within the state what was described as an "antiquated and overworked" system of power lines suddenly started performing like clogged arteries. A portion of the power grid lines (Path 15) running between Coalinga and Los Banos simply could not transmit adequate power north–south. A four-lane road was needed where only two lanes were present. Environmentalists likewise opposed any new power plants as harmful to flora and fauna. The insistence that power buys be on the "spot" market as opposed to long-term contracts (an idea that sounded good since that flexibility would provide the ability to take advantage of low prices when they came along) ended up costing billions as prices soared. Not to be overlooked was the fact the power usually available from the Northwest was less than usual due to a drought (less water flowing to turn turbines and generate electricity).

SMOKING GUN

(Rex Babin, *The Sacramento Bee*)

The reaction was several-fold. The governor called for more power plants and, at the same time, for conservation. The conservation message apparently got through. The multiple outages expected during the peak summer months simply never took place, due in large measure to reductions in demand. Californians in June 2001 used 12 percent less power than in June 2000. Rates skyrocketed of course leading to increased prices for all sorts of goods and services. Restaurants put an "energy surcharge" on their meals. The San Diego Zoo instituted an "energy assistance fee" for admission. Hotels increased room rates. Then there was the human factor. Blackouts threatened those on life support at home. Seniors who were most at risk if the air conditioning failed were given information on where to go—emergency centers where cool air would be assured.

Ultimately, the governor engaged in some behind-closed-doors negotiations for long-term contracts, contracts ranging from a few months to as long as 20 years. That seemed prudent at the time, but, as critics later pointed out, these contracts were entered into at a time when prices were at their highest. It was not too many months before the contracts that had been highly praised by the governor were being described as further price gouging. "Further" because as investigations proceeded it became apparent to many that the supply of power had been manipulated by power suppliers outside the state to maximize their profits.

By the end of the summer of 2001 the crisis had abated. In part this was due to belated action by the Federal Energy Regulatory Commission (FERC), which

Only God Can Make A Tree.....

..... But Only Man Can Make A Buck.

(Courtesy *McClatchy Newspapers*)

early on had pretty much said it wouldn't do a thing. You Californians, it said, got yourselves into this mess by refusing to build more power plants. Ignored at that stage was the fact that power prices had gone from $7.4 billion in 2000 to $27.6 billion in 2001 and showed no sign of stopping their upward surge. Eventually the commission reversed itself. It had been given power by Congress to prevent unfair and unreasonable charges and with megawatts going for, in some cases, more than $1,000 an hour they capped them at $92. Later memoranda from Enron showed markets that had been manipulated on several ways to get as much money from California customers as possible, a practice described by many as gouging.

With the construction of more power plants, more reliance on lower cost long-term contracts and some conservation the power picture improved greatly in 2002, though the record breaking heat that year (Sacramento hit 122, Redding and Red Bluff neared 120) led to alerts indicating reserves were dangerously low. Still, this crisis had been, at least for the time being, met. That left another crisis to be met, water. This of course has been perhaps *the* most pressing problem over the course of the state's history.

## WATER ALLOCATION ISSUES

California's water problem is due to the continuing press of the state's industrial and population growth upon its limited supply of water. In an average non-drought year, about 71 million acre feet of water fall on California, approximately 37 million acre feet of which are captured for agricultural, industrial, and residential use. The basic problem (even apart from drought years) is that statewide use-demand now exceeds the amount captured, which means that more dams and reservoir transport systems must be added to the state's mammoth water-harnessing network. But as so often has been the case when new water projects are being considered, efforts to increase the amount of captured water produce bitter disputes between Northern and Southern California, between farmers and city dwellers, between small farmers and large farmers, and between developers and environmentalists.

Population growth is one factor in what many experts are now warning will be a water crisis. By one estimate from the state's Department of Water Resources, urban demand for water, which was 8.5 million acre feet in 1995, will rise to 12 million acre feet in 2020. Compounding the problem in the long run, at least for those scientists who firmly believe in the phenomenon known as global warming, is the loss of a vital resource of water, the Sierra snow pack. One study undertaken at the University of California, Santa Cruz, and the Lawrence Livermore Laboratory has come up with what must be considered a worst case scenario. They estimate this snow pack will, by mid century, have declined by 82 percent! The impact of such a reduction or anything close to it is evident. It would be disastrous for agriculture, which depends heavily on it for irrigation. Urban areas such as Los Angeles and San Francisco would be starved for water. Electricity generated by hydro-electric power plants would diminish to a trickle. Should this take place it would make all the droughts of the past, such as the one between 1986 and 1992, pale to insignificance.

State, federal, and local governments have been active in constructing reservoirs and dams in California since the early part of the twentieth century. The Hetch Hetchy Aqueduct was built in the early 1920s to transport water from the Sierra down to storage reservoirs in San Francisco; the city of Los Angeles constructed a 283-mile aqueduct from the water-rich Owens Valley down to the semiarid valleys of the populous southland. Construction of Hetch Hetchy was controversial from the start. John Muir objected strenuously, comparing the valley to be covered by the resulting reservoir to the beauty of Yosemite. Two issues arose in 2005 when proposals to tear down O'Shaughnessay Dam at Hetch Hetchy arose once more: the cost involved and the difficulty of finding alternative sources of water for the 2.5 million residents of the Bay Area.

**Figure 11.2**   Water Allocation in California.

The increased demand for water by Southern California in the 1930s led to the construction of the spectacular Colorado River Aqueduct—the longest domestic water supply line ever built—which lifts water 1,600 feet by a series of five pumping plants before transporting it 242 miles across the desert to Lake Mathews, where it is stored for distribution to the five Southern California counties. In the late 1930s, in response to the drought and to stimulate the economy, work began on the mammoth $793 million Central Valley Project (CVP), constructed and operated by the U.S. Bureau of Reclamation to supply water for irrigation, municipal, and domestic uses; to provide hydroelectricity; to control floods; and to improve navigation on the Sacramento River. The CVP was conceived as a state project but was taken over by the federal government when the state proved unable to finance it. Today the main facilities in the CVP are five Northern California dams (Shasta, Folsom, Trinity, Friant, and New Melonas) from which water is delivered to farmers in the San Joaquin Valley through three canals (Delta-Mendota, San Luis, and Friant-Kern).

The largest California undertaking is the State Water Project, whose 750-mile course of dams and aqueducts, as completed, is the most spectacular water-harnessing system in the world. Originally estimated to cost $1.75 billion and to be built over a period of 25 years, the State Water Project cost more than three times that much by the time it was completed.

The North-South issues are the product of nature's dispensation: 75 percent of the precipitation falls in the northern one-third of the state, but 80 percent of the need for water occurs in the southern two-thirds of the state. In recent decades most of the large water projects have been designed to move the water from north to south. This has stirred northern resentment and fear—resentment at having to pay for facilities that disproportionately benefit the Southerners and fear that in times of drought the North will be left high and dry. This concern led to defeat of the Peripheral Canal to provide more water to the South from the Delta.

## Agriculture

If urban areas need adequate supplies of water, so does agriculture. Agriculture is, after all, a major contributor to the health of the state economy. It is estimated that gross farm income in 2001 amounted to $27 billion, making California for the fiftieth straight year the nation's biggest producer of agricultural products. Of the more than 200 crops grown and livestock nurtured in the state, California leads the nation in 53. Half the fresh fruit grown in the United States comes from California. The incredible variety of California agriculture is reflected in its top five cash crops— milk and cream, cattle, grapes, cotton, and hay.

The functioning of this rich cornucopia requires water, a great deal of water. With a population of 37 million, more than 92 percent of whom live in urban areas, many people are surprised to learn that between 80 and 85 percent of all the water used in California goes to agriculture. With a finite—even declining—amount available, conflicts between farmers and urban areas are to be expected. Agriculture cites its needs and the contributions it makes to the state's wealth; city leaders point to the waste that they say is inherent in the farmer's methods of using water. Farmers respond that they are careful in their use of water and that agriculture by its very nature requires great amounts of the liquid. They point to the number of gallons of water required to grow a pound of lettuce for the fall market (21 gallons), or a pound of sugar beets (28 gallons), or cotton (649 gallons). And a pound of almonds requires 681 gallons. A University of California study found it takes approximately 4,533 gallons of water to feed one person for a single day!

## Conservation

Most people pay little attention to water supply problems—until a crisis hits. They tend to take for granted their right to water their lawns as much and as often as they like. They assume a glass of ice water will automatically appear when they sit down in their favorite restaurant. The droughts of 1977–1978 and 1987–1994 led to bans on many kinds of water use in a number of areas of the state. San Franciscans, for example, were told they had to cut consumption 25 percent. Hosing down a driveway, if caught doing it once too often, resulted in the violator's water supply being completely cut off. In some areas watering lawns was prohibited, and drinking water in restaurants was available only upon request.

Three approaches to conservation predominate. One is the type of restriction on use just described. A second seeks installation of water-saving devices in showers or in toilet tanks, encouraged by rebates or mandated by building codes for new construction. The third might be termed the "disincentive system." It penalizes high use by making it cost more per unit once a certain level has been reached. Water meters in and of themselves can act as conservation instruments. Fresno and Clovis are neighbors in the Central Valley and enjoy identical climates. Clovis has meters, Fresno does not. Residential water use is 25 percent lower in Clovis. Opponents of meters claim they do not lead to conservation or, if they do, that lowered revenues will lead to increases in rates that would hurt seniors and others on fixed incomes.

## Supply vs. Demand

Increasing demands for water are hardly unprecedented, but at the beginning of the twenty-first century they became particularly acute. How to provide adequate water supplies for a rapidly growing population together with continuing demands from agriculture and industry while at the same time meeting the demands of the federal government such as found in the Miller-Bradley Act[1] proved to be a major challenge to state leaders. The federal government in 2002 instituted a plan that requires phasing down the amount of water the state receives from the Colorado River from 5.2 million acre feet a year to 4.4 million acre feet. Earlier the federal Department of the Interior had ruled three Indian tribes living on reservations along the Colorado River were entitled to 104,000 acre feet a year, enough to serve the needs of 500,000 Southern Californians for a year.

In meeting the state's recently developed needs, several approaches have either been instituted or contemplated. *Water marketing* was encouraged. This process involves those who hold water rights with their lands selling those rights to others, usually to urban and suburban buyers. Developed first in response to the drought of the late 1980s, some worried it might result in damage to the state's agricultural economy. However, that fear appears to have been unfounded. Another approach, one rejected earlier as too expensive, is *desalination*. This process involves the use of reverse osmosis by which ocean water is passed through a membrane that removes salt, making it safe for human consumption. Though some nations have made extensive use of this process (Saudi Arabia obtains all of its drinking water this way), the few attempts made here such as in Santa Barbara were quickly ended as too

---

[1]Miller-Bradley mandates that in normal rainfall years, 800,000 acre feet of water that previously had been available for the most part to agriculture had to be diverted to protect endangered species such as the Delta smelt and summer salmon. An acre foot equals the amount of water needed to cover an acre to the depth of one foot.

costly. However, new filtration technologies have reduced costs considerably, though the water produced is still four times as expensive as ground water. With increasing pressures to obtain more water, more plans are proceeding to build new plants. They have been proposed at El Segundo or Redondo Beach, Playa del Rey, and Dana Point. Of course, having enough water is crucial. Human beings and industry cannot run on a steady diet of soft drinks. But the quality of that water is also of great importance.

## Water Quality

Concerns over adequate water supply are often tied to issues of water quality. Providing water that is in ample supply but unsafe to drink is no solution. Contamination may come from toxic wastes improperly disposed of, from insecticides used in agricultural activities in the area, or even naturally occurring carcinogens such as selenium. Leaking gasoline storage tanks were a major source of contamination. In 1985 the State Water Resources Control Board reported there were 30,000 of these leaking tanks in the state. Laws requiring registration and testing of these tanks were followed by state mandates that resulted in "double hulling" (tanks with two walls) to prevent instances such as took place on Lake Arrowhead one morning when residents awoke to find gasoline polluted water coming from their taps. Over 40 wells were closed down in Fresno due to seepage of the agricultural pesticide DBCP into the water supply.

Of course pollution is probably better known to most in a different manifestation.

## AIR POLLUTION

Mention smog and most people immediately think of Los Angeles. A temperature inversion puts a pressure lid over the basin and traps pollutants that, after a few days, accumulate to the point that visibility is drastically reduced, eyes begin to smart, and noses wrinkle in distaste. Although some visitors are never aware of it, Los Angeles is located in a beautiful setting, mountains surrounding the city on three sides. However, for much of the year these moutains cannot be seen through the all-enveloping muck.

Los Angeles is, and has been for many years, the most polluted city in the state (and the country, for that matter, though in 1999 it briefly lost this "distinction" to Houston). However, it is by no means unique in having serious air pollution problems. North and south, along the coast and inland, Californians suffer the effects. Some 90 percent of the cities in the state are at one time or another in violation of permissible levels of ozone as set by the federal government. California's pollution, once considered the price that had to be paid for industrialization, provoked many jokes. Today, few find any humor in what has come to be recognized as a condition that is not just inconvenient or an affront to aesthetics but the cause of some major medical problems. It is estimated that some 80,000 Californians die from its effects on the heart and lungs every year. One study found that Southern Californians miss 15 million workdays a year due to air pollution-related illnesses. Another reported that the lung capacity of children living in Los Angeles was, because of air pollution, 10–15 percent less than that of children living in less-polluted areas. In 2002 a

(Courtesy *Frank Interlandi*)

study by the state's Air Resources Board found that air pollution in the form of "fine particulates," which are produced by vehicle emissions, power plants, unpaved roads, and wood burning stoves, are one-sixth the width of a human hair and cause asthma and lead to 9,300 deaths in the state each year. That is three times the number killed in car accidents. Clearly, smog debilitates and can kill. Economic costs are also high. Californians spend more for gasoline because devices to control automobile exhaust emissions, needed to limit the damage done to the quality of the air, reduce gas mileage. Regulations on industry, from power plants to paint shops, are often costly to business, and those costs are passed on to the consumer in the form of higher prices. Agriculture suffers as well. Smog causes an annual loss of approximately $1 billion in ruined crops. The yields from grapes, cotton, potatoes, and lettuce are reduced by between 25 and 60 percent, again leading to higher prices to the consumer.

The perpetually gloomy picture of Los Angeles' air quality is, to a degree at least, a bit unfair. It remains, it is true, the worst in the country, but conditions have improved a great deal over the years. Evidence of that improvement came from the federal Environmental Protection Agency in 2005. While listing Los Angeles as the most polluted area in the United States, the number of days it had exceeded federal clean air standards showed a remarkable decline, from close to half the year in 1976 to 129 in 2003 to 83 in 2005. One factor in the improvement: cars today are 98 percent less polluting than those of the 1970s.

The state legislature, in recognition of the fact that automobile exhausts were the biggest contributor to air pollution, passed the Motor Vehicle Pollution Control Act of 1960. It created a board to determine which pollution control devices should be mandated. In 1965 the federal government got into the picture with its Clean Air Act, which led the state to create its own Air Resources Board. In 1977 amendments to the Clean Air Act set penalties for states that did not make "reasonable progress" toward federally approved standards of air quality. When California failed to establish approved methods for smog inspections until August 1983, millions of dollars in federal highway funds and some sewage treatment funds were withheld.

Much of the credit for recent improvement was given to the introduction (and mandated use) of reformulated gasoline. The new product was estimated to improve air quality very substantially. The cost of gasoline went up, in part to reimburse oil companies that had spent $5 billion to convert their refineries to produce the new product. One complaint, that the new fuel resulted in substantially poorer gas mileage, appeared not to be true. Tests by the Automobile Club (AAA) showed a decrease of just 1 percent.

In an effort to attack the air pollution problem as it relates to automobiles, air quality officials in the San Joaquin Valley (an area deemed the third most polluted in the country) imposed hefty fees on developers under the rationale that better planned communities would reduce traffic. The fees are intended to encourage builders to locate banks, shopping centers, and other services such as markets and schools closer to homes or by creating bike lanes and walkways for car-less travel to education and jobs. This attack on urban sprawl is in its early stages with results to be determined. However, the Valley has the highest asthma rate in the state and has faced sanctions from the Environmental Protection Agency for its dirty air. Builders generally opposed the new fees on the grounds it would raise housing prices. However, one estimate was the increase would amount to around $1,770, seen as a modest cost by environmentalists when the average new home in the Valley ran around $300,000.

Many recent targets are so-called *small polluters*. These are polluting practices that, in a single case, may not be significant but when taken as a whole they are. In this category are volatile organic compounds, or VOCs. These are found in hair sprays, tile cleaners, air fresheners, and floor polish, among other products. Limits imposed in the South Coast Air Quality Management District (SCAQMD) were estimated to reduce these emissions by 45 *tons* a day. That compares with an average oil refinery, which emits between 1.4 tons and 3.9 tons of pollutants a day. Small polluters obviously do matter. Other targets of the SCAQMD include gasoline-powered lawn mowers, petroleum-based barbecue starter fluids, and drive-through windows serving hamburgers (idling cars pollute at length).

Still another approach involves what is termed *telecommuting*, the use of remote locations linked to the central office by telephone, computer, and/or fax machines. Typically this has been seen as a single person working out of the home, but some companies and government departments have set up area offices away from their central facility, allowing workers to work together yet with much-reduced travel time and fewer polluting miles driven.

## TRANSPORTATION

When Congress passed legislation in 1987 permitting the states to raise speed limits on interstate highways from 55 miles per hour to 65, those portions passing through urban areas were specifically excluded. For most Californians, that exclusion, at least

**TABLE 11.1    America's 15 Worst Highway Bottlenecks**

| Rank | City | Freeway | Location | Vehicles per day | Annual hours of delay (,000) |
|------|------|---------|----------|------------------|------------------------------|
| 1. | Los Angeles | US-101 | US-101 (Ventura Fwy) at I-405 Interchange | 318,000 | 27,144 |
| 2. | Houston | I-610 | I-610 at I-10 Interchange (West) | 295,000 | 25,181 |
| 3. | Chicago | I-90 | I-90/94 at I-290 Interchange ("Circle Interchange") | 293,671 | 25,068 |
| 4. | Phoenix | I-10 | I-10 at SR-51/SR-202 Interchange ("Mini-Stack") | 280,800 | 22,805 |
| 5. | Los Angeles | I-405 | I-405 (San Diego Fwy) at I-10 Interchange | 296,000 | 22,792 |
| 6. | Atlanta | I-75 | I-75 at I-85 Interchange | 259,128 | 21,045 |
| 7. | Washington (DC-Md.-Va.) | I-495 | I-495 at I-270 Interchange | 243,425 | 19,429 |
| 8. | Los Angeles | I-10 | I-10 (Santa Monica Fwy) at I-5 Interchange | 318,500 | 18,606 |
| 9. | Los Angeles | I-405 | I-405 (San Diego Fwy) at I-605 Interchange | 318,000 | 18,606 |
| 10. | Atlanta | I-285 | I-285 at I-85 Interchange ("Spaghetti Junction") | 266,000 | 17,072 |
| 11. | Chicago | I-94 | I-94 (Dan Ryan Expwy) at I-90 Skyway Split (Southside) | 260,403 | 16,713 |
| 12. | Phoenix | I-17 | I-17 (Black Canyon Fwy) at I-10 Interchange (the "Stack") to Cactus Rd. | 208,000 | 16,310 |
| 13. | Los Angeles | I-5 | I-5 (Santa Ana Fwy) at SR-22/SR-57 Interchange ("Orange Crush") | 308,000 | 16,304 |
| 14. | Providence | I-95 | I-95 at I-195 Interchange | 256,000 | 15,340 |
| 15. | Washington (DC-Md.-Va.) | I-495 | I-495 at I-95 Interchange | 185,125 | 15,035 |

during rush hours, hardly matters. Average speeds on city freeways in California at times when most are either going to or coming from work seem only grudgingly to edge into double figures. Rain, a minor accident, or even a car stalled on the shoulder can easily bring traffic to a crawl or a complete stop.

A number of factors have come together to create what is called *gridlock*, a condition that has become a frequent and frustrating reality for urban commuters. One of the most important—and obvious—factors is the number of vehicles on the roads, each typically carrying only one person—the driver. There are over 21 million automobiles registered in the state and another nearly 6 million trucks. Joining them are 2.5 million trailers. The result is traffic overload, which leads to quips such as the one describing the Hollywood Freeway at rush hour as "the longest parking lot in the world."

It was generally recognized from the outset that extensive and efficient transportation was essential to California's economic growth. At the same time it has been a part of the problem of runaway growth, as manifested in issues of energy use, air pollution control, and land use. After World War II the state launched a huge freeway construction program, financed by taxes on motorists. The state Department of Public Works in 1959 recommended a comprehensive system of freeways that by 1980 would connect every section of the state with 12,000 miles of roads, touching almost every town with a population of more than 5,000. The motorist in a hurry to reach San Francisco from Los Angeles would have a choice of five routes, and the nature lover would be able to cross the Sierra Nevada in about ten places. The legislature acted to implement this recommendation by passing the Collier Master Plan for Freeways, which established the California freeway and expressway system and incorporated into it practically all of the important state highways then in operation or projected for the next 20 years.

Congestion remains, however. In a 2005 survey, four of the ten worst clogged freeway interchanges in the country were in California. Indeed, the worst in the whole country was the one joining the Ventura and San Diego freeways. Some 318,000 vehicles use that interchange each day with an average of 27,144 hours of delay due to traffic jams. Fifth worst: the San Diego-Santa Monica interchange (280,000 cars and 22,792 hours of delay).

In 2005, a survey by the Texas Transportation Institute found Los Angeles, for the eighteenth straight year, to have topped the nation as having the most congested streets and highways. Drivers there spent an average of 93 hours a year stuck in slow or not moving traffic. Nor were Angelenos alone. San Francisco won the dubious distinction of having the second worst congestion with San Diego fifth. This experience is not just frustrating, it is costly. The study estimated it cost those driving in Los Angeles over $1,668 a year in wasted time and gasoline.

To top all this off, another study found California roads to be the worst in the nation. Some 37 percent are in poor condition according to the Federal Highway Commission. This may be due in some measure to the fact the state spends less per capita on road maintenance than any other state except New Hampshire (in 2004 just $137 vs. the national average of $218). The Public Policy Institute of California found that real capital outlays had declined 79 percent from 1960 to 1980 and have remained constant since. More telling, from 1980 to 2000 California added just

(Courtesy *Frank Interlandi*)

6 percent in highway miles when there was an increase of 87 percent in the number of miles driven. By one estimate, shoddy roads cost California drivers an average of $705 a year in repairs, vehicle deterioration, and fuel.

## Freeway Shortcomings and Some Alternatives

Many transportation experts have concluded that building more freeways will not, in itself, solve the transportation problems facing the state. They stress three main points. The first is that it is impossible to build freeways fast enough to keep up with the increases in the number of vehicles projected for the next 20–30 years.

Second, freeways are expensive. The Century Freeway, completed in 1993, cost $127 million per mile, or $2.2 billion. It *is* state of the art with roadbed sensors and television cameras to monitor traffic flow and it has a light rail line (the Green Line) designed to carry 100,000 passengers a day running down its median. The funds required to pay for rights-of-way to help those living in the path of the new freeway to relocate and for erecting sound barriers to protect nearby residents from noise pollution all add to the expense.

Third, other means of moving people are more efficient and practicable. Instead of building more freeways, many urge steps be taken to encourage the use of alternative ways of "getting from here to there."

## Carpooling

The logic behind carpooling is straightforward enough: If more people shared rides, fewer cars would be on the road. Fewer cars mean less congestion. One move to encourage ride-sharing, the famous (or infamous) Diamond Lane experiment that reserves a lane for cars carrying two or more people, has met with considerable resistance and a good deal of cheating. (Several drivers were caught using dummies propped up on car seats to fool patrolling police.) At least part of the problem lies with a desire for autonomy ("I want to go where I want to go when I want to") and the fact that a widely dispersed population makes ride-sharing difficult and even impossible as employees converge on their workplaces from so many different locales.

A state law requires that all businesses with more than 100 employees at a single location make every effort to convert solo drivers into carpoolers. As the state neared the end of the twentieth century, however, there was little evidence of major increases in joint ridership. Increases in the mid–1990s across the state were minimal.

Despite the efforts to increase ride-sharing, the percentage of Californians who carpool has remained relatively low. During the 1990s, the number of carpool miles increased from 149 miles to 1,011. Yet the percentage of the state's drivers going to work alone rose slightly, from 71.6 to 71.8 percent. There was an unexpected dividend for one pooler, however. A matchmaker in his pool set him up with his future wife.

## Mass Transit

Most urban planners contend that new mass-transit systems are increasingly necessary not only to relieve freeway congestion but also to provide low-income, non-car-owning families with wider access to jobs, shopping, and recreation in California's cities.

This brings forward other issues: What means of transportation should be used—buses, trains on fixed rails, vehicles operated on air cushions? How shall the routes be determined? Above all, who should pay for transportation—property owners through higher real estate taxes, automobile users through gasoline taxes or license fees, or the general public through increased sales or income taxes?

Proponents of the public's greater reliance on mass transit generally agree that buses, although essential in any comprehensive transportation system, are insufficient for moving millions of people over the long distances of California's great metropolitan areas. They prefer some kind of fixed guideway system: two rail, monorail, air cushion, and so on.

California is not without experience in building rail systems. In the first third of the twentieth century, many of the state's major cities had extensive streetcar lines. In Northern California the electric trains of the Southern Pacific, the Key System, and the Sacramento Northern Railway connected San Francisco with many communities of the Bay region. In Southern California the Pacific Electric was hailed as the world's largest and best interurban railroad, and in 1930 it operated 88 trains daily in each direction from downtown Los Angeles to Glendale and 109 to Pasadena. Northern California was connected to Southern California by almost a dozen daily passenger trains on the Southern Pacific and Santa Fe.

After World War II, however, public transportation systems were allowed to deteriorate, and no efforts were made to replace them; service became less and less frequent, and fares increased; line after line was discontinued. By the 1960s hardly a single streetcar, except San Francisco's cable cars, was operating in California. Today buses are supposed to provide the public with the mobility once gained from streetcars and trains, but passengers often have to wait an hour in the hot sun on a noisy street corner for a bus, and in many areas there is no public transportation at all.

The San Francisco Bay region was the first to meet the new demand for rapid public transit. In 1962 the voters in San Francisco, Alameda, and Contra Costa counties created the Bay Area Rapid Transit (BART) District by approving a $792 million bond issue. The directors of BART decided on the traditional system of cars with steel wheels riding on steel rails with cars operated automatically by computers. The entire system was expected to be completed by July 1, 1971, at a cost of $995.9 million, the debt to be paid off by fares and by a special sales tax levied throughout the district. These targets were missed by a wide margin. The cost mushroomed to $1.3 billion, and it was not until September 1974 that BART trains began to run between Oakland and San Francisco under the Bay (although limited service between Oakland and Fremont began in the fall of 1972).

On a number of scales of performance, the system works quite well. Average ridership runs well over 300,000. The trains ride smoothly, frequently, and are generally reliable as they move along the 104 miles of track connecting 43 stations. Maximum speeds can reach 80 miles per hour with the average at 36 mph. Stops are usually about 20 seconds long, and trains are on schedule just over 95 percent of the time. A long sought after leg of the system was completed in 2002. It is an 8.7 mile-long extension to the San Francisco International Airport. Other extensions under study include one to take BART into San Jose. Its nine-member, popularly elected board of directors, representing the localities of the Bay Area, constitutes a working regional metropolitan government with legislative and taxing powers for its specific functions.

Attempts to match or even approach the Bay Area's efforts in Southern California met with a good deal of voter opposition. A bond issue to finance an 89-mile rail system was defeated in 1968, and other proposals to be funded from increased sales taxes were rejected at the polls in 1974 and 1976.

Undaunted, transit advocates continued their efforts to improve transportation facilities in Los Angeles. A plan the voters approved in 1980 was scaled down from earlier proposals and is financed by a half-cent sales tax supplemented by federal and state funds and some private financing. Monies are used to improve and expand existing freeways and to build two new rail systems. One is a subway system, known as Metro Rail. The first phase, a 4.4-mile segment called the Red Line, opened in 1993. A second phase was completed in 2000. It connects Union Station with North Hollywood. Lovely stations filled with art, clean and graffiti free, sleek, fast trains that run on time, this is surely a model for the future. Or is it? The cost of construction ($4.7 billion or $270 million a mile) and operation have turned many former enthusiasts off. One study found it cost $1.15 a mile, which translates into $20.01 for the run from Union Station to North Hollywood. The fare? $1.35.

The only line to live up to its projected use is the Blue Line that runs from Long Beach to Los Angeles. It carries approximately 70,000 passengers a day. The third or Green Line serves some 27,000 people daily. In all likelihood the completion of the Red Line marked the end of subway construction in the area. The mayor at the time, Richard Riordan, summed up the feeling of many when he said, "I wish we had never started the whole thing. . . . Fixed rail is not the answer to the transportation needs of our city."

The Tijuana Trolley in San Diego, Sacramento's Metro, and Cal Train (San Mateo and Santa Clara counties to San Francisco) are examples of mass transit systems elsewhere in the state, none of which pay for themselves.

## Other Approaches

Some efforts to improve the efficiency of California's transportation system have turned to advanced technology. From "traffic alerts" broadcast on radio and electronic warning signs along freeways (which skeptics maintained often warned of a problem only after you were already in it) to magnetic sensors implanted in roadbeds and remote control television cameras to monitor traffic, advanced technology is being used more and more to regulate movement along urban freeways. A very different kind of experiment was undertaken in Orange County where four toll roads (sometimes described as "un-Californian," "highway robbery," "unfreeways," and worse) have been built to relieve pressure on the freeway system. Part of their high-tech image comes from the use of *smart cards,* which are inserted into dashboard-mounted transponders that "tell" the tollway computers that the car is using the road, allowing drivers to bypass tollbooths with charges deducted from a pre-existing account.

The first of these toll roads to become operational was a ten-mile stretch that runs along the middle of I-91, the Riverside Freeway. Four lanes wide, it has proved very attractive to many commuters normally stuck in rush hour traffic. At peak hours the cost was $2.50; losses to the private company operating the toll road led to the price being increased to a maximum of $3.

Another new approach brought focus on a possible conflict between two of southern California's needs: improving transportation and earthquake safety. The original estimate of the number of cars using the Riverside Freeway rose dramatically from the 225,000 a day it was engineered to handle to 268,000 in 2005 with official estimates that that figure would rise to 500,000 by 2050. To address this need, a project was proposed that would cost $9 billion and create the world's second longest tunnel (11 miles in length) linking the rapidly growing Inland Empire with the lucrative jobs offered in Orange County. The only problem (other than cost)?

The tunnel would run through active earthquake country. In one version the tunnel would begin barely one mile from a fault that produced a 6.0 earthquake, though it had taken place a hundred years before. As one vocal critic asked, noting a proposal to double deck the freeway had been rejected because of the earthquake issue, ". . . would you want to be in that tunnel?" Answer pending.

In the really high-tech category are *smart cars* equipped with on-board computers and television screens displaying maps that tell the driver the least-trafficked way to get from here to there. Then there is the *automated highway*, on which computers and car radars actually control the driving along freeways focused on magnetic sensors in the roadbed (that's *really* leaving the driving to us—or Caltrans). At the other end of the technological scale is the antigridlock law that went into effect January 1, 1988. It imposes fines on motorists who become stuck in the middle of intersections, impeding traffic. Intended to improve conditions on surface streets, fines of up to $500 may be imposed for the third offense.


## EARTHQUAKES

Predictions that within the next 20 years or so California will experience a "catastrophic" earthquake—often referred to as the "Big One"—have generated a number of novels and motion pictures depicting the likely consequences of such a massive upheaval of the earth's surface. The descriptions typically feature tall buildings crumbling to the ground, fires fed by broken natural gas lines raging everywhere, structures and people slowly sinking into ground shaken so badly it turns into the equivalent of quicksand, and a tsunami, or tidal wave, crashing across the shoreline, inundating coastal communities. For some, the image of "the late great State of California" slipping beneath the Pacific Ocean apparently holds a certain grim fascination.

The causes of earthquakes are reasonably well understood. Some result from the collapse of underground caverns and others from volcanic action. The "Big One," when it comes, will be through the action of what are known as tectonic plates—huge rigid coverings on the planetary surface that float on a soft, plasticlike interior. As these plates move, they push against one another; the pressures generated create mountain ranges—and earthquakes. The most famous example of this in California is the San Andreas Fault, which runs 650 miles along the western edge of the state from Southern California to Mendocino. It was this fault that caused the disastrous earthquake of 1906 in San Francisco. The San Andreas fault is, however, only one of many that crisscross the state, each posing in varying degrees the danger of significant damage should the pressures along it grow too great.

Most "adjustments" of the earth's surface do little or no damage. There are frequent temblors of less than 4.0 on the Richter Scale that result in nothing more than a call to the local fire station or television newsroom. Even those measuring up to 5.5 often result in nothing more than a few broken dishes or soup cans in supermarket aisles. When contemplating the "Big One," a figure of 7.5 or higher is usually predicted. A common misconception is that the figures on the Richter Scale are arithmetic; they are logarithmic. The Palm Springs earthquake of 1986 measured 6.0 on this scale, whereas Eureka's in 1980 at 7.0 was ten times as severe.

## Number of quakes since 1800

Number of quakes of more than 5.0 on the Richter scale by decade*

|  |  |
|---|---|
| 1800–'09 | 1 |
| '10–'19 | 1 |
| '20–'29 | 0 |
| '30–'39 | 2 |
| '40–'49 | 0 |
| '50–'59 | 1 |
| '60–'69 | 2 |
| '70–'79 | 1 |
| '80–'89 | 0 |
| '90–'99 | 0 |
| 1900–'09 | 1 |
| '10–'19 | 0 |
| '20–'29 | 2 |
| '30–'39 | 1 |
| '40–'49 | 2 |
| '50–'59 | 4 |
| '60–'69 | 0 |
| '70–'79 | 6 |
| '80–'89 | 11 |
| '90–present | 6 |

*Each "multiple quake" - in which two or more quakes occur extremely close in time and space, such as the Landers and Big Bear quakes of June 28, 1992 - is treated here as a single quake

## Location of quakes more than 5.0

Quakes since 1980

## Deaths and injuries

Number of deaths and injuries for the top 10 quakes since 1800.

| Location, year | Deaths | Injuries |
|---|---|---|
| 1. San Francisco | 700–800 | Unkown |
| 2. Long Beach, 1933 | 115 | Hundreds |
| 3. Loma Prieta, 1989 | 63 | 3,757 |
| 4. San Fernando, 1971 | 58 | 2,000 |
| 5. Northridge, 1994 | 55 | 5,000 |
| 6. San Juan Capistrano, 1812 | 50+ | Unknown |
| 7. Hayward, 1868 | 30 | Unknown |
| 8. Owens Valley, 1872 | 27 | 56 |
| 9. Santa Barbara, 1925 | 12–14 | Unknown |
| 10. Kern County, 1952 | 12 | 18 |

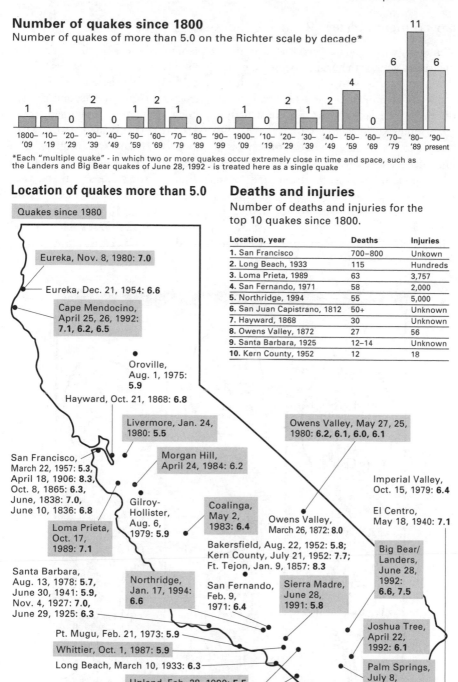

Eureka, Nov. 8, 1980: **7.0**

Eureka, Dec. 21, 1954: **6.6**

Cape Mendocino, April 25, 26, 1992: **7.1, 6.2, 6.5**

Oroville, Aug. 1, 1975: **5.9**

Hayward, Oct. 21, 1868: **6.8**

Livermore, Jan. 24, 1980: **5.5**

Owens Valley, May 27, 25, 1980: **6.2, 6.1, 6.0, 6.1**

San Francisco, March 22, 1957: **5.3,** April 18, 1906: **8.3,** Oct. 8, 1865: **6.3,** June, 1838: **7.0,** June 10, 1836: **6.8**

Morgan Hill, April 24, 1984: **6.2**

Gilroy-Hollister, Aug. 6, 1979: **5.9**

Coalinga, May 2, 1983: **6.4**

Owens Valley, March 26, 1872: **8.0**

Imperial Valley, Oct. 15, 1979: **6.4**

El Centro, May 18, 1940: **7.1**

Loma Prieta, Oct. 17, 1989: **7.1**

Bakersfield, Aug. 22, 1952: **5.8**; Kern County, July 21, 1952: **7.7**; Ft. Tejon, Jan. 9, 1857: **8.3**

Santa Barbara, Aug. 13, 1978: **5.7,** June 30, 1941: **5.9,** Nov. 4, 1927: **7.0,** June 29, 1925: **6.3**

Northridge, Jan. 17, 1994: **6.6**

San Fernando, Feb. 9, 1971: **6.4**

Sierra Madre, June 28, 1991: **5.8**

Big Bear/ Landers, June 28, 1992: **6.6, 7.5**

Pt. Mugu, Feb. 21, 1973: **5.9**

Whittier, Oct. 1, 1987: **5.9**

Long Beach, March 10, 1933: **6.3**

Upland, Feb. 28, 1990: **5.5**

San Juan Capistrano, Dec. 8, 21, 1812: **7.0**

Oceanside, July 13, 1986: **5.3**

Joshua Tree, April 22, 1992: **6.1**

Palm Springs, July 8, 1986: **5.9**

San Diego, Nov. 22, 1800: **6.5**

Imperial County, Nov. 23, 24, 1987: **6.2, 6.6**

**Figure 11.3**  Significant California Quakes.

## Government Policies: Reducing the Risks

There are two major aspects to government planning for earthquakes. The first focuses on actions to be taken before one hits and is designed to minimize its effects; the second deals with the effects after it occurs. Minimizing the effects of earthquake damage involves three factors: land use, structural requirements, and prediction. Land-use laws restrict new construction in known fault areas. The Field Act of 1933 followed the highly destructive earthquake of that year, which destroyed or badly damaged a large number of schools in Long Beach and Los Angeles. The Hospitals Act of 1972 was patterned after the Field Act in that it requires that all plans for new hospitals be submitted to the Office of the State Architect, who reviews them in light of the geology of the site. The Alquist-Priola Act of 1972 bans construction of any "building for human habitation" within 50 feet of a known, active fault. Structural requirements are imposed by the California Health and Safety Code. All new buildings must be constructed so as to maximize their ability

(Courtesy *Frank Interlandi*)

to withstand the swaying and twisting forces associated with earthquakes. Prediction focuses on trying to anticipate when an earthquake will take place, with the objective of evacuating those in danger before it hits. Although there have been advances in this area (lasers are used to measure minute earth movements, for example), prediction is still far too uncertain. Given the economic and psychological costs of being wrong, officials are unlikely to order an evacuation. One effort to make prediction more reliable is underway near Parkfield in central California. There scientists are drilling a hole a mile and a half deep to allow them to lower a number of tiny seismometers into the San Andreas fault area to better learn what precedes a quake and, accordingly, how to predict one.

## Government Policies: Dealing with the Effects

When dealing with what is termed emergency response planning (ERP), the question shifts from limiting the effects of an earthquake to what to do after one takes place. Those images from the disaster movies are the stuff of policy planning. The Federal Emergency Management Agency (FEMA) lists the many tasks state and local governments should be prepared to perform. With communications disrupted, power generators out, natural gas mains broken, roads obstructed by debris, and structures either badly damaged or destroyed, well-developed plans for dealing with the aftermath of a temblor are essential. Among FEMA's list of tasks are restoring communications to assist in directing postquake activities, clearing roadways so that fire apparatus and medical teams can move quickly to where they are most needed, and providing food and shelter to those whose homes have been destroyed or who are stranded. Local disaster councils are aided by the State Office of Emergency Services in preparing plans for dealing with the effects of a major temblor.

A good deal has been done to prepare for earthquakes in California. There is a consensus, however, that much more needs to be done. But the public has been, for the most part, apathetic when it comes to earthquake preparedness, feeling that when one comes the chances they will be affected are probably slight. More immediate issues such as taxes, pollution, crime in the streets, and potholes are far more likely to capture the public's attention.

A crack in this general apathy was evident in the overwhelming approval voters gave Proposition 77 in the June 1988 election. Titled the California Earthquake Safety and Housing Bond Act of 1988, it authorized the sale of $150 million in bonds to improve the ability of unsafe structures to withstand earthquakes. Specifically targeted were apartment buildings constructed of unreinforced masonry (brick, cement block), which are most likely to be damaged in a quake. That they are most "at risk" was shown by the Whittier earthquake in 1987. Of the 700 structures damaged, 80 percent were of unreinforced masonry. The money from sale of the bonds aids local governments in identifying these hazardous structures as mandated by a state law passed in 1987. The program is administered by the State Department of Housing and Community Development, which makes loans to apartment house owners whose buildings have been found unsafe.

The funds came too late to help prevent massive destruction. In October 1989, just as the third game of the World Series between the San Francisco Giants and the

Oakland A's at Candlestick Park was about to begin, a major earthquake struck the Bay Area. The Loma Prieta quake measured 7.1 on the Richter scale and wreaked heavy damage, especially in San Francisco, Oakland, and down the peninsula. There were 89 lives lost and $7 billion in property damage. The state passed a quarter-of-a-cent increase in the sales tax to assist local rebuilding efforts, though the amount raised—about $70 million—fell far short of the losses suffered. Much of the damage was to unreinforced masonry buildings, as had been expected. As many as 2,000 such buildings remained in San Francisco in 1994, but the city's voters passed a $150 million bond issue in 1992 to fund retrofitting them.

The collapse of the Cypress Freeway in that quake led the state to undertake a major retrofitting of all freeway overpasses throughout the state. The $1.5 billion effort apparently paid off in the devastating Northridge earthquake in January 1994 when all 114 of those retrofitted overpasses survived.

The massive damage that nonetheless resulted from the Northridge earthquake was, in a sense, worse than the Loma Prieta quake. Though fewer lives were lost, 61, the economic costs were far greater. The severe damage done to the freeway system that dominates the lives and economy of the Los Angeles area cost millions in lost time for commuters and truckers forced onto surface streets. Among the six freeways put out of commission were the Santa Monica (the world's busiest and scheduled for retrofitting only weeks later) and the I-5, the state's major north-south artery. Overall, the losses to homes, businesses, schools, and other public facilities were estimated to be as high as $40 billion, making this the greatest natural disaster in the history of the United States until Hurricane Katrina struck the South in 2005. The one beneficiary of the Northridge temblor: the construction industry.

The long-term impact was limited by the speedy response of government at all levels. Federal aid together with state action saw all freeways restored to full operation less than a year after the quake hit. The Santa Monica, which was one of the most badly hurt, was open again within three months.

Reverberations from the enormously powerful earthquake that caused the tsunami that killed thousands in Asia in 2004 were felt in California as well. A report by the state's Seismic Safety Commission in 2005 warned that a large temblor off the state's shores would threaten at least a million coastal residents living in low lying communities such as Santa Barbara and Crescent City and could inundate the largest port at Los Angeles and Long Beach. A two-month shutdown would, it said, cost an estimated $60 billion.

## REVIEW QUESTIONS

1. What are the primary causes for California's problems and how are these problems manifested? (pp. 201–202)
2. Identify the causes for the energy crisis of 2001. What actions helped to ease it? (pp. 202–205)
3. The state's water allocation problems have been compounded by several court decisions limiting some traditional sources. Explain. How is this issue related to water marketing? (pp. 208–209)

4. What are the primary sources of air pollution? What effects does this pollution have and what policies have been adopted to reduce smog? (pp. 209–212)

5. What are some of the solutions that have been introduced to relieve congestion on the state's roads and highways? (pp. 214–218)

6. What are the steps that have been taken to prepare for a major earthquake? To deal with the aftereffects of one? (pp. 220–221)

## SELECTED WEB SITES

There are three sites of interest when looking at earthquakes. One, the Office of Emergency Services, may be found at www.oes.ca.gov. It provides information on earthquake preparedness, proper ways of disposing of toxic wastes, and measures that may be taken to prepare for flooding. A second, the Seismic Safety Commission, is devoted to preparation for earthquakes and the ways damage may be limited. It is located at www.seismic.ca.gov. Last is the web site dealing with the drilling near Parkfield, www.icdponline.de/html/sites/sanandreas/index/index/html.

Some other sites of interest:

California's Air Resources Board, www.arb.ca.gov, details plans to deal with air pollution, provides information to consumers on ways to improve air quality, and lists laws and regulations to achieve that end.

The Department of Water Resources, www.water.ca.gov, provides information on the state water project, current river flows, and reservoir storage.

The Department of Transportation (Caltrans) provides information of road conditions, and construction as well as answers to frequently asked questions such as the proper use of call boxes, the extent of freeway congestion, and how to obtain department publications.

The Department of Motor Vehicles (DMV) provides updates on new laws governing the operation of motor vehicles in the state as well as consumer information such as what to do if you find you have purchased a "lemon" (the lemon law). This may be found at www.dmv.ca.gov. Legislative committees dealing with subjects treated in this chapter include the senate committee on agriculture and water resources (note that all senate committees have similar web sites that begin with www.senate.ca.gov/ftp/senate/committee/standing). For the agriculture committee the last part of their address is ag_water/home/profile.htm. The transportation committee's site ends transportation/home1/profile.htm. On the assembly side, sites are also standardized, beginning in all cases www.assembly.ca.gov/newcomframesetasp?committee= and ending in a number. The agriculture committee's number is 53, water parks and wildlife is 26, and transportation 24.

## SELECTED REFERENCES

Anon., Department of Water Resources, "California Water Plan Update," Sacramento, 2005.

Assembly Office of Research, California 2000, *Paradise in Peril*, Sacramento: State Printing Office, 1987.

Barber, Elisa, "Time to Work: Commuting Times and Modes of Transportation," Public Policy Institute of California. 2006.

Bathen, Sigrid, "Gridlock and Beyond," *California Journal*, November 1998.

Bowman, Chris, "State Losing Farmlands to Salts, Urbanization," *Fresno Bee*, December 29, 1987.

Bowman, Chris, Russell Clemmings, and Alvie Lindsay, "Air Carries Toxic Chemicals Far from Farms," *Fresno Bee*, November 15, 1993.

Brinkerhoff, Noel, "Water Marketing: Let's Make a Deal," *California Journal*, August 1999.

————, "Whose Minding the Aquifer?" *California Journal*, July 2001.

California Seismic Safety Commission, "California at Risk," Sacramento 1988.

*California Tomorrow*, a journal dealing primarily with environmental issues, quarterly, Sacramento.

Carson, Dan, "Water Wars," *California Journal*, April 1993.

Cone, Marla, "State's Air Quality Among Nation's Most Toxic," *Los Angeles Times*, March 22, 2006.

Davis, Phillip, "Omnibus Western Water Law," *Congressional Quarterly Weekly Review*, November 21, 1992.

Flanigan, James, "Decision Forces New Water Era on California," *Los Angeles Times*, June 7, 2000.

Herzog, Steven J., "California Water: The New Gold," *Appraisal Journal*, April 1996.

Kahrl, William, "Court to L.A.: Go Fish on Water Rights," *Los Angeles Times*, July 3, 1988.

King, John, "The Great Earthquake of 1906–2006," San Francisco, April 16, 2006.

McKim, Jennifer B., "For Whom the Road Tolls," *California Journal*, June 2001.

Nemec, Richard, "Electricity in California," *California Journal*, January 2001.

Olszewski, Lori, "Thirsty Cities Covet Water Used by Farms," *San Francisco Chronicle*, April 17, 1991.

Reisner, Marc, *Cadillac Desert: The American West and Its Disappearing Water*, New York, Viking Press, 1986.

Sotero, Ray, "Not Your Average Pothole," *California Journal*, September 1996.

Stanton, Sam, "Power Crunch: How Californians Got Burned," *Sacramento Bee*, May 6, 2001.

Teitz, Michael B., "California Growth: Hard Questions, Few Answers," in John J. Kirlin and Jeffrey I. Chapman, eds., *California Policy Choices*, Vol. 6, Los Angeles: University of Southern California School of Public Administration, 1990.

Vogel, Nancy, "Tapped Out in California," in Thomas R. Hoeber and Charles M. Price, eds., *California Government and Politics Annual, 1991–92*, Sacramento: California Journal Press, 1991.

Wyner, Alan J., and Dean E. Mann, *Preparing for California's Earthquakes*, Berkeley: Institute for Governmental Studies, 1986.

Chapter

# 12

# Major Political and Social Issues

Politics has been described as the art of compromise, a process of give and take. The greater the diversity of the population, the greater the number of competing interests involved in this process. That is particularly true of California where the population is not just growing but growing ever more heterogeneous. Evidence of this increasing diversity can be seen in large areas of most California cities where signs are almost exclusively in a foreign language and shops and restaurants cater to the needs and wants of the foreign born.

If those newly in the country face problems of adjustment and assimilation for which they seek help from government, others, also considered "different" because of the color of their skin or their accent or their sexual preference, increasingly have been turning to the political process in an effort to eliminate discrimination against them. Foremost among their goals is equality. If members of these groups have an interest in reducing pollution or preserving the coastline or ensuring adequate water supplies, and they do, they have an even more immediate interest in pressing for reform in those social and political arenas where they have felt the effects of bias. Their efforts in many cases have not been welcomed. Affirmative action in hiring has been resisted as "reverse discrimination." Or special admissions to colleges and universities to provide greater educational opportunity for minorities have been decried as a lowering of standards. Demands for gay rights have been opposed by those for whom that lifestyle is repugnant.

If the battle continues for blacks and Hispanics and gays, it is for the most part just beginning for others who have seen progress pass them by. They either have chosen not to join in it or do not possess the skills to do so. Many are now turning to "the system," attempting to bring pressure on government for help. Lobbies for the underprivileged, the poor, the unemployed, and the homeless have emerged.

Then there are those who have rejected the system and the society it regulates. They have gone outside the law (are literally outlaws) and have declared war on society. Norms of behavior are ridiculed, and violence escalates as profits roll in. Questions of how to deal with criminals and the root causes of their actions are major concerns of public policy.

## THE SITUATION OF RACIAL MINORITIES

On the basis of demographics alone, California is a multiracial society. In 2004, the California Secretary of State's office estimated 46 percent of the population of the state or 12.4 million was non-Hispanic white, 34 percent was Hispanic, 12 percent Asian-Pacific Islander, and 7 percent African American. The non-Hispanic white population ceased to be in the majority in 2000. The rapidly growing Hispanics were projected to be 41 percent by 2025. Non-Hispanic whites, on the other hand, were seen as declining to just 37 percent. These figures were not as dramatic as those forecast by the Federal Bureau of the Census, which had Hispanics and non-Hispanic whites at 47 percent and 30 percent respectively in 2025. The Asian-Pacific Islander population has also been growing rapidly, more rapidly in percentage terms than any other. They, according to Department of Finance estimates, will increase to 15 percent of the population by 2025. Holding relatively steady? Blacks with 7 percent and Native Americans with 1 percent. Los Angeles has long been a city of minorities. Hispanics in 2004 numbered 4.6 million with non-Hispanic whites standing at under 40 percent and Imperial County has for many years boasted a *Hispanic* majority of some 70 percent.

### The Evolution of Black Power

The period from the late 1950s to the late 1970s witnessed an evolution in the political role of California's black population: From a minority that felt itself essentially a victim of injustice, it has grown into a highly activated community at the center of the state's political life. This change has been reflected not only in the methods by which the 2.5 million blacks have pressed their demands on the majority of the population, but also in the responsiveness of California's institutions to these demands.

In 1965 Californians were shocked by the violence of the Watts riots. The focus of black concerns shifted from basic civil rights, school integration, and housing to economic deprivation. The tree-lined streets in Watts with their pleasant, pastel-colored homes and neatly trimmed yards hid the fact that many living there were out of work and living on welfare, that the prices charged in local stores were exorbitant, that there were no motion picture theaters, and mass transit hardly existed.

The shock from the riots was made all the more forceful because Californians had believed their state had one of the best civil rights records in the country, both in the degree of integration and in the upward mobility being achieved; there were more black doctors and lawyers per capita than in other states and more blacks owned their own homes. With their new awareness a number of studies were undertaken. New job-creating and skill-expanding programs by both government and private industry were urged. The hiring of more black teachers in the schools, having labor unions integrate their memberships, and improvement in police-minority community relations were all part of the proposed changes. But the massive programs to build needed housing, schools, hospitals, neighborhood centers, and transportation facilities, which had been recommended by black leaders, did not get sufficient backing.

The problems of south central Los Angeles festered for two decades, to explode in the Rodney King riots in 1992. These riots were set off by the verdict in a case involving a videotaped episode in which it appeared police officers had used unnecessary force in beating a black man who had been speeding and refused to stop.

Former Mayor of San Francisco, Willie L. Brown. (Photo Courtesy Speaker Brown's Office)

When a jury in Simi Valley (the case had been moved due to pretrial publicity in Los Angeles) acquitted the four police officers involved on all counts, much of Los Angeles—and especially south central Los Angeles—exploded. Smoldering anger concerning allegations of a pattern of police brutality against minorities and suspicion that justice in the courts had a double standard, one for minorities and one for whites was, in many minds, confirmed. (Some whites felt much the same when two black men who had been videotaped beating a white truck driver to near death were later acquitted of all but the most minimal of the charges brought against them.) The old Watts era concerns over price gouging were renewed as many Korean shopkeepers became targets (rightly or not) of black anger. Hundreds of businesses were burned to the ground; looters ran wild, many less interested in the King verdict, it was claimed, than in getting loads of free goods. Clearly racial animosity was not directed solely toward non-Hispanic whites.

The 1970s, in the aftermath of the Watts riots, saw blacks make a renewed effort to use the electoral process to obtain power and status and to bring pressure on government programs. The first major breakthrough was the election of Wilson Riles as superintendent of public instruction in 1970. Riles was reelected in 1974 and again in 1978. The election of Mervin Dymally as lieutenant governor in 1974 made California the only state with two black statewide elected officials.

Blacks made other significant gains in later years, in Congress and the state legislature. Yvonne Brathwaite Burke was the first black woman elected, first to the state assembly in 1966 and later to Congress in 1972. Diane Watson in 1978 became the first black woman to sit in the state senate. Without doubt, however, the most visible and most powerful black politician to date has been Willie Brown, who was first elected to the assembly in 1964 and chosen speaker of the assembly in 1980, a post he held longer than any other person. Forced to seek other office by term limits, he was elected mayor of San Francisco in 1996.

Blacks also began to have considerable success in running for local office. Most impressive was the election of Tom Bradley as mayor of Los Angeles in 1973 (a spectacular comeback after being defeated in his 1969 bid). Three blacks were also elected to the Los Angeles City Council. In the northern Bay Area, Berkeley, Oakland, Richmond, and Albany each elected a black mayor, and Berkeley elected a city council with a black majority.

Meanwhile, mainly as a result of appointments by Governor Jerry Brown, the number of black judges on the state bench expanded to more than 45. Of particular note was Brown's appointment of Wiley Manuel as the first black supreme court justice in 1977, but he died of cancer only four years later. Brown later named Allen Broussard, another black, to the high court in 1981. The first black woman justice, Janice Rogers Brown, was appointed by Governor Wilson in 1996. These actions had considerable symbolic significance because they gave integrity to the system of law and order that touched the daily lives of blacks. However, for some, the Rodney King riots demonstrated there is much ground yet to cover before full credibility will be accorded the court system.

Black political power was struck a significant blow with term limits forcing many senior black officials from office. The most obvious example: Willie Brown being forced to vacate what many regarded as the second most powerful position in state government, the Assembly speakership. Oakland, once described as the capital of black California, elected a white mayor, Jerry Brown, and in 2000 was represented by whites in both the state senate and the assembly. On top of term limits is the unmistakable fact that the increasing clout of Hispanics has come, at least at times, at the expense of black politicos.

## Hispanic Political Power

"It's our turn. It's been 150 years." The rallying cry was that of Mexican-American Abe Tapia, candidate for the Democratic nomination for lieutenant governor in the June 1978 primary against the black incumbent Mervyn Dymally. Tapia lost, but the challenge of this respected political organizer who had loyally stumped the state in previous elections on behalf of the Kennedys, Hubert Humphrey, Jimmy Carter, and Jerry Brown symbolized the rising determination of Hispanic leaders in California and throughout the southwestern United States to take political advantage of the fact that they, not the blacks, are the largest racial minority and that on most indexes of socioeconomic deprivation their situation is worse in California.

Although there are more than four times as many Hispanics as blacks living in California, blacks historically outnumbered Hispanics in the state legislature and on California's congressional delegation. However, with the redistricting of legislative seats following the 1990 census, the number of Hispanics elected to office exploded. Following the 2000 census, for example, there were 27 Hispanics serving in the state legislature. Another mark of the growth of Hispanic influence was the election of Cruz Bustamante of Fresno as speaker of the assembly. He was followed by Antonio Villagarosa of Los Angeles, another Hispanic who later ran successfully for mayor of Los Angeles.

A major center of political influence for many years was the United Farm Workers (UFW) union and its charismatic leader, the late Cesar Chavez. He was highly successful in his early efforts to organize farm workers and was supported by Governor Jerry Brown in his push for better working conditions for farm laborers. Other organizations have worked toward improving the lot of Hispanics in recent years. The Mexican-American Legal Defense and Education Fund (MALDEF), though headquartered in Texas, has been active in the state as has the League of United Latin American Citizens (LULAC). The Mexican-American Political Association (MAPA) has perhaps been most active in working to promote the participation of Hispanics in politics.

The history of Hispanics in California politics has been, at times, frustrating for those who believe such participation is the key to their future progress there. Despite major efforts to increase Hispanic voting, for example, typically Hispanic turnout is roughly half that of non-Hispanics and blacks. That has been due in part to two factors: age and citizenship. Hispanics, with 34 percent of the population, cast just 10 percent of the votes in 2002. That figure actually constituted a decline from 1998 when Hispanics cast 14 percent of the vote, but rose again in 2004 when Hispanics cast 18 percent of votes.

In the late 1960s a Chicano militancy, patterning itself on the militancy of black-power activists, flared up in California under the leadership of organizations

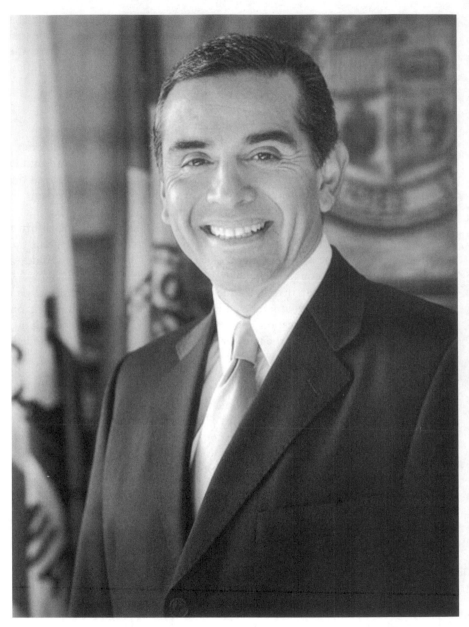

Mayor of Los Angeles, Antonio Villaragosa. (Photo Courtesy Villaragosa's Office)

like La Raza Unida Party and the Brown Berets. Thousands of Mexican-American high school students staged a march in 1968 to protest the inferior educational opportunities provided them in the schools of East Los Angeles. The Mexican-Americans had their own "mini-Watts" in East Los Angeles in 1970, when Ruben Salazar, a *Los Angeles Times* columnist and the news director of KMEX-TV, was killed. Police disruption of a march of 20,000 Mexican-Americans who were protesting the Vietnam War led to the violence, which in turn provoked a virtual police occupation of the area for over a month. Since then Mexican-American militants have found it more difficult to mobilize followers for direct confrontations with official power.

Though Hispanics still lag well behind non-Hispanic whites and blacks in voter participation and the holding of public office, progress is being made. It is somewhat ironic that this is the case inasmuch as Hispanics held high offices early in the state's history. Romualdo Ramirez was elected governor in 1875. Pablo de la Guerra was chosen lieutenant governor in 1861. Andreas Pico was elected to the assembly in 1851. It was not until 1982 that a Hispanic woman was elected to the assembly, Gloria Molina, the same woman who later broke new ground when she was elected to the Los Angeles Board of Supervisors.

A major breakthrough for Hispanics took place in 2005 with the election of former assembly speaker and city council member Antonio Villagarosa as the first Hispanic mayor of Los Angeles since 1872. Elected on a liberal platform that included amnesty for illegal immigrants and allowing them to have driver's licenses, he polled an impressive 48 percent of the black vote compared with the 20 percent he had gained four years earlier.

While Hispanics greatest success has been at the local level in contests for city councils, boards of supervisors, school boards, and the like, in recent elections there has been more success at the state level as well. Accompanying the election of Ron Gonzalez as mayor of San Jose (the largest city in the state headed by a Hispanic and with a population just 14 percent Hispanic), as noted earlier there were 27 Hispanics elected to the legislature, four of them assembly Republicans. The election of Cruz Bustamante as lieutenant governor in 2000 made him the highest Hispanic elected official of the state.

There have been, and to a degree still are, obstacles to overcome if this segment of the population, referred to for many years as California's "sleeping giant," is to become the potent force it could be.

Language remains a continuing obstacle to Hispanic participation in the political process. The 2000 census found that over a quarter of the state's population speak Spanish in the home. A second study, this by the National Council for La Raza in 2000, estimated that 26 percent of Hispanics do not speak English fluently. Despite provision of bilingual ballots and the presence of Spanish language radio and television stations, full participation requires a reasonable proficiency in the use of written and spoken English.

A second reason for the rate of Hispanic participation is simply that many are too young. The long range prospects for Hispanic influence are excellent, however. A study by the University of California, Los Angeles, found that Hispanic women gave birth to nearly half of all children during the 1990s, 47.5 percent. By contrast, non-Hispanic white births constituted just 33.9 percent followed by Asians with 10.7 percent and blacks 5.8 percent. This high birth rate among Hispanics is reflected in the median ages of the various ethnic groups in the state with Hispanics at 25 and non-Hispanic whites at 40.3.

The aforementioned National Council of La Raza study identified a lack of education as the most significant barrier to Hispanic progress. Employment is high but in low paying jobs that typically do not carry with them either health insurance or pensions. Those who have completed college do well, but only one in ten Hispanics has earned a college degree compared with four in ten non-Hispanic whites.

The political implications of this are mixed. Though Hispanics have traditionally favored the Democratic Party, those who have "made it" economically tend to shift toward the Republican Party. The Southwest Voter Registration and Education Project found that 82 percent of Hispanics making under $10,000 a year voted for Walter Mondale in 1984 whereas 70 percent of those earning over $50,000 a year cast their ballots for Ronald Reagan.[1]

Immigration, as we will see shortly, became a major issue with the onset of the recession of the 1990s. While polls showed Californians of all ethnic backgrounds, including Hispanics, opposed illegal immigration, there was concern that cracking down on these (for the most part Mexican) immigrants could raise animosity toward those of Mexican descent, especially among employers who faced heavy fines if they "knowingly" hired illegal aliens. The fear was that, to be on the safe side, employers would simply not employ any Mexican-looking applicant. One factor in the increased Hispanic participation in the electoral process in 1996 was thought to be new federal legislation denying legal immigrants a variety of welfare benefits and the earlier approval by California voters of the anti-illegal immigrant Proposition 187 (see Chapter 3). Several Democratic victories were attributed to Hispanic displeasure over what was perceived to be anti-immigrant policies of the national Republican Party. Best known of these: Loretta Sanchez' victory over Congressman Bob Dornan in an increasingly Hispanic district in Orange County. (Her sister joined her in Congress in 2002, the first sister act in that body's history.)

Another factor in the greater number of Hispanics voting was the action of the Mexican government in passing a law permitting dual citizenship. Many Mexican residents of California had been reluctant to take up United States citizenship for fear of losing Mexican citizenship in the process. That ceased to be a barrier in 1996.

Another emotional issue is bilingualism. Because Spanish is the native tongue of so many Californians, and sometimes the only functional language, an important political and constitutional issue is the extent to which Spanish should be used as a medium of general instruction in public schools. The voters rejected bilingual education when they overwhelmingly approved Proposition 227 in 1998 (see p. X). A fairly large majority of Hispanics (62 percent) voted against the proposition, but polls showed they placed a high priority on having their children learn English. The issue for many was not whether to learn it but how. A related issue is the use of Spanish on official state and local documents (especially election ballots, public signs, and announcements of laws and regulations). Under the federal Voting Rights Act of 1975, California counties with a sizable portion of Hispanics have the option of asking voters whether they want their mailed sample ballot printed in Spanish or of simply mailing all voters both Spanish and English ballots. But the counties *must* provide an *opportunity* to voters to receive the Spanish version. In some counties voting officials have had to contend with a nasty backlash from whites who

---

[1]*Los Angeles Times,* December 26, 1987.

complain that Hispanics who have not learned English are not fit to be American citizens.

The Hispanic community is vitally interested in a wide variety of other public policy issues. Some are specific to their particular interests, but most Hispanics see themselves as part of the larger community as well. They are concerned not just with affirmative action policies, housing discrimination, and other "minority" issues, but with such "general" problems as assuring a quality educational system, improving transportation, and combating crime. As their numbers increase, so will their stake in the resolution of these problems—and their influence in determining how they are to be addressed.

## Other Minorities

Californians of Asian ancestry, numbering approximately 4.2 million, have been systematically denied equality of opportunity at various periods in the state's history: the Chinese in the last decades of the nineteenth century and the Japanese during World War II. A degree of militancy was generated in efforts to gain a measure of recognition and restitution from federal and state authorities for the forced relocation of Japanese-Americans during World War II. Those efforts met with success when, in August 1988, President Reagan signed into law legislation tendering an official apology for the action and awarding $20,000 in reparations to each of the surviving 60,000 former internees. Two of the leading cosponsors of the bill were the only two members of Congress interned during the war, Robert Matsui of Sacramento and Norman Mineta of San Jose. State action followed, which made the payments exempt from taxation.

Asian-Americans have served in a number of prominent positions in the state. March Fong Eu was the first Asian-American to serve in a statewide office (secretary of state). Her son, Matt Fong, became the second Asian-American to hold statewide office when he was elected treasurer in 1994, though he did it as a Republican. Joyce Kinnard in 1989 became the first to be a member of the state supreme court. She was followed onto the court by Ming Chin in 1996. In 1992, Jay C. Kim, mayor of Diamond Bar and a native Korean, was elected to Congress where he joined Robert Matsui of Sacramento and Norm Mineta of San Jose (President George W. Bush later named him Transportation secretary) as three of the four Asian-Americans in the House of Representatives (Patsy Mink of Hawaii who died in 2002 was the other). Kim was later defeated for reelection following conviction for campaign finance irregularities.

The original Californians, the Indians, were for many years considered the most badly treated of the state's minorities. As described in Chapter 1, when the Spaniards ruled California the Indians were suppressed within the mission system; under American rule all Indians were deprived of their lands and were forcibly confined to reservations, where they became wards of the national government. Beginning in the early 1970s, these "forgotten Americans" began to seek ways of pressuring the larger society to rectify the historic inequities foisted on them. The Indians' symbolic occupation of Alcatraz Island, like the confrontation at Wounded Knee, South Dakota, was an early sign of the inevitable growth of militancy among the Indians. Today they have made enormous progress due to the casino gambling revenues generated on their lands. Their political clout, as indirectly indicated by the millions of dollars spent in support of ballot propositions and political candidates, has made a quantum leap upward. (See Chapter 3 on the casino gambling controversy.)

## GAY RIGHTS

The nationwide emergence of a gay-rights movement and the resulting backlash finds California, not untypically, a major storm center. Starting in the early 1970s, homosexuals began to organize for political activity. They recognized that their numbers were sufficient to effect an enlargement of civil rights for themselves if only they would follow the example of the blacks, Hispanics, and women and function as a special-interest constituency, supporting candidates for public office who would act to repeal antihomosexual legislation and generally help gays to overcome their status as pariahs in society. The gays' activist stance, however, has stimulated antigay agitation by elements in the population with more traditional moral views, who believe that equal rights and equal status for gays will weaken the fabric of essential social institutions, such as marriage and the family, and will make it more possible for gays to serve as role models for impressionable children.

Initially operating out of homosexual Democratic clubs in the San Francisco area, by the mid–1970s the gay activists were able to take credit for local ordinances and resolutions that extended fair-employment practices to homosexuals in San Francisco, Berkeley, San Jose, Palo Alto, and other communities.[2] They elected one of their own, Harvey Milk, to the San Francisco Board of Supervisors. Supervisor Milk and George Moscone, the mayor of San Francisco and not a gay, were both shot and killed by an ex-supervisor, Dan White, in 1978. At issue was White's ouster from the Board of Supervisors and his opposition to the political power of gays in San Francisco.

In 1978 the gays received a blessing in disguise: a statewide ballot initiative that attempted to prevent them from teaching in the public schools. The statewide interest and debate over the ballot proposition, like Anita Bryant's campaign in Florida to limit the rights of homosexuals, only allowed the gays to "legitimatize" their cause before the general public and meanwhile intensified their political organizational work in localities more resistant to gays than the San Francisco area.[3]

In 1979 Governor Jerry Brown issued an executive order prohibiting discrimination in public employment based on sexual preference. Since that time California has become among the leaders nationally in adopting policies guaranteeing equal rights for gays.

In 1986 and 1988 the voters defeated initiatives, which both gays and the medical profession opposed, that would have required disclosure of the names of those

---

[2]Nancy Friedman, "Gay Power: From Closet to Voting Booth," *California Journal* VI, 10 (October 1975), pp. 341–344.

[3]Interviews with Harvey Milk, May 25, 1978, and with Jim Foster (a gay activist on the California Democratic Party Executive Committee), May 4, 1978.

with the AIDS virus. (Results of these tests are now confidential.) In his campaign for governor in 1990 Peter Wilson appeared to promise he would sign a gay-rights bill. However, in 1991 he vetoed such a bill barring discrimination against gays in employment and housing and making violations a criminal offense. Gays' violent protests broke out across the state. A more limited bill was signed into law in 1992 that banned discrimination in the workplace only with penalties enforced through civil law. Wilson's signature made little actual difference because a state appellate court ruled in 1991 that discrimination based on sexual orientation was illegal.

Another and growing controversy has been over gay efforts to gain recognition of same sex marriages. Voters rejected the right of members of the same sex to marry in 2000 when they overwhelmingly approved Proposition 22 banning the practice. However, the battle heated up in January 2004 when newly elected mayor, Gavin Newsome, challenged the law, announcing the city would allow same sex couples to apply for marriage licenses. On the first weekend after that announcement 2,000 couples applied. The question became one for the courts: could a city defy/flout state law. The answer came quickly from both federal and state courts: a resounding no!

Following that rejection, pressure mounted on the state legislature to reverse these decisions and the lawmakers responded, becoming the first legislative body in the country to legalize same sex unions as marriages. Governor Schwarzenegger vetoed the bill citing public approval of Proposition 22 and his belief the proper venue for this decision was the courts. This action left in place the state-authorized registry for same sex couples as "domestic partners," which have many if not all of the same rights, including hospital visitation, the right to serve as conservators, and other rights married couples enjoy.

## THE MEDICINAL MARIJUANA CONTROVERSY

In recent years, the AIDS crisis has been foremost in the minds of the gay population. This disease knows no cure and is, without exception, fatal, though advances in medical science have led to longer life spans for many. Those afflicted by it are for the most part, though not exclusively, homosexuals and intravenous drug users. While gays suffering from AIDS were in the forefront of efforts to legalize the use of marijuana for medical purposes, others afflicted with problems associated with the disease rallied to the cause. Cancer patients undergoing chemotherapy maintained their nausea was alleviated and those suffering from glaucoma said pressure on the eyes was lessened when smoking pot.

In 1996 voters approved Proposition 215 legalizing marijuana for medical purposes. This put the state in direct confrontation with the federal government, which held use of this drug for any purpose is illegal. Opponents cite claims that legalization of pot, no matter the objective, increases its use and provides entry to more serious drugs such as cocaine and heroin. The Federal Drug Enforcement Agency (DEA) under both presidents Bill Clinton and George W. Bush has vigorously acted to discourage legalization, citing cases involving drug traffickers who have hidden behind Proposition 215 where there is no evidence of medical need. Law enforcement cites problems of distinguishing between legal and illegal pot.

Those supporting medical uses cite studies they claim show that legalization has decreased usage in states where the drug has been approved for medical use, instead of causing an increase. Advocates say California has seen a drop of as much as 50 percent in some categories. Anecdotal data are said to demonstrate the drug's effectiveness in relieving nausea among those suffering from AIDS as well.

Decisions in court cases have been varied. The Supreme Court in June 2005 held that medical marijuana laws in a dozen states do not protect users or pot suppliers from federal prosecution. However, legislation has been introduced in Congress to remove medicinal marijuana from the prohibited category.

Meanwhile, policy among state officials seems to have sided with the proponents of pot use. In August 2005 the California Highway Patrol (CHP) ordered its officers to stop confiscating medical marijuana during routine traffic stops. A new policy was announced that set a standard that allows patients who use pot with a doctor's authorization to travel the state's highways with up to eight ounces of the drug. And the controversy continues.

## EDUCATION

In many ways the state of California's public schools can be summed up in the often used observation: there's good news and there's bad news. The good news is that student performance has improved in recent years. The bad news is that performance remains well below that in other states and far below what is needed for California to remain an economic and social bell weather for the nation.

On the good side of the slate is the greater number of students achieving proficiency in math at every grade level. This has been accomplished along with more modest gains in English and the language arts. Test results showed increases in the proficiency of fourth graders from 33 percent in 2004 to 47 percent in 2005. Comparable improvements were seen in math but for other grade levels the changes, though positive, were less.

Other good news focused on improvements made by those for whom English is not their primary language (known as English learners or ELs). (More on this later.) In addition, SAT scores are improving and more public schools, 86 percent, are offering advanced placement classes. More students are eligible to attend the University of California, with one national organization ranking the state as one of the top three in improvements over the last ten years in students attending college.

On the negative side, the prestigious RAND Corporation, a nonprofit think tank in Santa Monica, found the state's school system "lags behind most of the nation in almost every objective measure of student achievement, funding, teacher qualifications and school facilities." Among the negatives cited were performances on national tests where California's student ranked just ahead of Louisiana's and Mississippi's and thus forty-eighth in the country. Also cited was the high student/faculty ratio (this despite lowering of the ratio in kindergarten through third grade) and the percentage of school districts requiring their teachers be credentialed in the subjects they teach, just 46 percent as opposed to an average of 82 percent nationally. Compounding the problem is a looming shortage of teachers. It is esti-

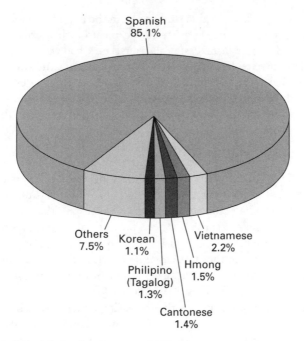

Spanish
85.1%

Others
7.5%

Korean
1.1%

Philipino
(Tagalog)
1.3%

Vietnamese
2.2%

Hmong
1.5%

Cantonese
1.4%

**Figure 12.1**  California's English Learners, 2003–04.

mated that, with resignations, retirements, and higher enrollments, the state will need an additional 200,000 teachers by 2010.

Still another problem is the state's dropout rate. Just how much of a concern is an issue? State figures show 87 percent of students in high school graduate. A Harvard University study released in 2005 found only 71 percent did. Regardless, most agree the problem lies with students from poor families, in overcrowded classrooms, and in underperforming schools with less well-prepared teachers. These tend to be concentrated in areas with large minority populations. The Harvard study found graduation rates substantially lower among minority students with just 56.5 percent of blacks and 60.3 percent of Hispanics completing high school.

One "answer" to the problem of dropouts has been a practice known as social promotion—promoting students regardless of the performance in class. Public and legislative distress over this practice led to pressure to discourage it, though in some cases space limitations almost mandated it. To insure graduates are qualified to receive diplomas, the state has mandated all students pass a so-called "exit exam" by the end of their senior year. That requirement was postponed from 2004 to 2006 when it became apparent tens of thousands of seniors would not pass the test and would not graduate. Issues arose, even then as thousands faced graduation without passing the test. What about special education students (those with special needs such as the hearing or sight impaired or those suffering from dyslexia)? Others urged those whose native tongue was other than English be given a break. The reaction was more favorable for the special ed students with line holding firm on the English requirement. Legislation adopted in January 2006 exempted between

25,000 and 30,000 special education students from the requirement for that year. For those not passing the exit exam, some districts came up with alternatives intended to replace diplomas. In some instances, if all coursework had been completed, certificates of completion were planned. In some cases that meant the students with these certificates could participate in graduation ceremonies, in other cases, they could not. In many cases there was no recognition at all. An Alameda superior court judge ruled just days before the commencement ceremonies were to begin, that since some schools provide fewer opportunities for learning, no student should be denied a diploma if all other graduation requirements had been met. It was simply a fact, the judge wrote, that ". . . scarcity of resources continues to fall disproportionately on English learners, particularly with respect to the shortage of teachers who are qualified to teach these students." Critics of this decision said it was unfair to the thousands of students who had studied hard to pass this exam, that special classes and individual tutoring at state expense had been provided along with multiple opportunities to pass over three years. If Round 1 went to the exam's opponent, Round 2 was won by its supporters when the state supreme court, in a split decision, restored it. Round 3? Finally, they noted the level of achievement to be demonstrated was at the 10th grade level for English and the 9th grade level for math.

Compounding the problems was the increasing diversity of school populations. For example in 1981–1982, the ethnic breakdown was 56 percent non-Hispanic whites, 26 percent Hispanic, 10 percent African-American, and 5 percent Asian. In 2002–2003 the comparable figures were 33.7 percent non-Hispanic white, 45.2 percent Hispanic, 8.3 percent African-American, and 8.3 percent Asian.

Despite the relatively dismal picture (low scores on standardized tests, high dropout rates, large classes, too few computers, etc.) matters had, in some respects, improved. California remained in 2005 nearly at the bottom of states in terms of students per teacher and close to or at the bottom when it came to students per computer and per librarian. But it has risen close to the national average in per student expenditure and is ranked first in the nation in teacher salaries averaging

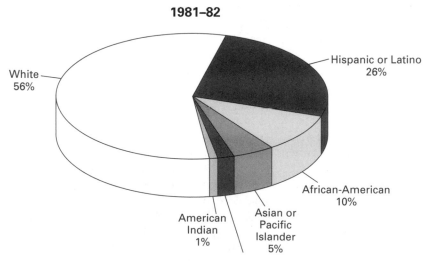

**1981–82**

White
56%

Hispanic or Latino
26%

African-American
10%

American
Indian
1%

Asian or
Pacific
Islander
5%

**Figure 12.2**    California's Changing Ethnic Makeup, 1981–82.

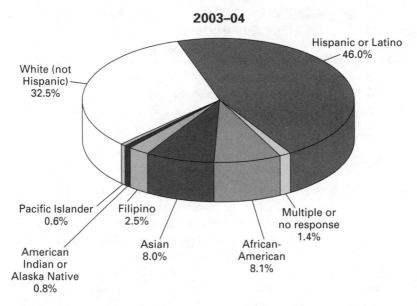

**2003–04**

Hispanic or Latino
46.0%

White (not
Hispanic)
32.5%

Pacific Islander
0.6%

Filipino
2.5%

Multiple or
no response
1.4%

American
Indian or
Alaska Native
0.8%

Asian
8.0%

African-
American
8.1%

**Figure 12.3**    California's Changing Ethnic Makeup, 2003-04.

$57,786 according to the National Education Association (though sixteenth in purchasing power given the high cost of living). The governor's budget for 2006–2007 proposed spending $11,000 per student, a record for the state.

This was at the heart of the debate over Proposition 227 that voters approved in 1998. It targeted the 1.4 million students who were not proficient in English, many enrolled in bilingual programs where non-English instruction took up as much as 90 percent of the time. Critics pointed out that only 5 percent of students in bilingual programs were mainstreamed (moved into regular instructional programs) each year. Those opposing Proposition 227 said its "one size fits all" approach was too rigid and the one-year time limit to learn the language too short. Though parents had the right to request their children remain in bilingual programs, most did not. Some 90 percent of English learners in the Los Angeles Unified School District entered immersion programs in the first year, for example. Results of the change have been, for the most part, positive. Only about 20 percent of students who remained in bilingual classes where they learn academic subjects in their native languages and English on the side rated "advanced" or "early advanced" in 2005, unchanged from a year earlier. This is less than half the rate of the general student population, including those in so-called emersion programs.

One approach that has proved popular as a way to improve education is the charter school. A charter school is one the state allows to break away from its district (with the district's approval), formulate its own goals, and manage its own affairs, apart from the multitude of state regulations. Volumes containing thousands of regulations weigh close to 40 pounds and deal with matters from the fundamental to the trivial such as the kind of paint to be used in school bathrooms. The explosion in these schools' numbers shows their popularity. By 2006 there were 572 charter schools enrolling 212,000 students. Curricula vary enormously. A school in Oakland emphasizes bilingual education; a Los Angeles area school focuses on personal health and family relationships along with academic subjects. Not all was what had been hoped for, however. Some 50 charter schools failed for a variety of reasons. In one case a school had run up $1.3 million in debt. Another hired convicted felons as teachers. Still another was found to have used school funds to lease a sports car for its principal. Such cases led to several bills in the legislature to assure accountability, but despite the problems the concept remains very popular with the public and politicians alike.

## HIGHER EDUCATION

As the population of the state renewed its rapid growth entering the twenty-first century, the pressure on the state's institutions of higher education grew as well. Estimates from California's Postsecondary Education Commission in 1999 were that the number of students would grow from just under 2 million in 1998 to over 2.7 million in 2010. Causes? There are more people and more demand for college-level skills in the economy. Yet space may simply not be available. The estimate is that meeting this increased demand would require the state spending $1.5 billion a year for the next ten years; it is spending half that amount.

A major controversy arose in 1995 in the successful push by Governor Wilson, Regent Ward Connerly (an African-American), and others to abolish affirmative action programs at the University of California. Those favoring this move argued that the only criterion for admission or hiring should be qualifications and not race or gender. Those opposed held that elimination of such programs would severely limit minority enrollments, reduce educational diversity, and result in major reductions in the number of blacks and Hispanics enrolled. They pointed out that 95 percent of UC students have grade point averages and test scores that place them in the top 12.5 percent of high school graduates, qualifying them for admission under the Master Plan. Those seeking abolition of affirmative action admissions simply replied it was unfair for a nonminority to be barred from admission in favor of a less-qualified minority. The courts have generally upheld elimination of race-based qualifications and, though many academics favor some form of affirmative action, they have not found recent court actions supporting them.

That Master Plan was adopted in 1961 and is supposed to govern all three public systems of higher education. The Master Plan sets down different functions for the University of California, the California State University system, and the community colleges. UC was designated the primary research institution, the CSU system has teaching as its primary role, while the community colleges are to provide vocational instruction, an opportunity for those who do not qualify for entry into the other two systems to prove they can do college work, and the chance to transfer upon completion of two years of study. UC takes the top 12.5 percent of high school graduates, the CSU system the top third, and community colleges accept anyone over the age of 18.

A new concern arose at the end of the nineties: the increasing need of four-year institutions to provide remedial instruction, especially in English and mathematics. In 1998, 54 percent of students entering the state university system as freshmen failed to meet minimal competency requirements in math and 47 percent were unable to meet such standards in English. For years the University of California pro-

(Ramirez, *Los Angeles Times*)

vided sections of so-called "bonehead English," this for the top 12.5 percent of high school graduates. The CSU Board of Trustees adopted a policy that will, if fully implemented, reduce remediation for all but 10 percent of entering freshmen by 2007. However, by 2005 nearly half of entering freshmen still failed math and English entry examinations, placing that policy in jeopardy.

Among other changes that have taken place recently was the construction of a new UC campus in Merced, which opened in 2004, a location some found questionable because it is far removed from the major population centers of the Central Valley it is to serve. No less controversial was the move by the University of California to drop use of the Scholastic Aptitude Test (SAT) as a criterion for admission. In a move to meet criticisms of the test, the College Board developed a written segment for use in 2005 as a better means of measuring student ability. In the CSU system, on the other hand, a new campus, the Channel Islands campus, was opened with much celebration and little controversy in 2002.[4]

Education at all levels is extremely important for everyone and a good educational system is vital to a growing and vital economy. Particularly in need are those at the lower end of the economic ladder, people on welfare, immigrants, and the homeless.

An area that has been hotly debated has concerned education for those who have recently entered the country.

---

[4]It should be noted that the new campus, despite its name, is not located on an island but on the mainland in Ventura County. No row boat or canoe is needed to attend class.

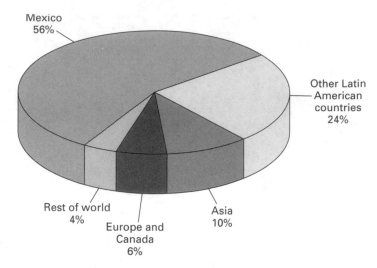

**Figure 12.4**   Most Illegal Immigrants Are from Latin America (Courtesy Public Policy Institute of California).

## IMMIGRATION

They are Laotian and Hmong, Filipino and Salvadoran, Korean, Guatemalan, and Japanese, Nicaraguan and Mexican. Theirs are the fear-filled faces of peoples fleeing war in their homelands and the hopeful countenances of those seeking freedom and economic opportunity in another land. They are contributing in a major way to California's recently booming population growth. They are the new immigrants.

There are of course two types of immigrants, legal and illegal. There are also two ways of looking at them: (1) as peoples who can and do contribute to the economic growth and cultural vitality of the nation or (2) as likely to add to the burdens of Americans, who have to compete with them for jobs (and allegedly experience lower pay scales in the process), and as recipients of welfare benefits provided out of their tax dollars.

Just how many immigrants have settled in California in recent years is difficult to determine. However, in 2006 it was estimated that of the eleven to twelve million illegal aliens in the country, 2.4 million lived in California, or 6.3 percent of the state's population. Most have settled in Southern California. Immigrants, legal and illegal, together make up well over 22 percent of the state's population. An estimated 200,000 legal immigrants arrive annually; another 100,000 are believed to come illegally. The continued growth in the number of illegal immigrants entering the state would seem to indicate that voter approval of Proposition 187, the anti-illegal immigrant proposition, in 1994 has had little if any effect on the flow of such immigrants into the state. One study, by the Kaiser Family Foundation, concluded that jobs, not benefits, motivated most to come, even in the face of increased surveillance at the border and increased danger in crossing. Enhanced security at San Diego, titled Operation Gatekeeper, resulted in many who tried to enter illegally using border crossings that were much more dangerous. While deaths were reduced in San Diego County, they went up in Imperial County.

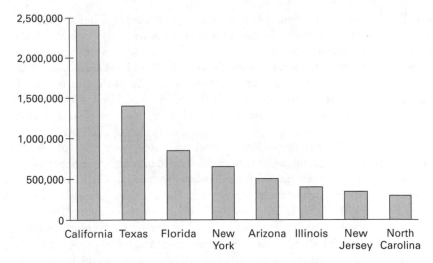

**Figure 12.5**    California Illegal Immigrants (Courtesy Public Policy Institute of California).

Why do they come? There are both what are called "push" factors and "pull" factors. "Push" refers to living conditions that are so bad people are "pushed" into leaving their home countries. Immigrants from Mexico are pushed by high unemployment, whereas those from Southeast Asia and Central America have fled homelands torn by war. "Pull" factors generally refer to opportunities to better oneself economically, though the freedoms associated with the American way of life are significant for some.

The subject of illegal immigrants became a "hot button" topic with the onset of the recession and became even hotter in 1993 with the sudden influx of Chinese being smuggled into the country by ship. The issue of immigration is complex and involves a number of tradeoffs. Migrants of all types add greatly to the cultural richness of the country. They also in many cases take low-paying jobs that native-born Americans do not want. Some 92 percent of farm workers in California are foreign born, with one estimate that nearly 90 percent of them are in the country illegally. Without them the state's $5 billion in perishable crops would be threatened. Seventy-five percent of the employees in Los Angeles's furniture manufacturing and textile industries are immigrants, many illegal. The hard-working and legal immigrants who have been here more than ten years are slightly less likely to be on welfare than those born here. Hispanic and Asian immigrants have fewer drug-influenced babies, are less likely to have heart attacks or strokes, have fewer out-of-wedlock babies, are much more likely to have two-parent families, and live longer than native borns. Because they will work for lower wages, the costs of much that we consume are lower and thus benefit the rest of the population. So what, then, is the problem (aside from the fact that many illegals are unscrupulously exploited by employers who know they cannot complain)?

The costs of illegal aliens became a major issue in 1993 when the federal government was asked to pick up the tab for the cost of educating and providing health care for those illegally in the state. Because immigration is a federal responsibility, that request seemed reasonable to many. It was, however, ignored. What are these costs? Estimates vary and figures change quickly, but there is some agreement that health care costs run close to $1 billion a year. Educating the children of illegal immigrants enrolled in public schools, estimated to number nearly 500,000, runs another $2 to $3 billion. Then there are the over 20,000 illegal aliens being held in state prisons at a cost of over close to $1 billion a year. That the public is concerned, long after Proposition 187 was approved, is shown in a Field Poll taken in September 2005 where 81 percent of those interviewed were "concerned" and 49 percent were "alarmed."

A bill passed by the house Representatives roused both sides of the illegal debate. It declared illegal immigrants to be felons and urged they be deported. Such people were seen by proponents of this bill as law breakers who had, in effect, cut in line ahead of the many who patiently go through the laborious processes involved in gaining entry legally. Early in 2006 a series of demonstrations took place opposing this bill. More than 500,000 turned out in Los Angeles with large numbers reported from San Diego and Fresno. A different approach to the issue, proposed by President Bush and endorsed by a bipartisan group of Senators, sought to create a so-called "guest worker" program that could, over time, lead to citizenship if they had lived in the country for five years, paid their taxes, paid a fine and learned English. This proposal seemed to find favor with Californians. A Field Poll in April 2006 found that 76 percent supported this idea with only 21 percent opposed. A nationwide boycott backing the expanded rights of illegal immigrants took place May 1, 2006. Illegal immigrants, their supporters and children took to the streets pledging not to work, go to school or make any purchases that day to illustrate their contributions to the economy.

Two controversial measures dealing with illegal immigrants surfaced in the early 2000s. One involved those of college age. The assertion made was that these young men and women, in the country illegally because of the actions of their parents, were being penalized by having to come up with out-of-state tuition payments, thus effectively denying them a college education. Opponents pointed out if those illegally in the country were given in-state status they would be given preference over students from Nevada or Utah, for example. Governor Davis signed a bill that allowed those illegally in the country to qualify for in-state tuition provided they had lived in the state for three years and had graduated from a state high school. A Field Poll in 2006 found Californians approved of this policy, though narrowly, with 51 percent in support.

The other issue was in a sense more complicated. It involved whether undocumented workers should be allowed to obtain driver's licenses. An alliance of insurance companies, immigrant rights groups, and others supported this move on the grounds that obtaining a license would assure these drivers were qualified to be on the state's roads, a safety issue. Those in opposition noted that drivers' licenses had been used by the men who flew airplanes into the World Trade Center and Pentagon to legitimize their status in the country. For them the issue was crime control. The last argument was cited by Governor Davis in his veto message in September 2002. Governor Schwarzenegger agreed, vetoing similar legislation in his first year in office. The public seems to agree. The same poll cited above determined that the residents of the state reject allowing illegal immigrants to have driver's licenses by a two to one margin (64–32).

## DEALING WITH CRIME AND THE CRIMINAL

"Two Killed in Drive-by Shooting," "Judge Orders Early Release of Felons Due to Overcrowding," "Epidemic of Crack Use Reported," "Gang-related Violence Escalates." Headlines like these have become almost commonplace. Carjackings are no longer news unless someone dies. Gang turf wars have "graduated" from tire irons and chains to AK-47s and Uzis as members fight over the buying and selling of drugs. Violent crime has often topped the list of things Californians worry about. What to do about it became the big issue of the mid–1990s.

### Three Strikes and You're Out

As with immigration, politicians often seek to outdo one another in their concern for and toughness on crime. The kidnapping and subsequent murder of 12-year-old Polly Klass from her home in Petaluma in 1993 shocked the nation, raising concerns that even the most "secure" spots were not very secure at all anymore. The fact that her admitted killer was a convicted felon recently released from prison after serving eight years of a 16-year sentence for, yes, kidnapping, gave momentum to a number of efforts to come down hard on repeat offenders. One such effort was the "Three Strikes and You're Out" proposal. Patterned after a similar initiative adopted by the voters of the state of Washington and pushed by the father of a Fresno teenager, Kimber Reynolds, who was killed by another repeat offender in 1992, it received

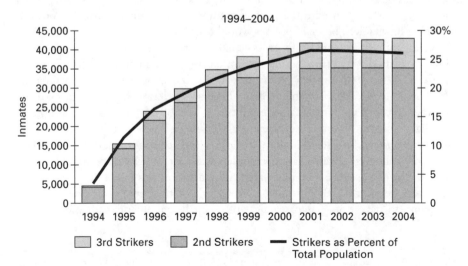

**Figure 12.6** Growth in the Three Strikes Inmate Population in State Prison.

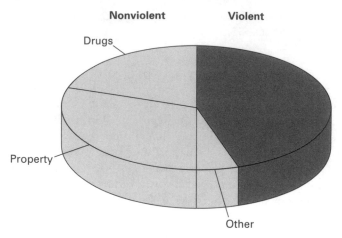

**Figure 12.7**    Prison Population by Type of Offense.

strong public support. The legislature passed three strikes legislation and Governor Wilson signed it into law in March 1994. It doubles the sentence for a second offense and for the third felony the effective term is life without possibility of parole. It, along with other proposals, substantially reduces the amount of time a prisoner can get off his or her sentence for good behavior. Had it been in effect, neither of the men involved in the two murders just cited would have been on the streets. Opponents pointed to the fact the law does not require the third conviction be for a *violent* felony, claiming that writing a bad check could result in a life sentence. Others noted that the overwhelming majority of felony cases were settled out of court by plea bargaining.[5] With a third conviction automatically resulting in life behind bars, few, they said, would opt for a plea bargain to a lesser felony. The results, the critics said, would be to overwhelm the court system, with an incredible backlog of cases becoming inevitable. They said prisons would overflow.

Court rulings changed and/or clarified the original law. One found that a felony conviction for a crime in another state could be counted as a "strike" in California. That made supporters of the law happy, but another set of decisions did not. These allowed considerably greater judicial discretion in application of the law when dealing with what are described as "wobblers" (actions that might be considered misdemeanors or felonies). A 1996 decision held this to be true for cases involving public safety (a felony if it did, a misdemeanor if it did not). A January 1997 ruling expanded that to include cases that could be felonies or misdemeanors but did *not* involve public safety. The decision was based on a case where a man was riding a skateboard on the wrong side of the street and, when arrested, was found to have drug paraphernalia and a small amount of methamphetamine

---

[5]Of the 1,700 violent felony cases in Alameda county in 1993, between 100 and 150 went to trial, the rest were plea bargained. Approximately 90 percent of such cases were plea bargained in San Francisco that same year.

on his person. The court found application of a misdemeanor more appropriate "in the interests of justice." Two cases reaching the Supreme Court in 2002 involved two men who stole, respectively, a set of golf clubs and video tapes. The issue? Does application of three strikes in such cases constitute cruel and unusual punishment? The court in a 5–4 decision decided it was not, saying society has a right to protect itself from career criminals. A move was made in 2006 to require the third strike be for a serious or violent felony, the issue to be placed on the November ballot.

## The Death Penalty

For many years perhaps the central focus of the law-and-order debate in California was the propriety of the death penalty. His avowed opposition to it hurt Pat Brown in his attempt to gain a third term as governor in 1966. His son Jerry, equally opposed, might have suffered the same electoral fate as his father had he faced stronger opposition in 1978. Those favoring capital punishment contend that, as the ultimate sanction, it deters crime. It also, and obviously, insures absolute protection to society from dangerous and violent criminals who might otherwise be paroled. Opponents deny that the death penalty deters crime, citing studies comparing states with and without it, studies that appear to show it has no effect. They point out that because humans make decisions, mistakes occur and they cannot be rectified once this most severe of sentences is carried out. Nor, they say, do most murderers kill again. While Californians remain in favor of the death penalty, there was some erosion in its popularity in 2002 following revelations that a number of men on death row in other states, most notably Illinois, had been found innocent as a result of DNA testing. Indeed, a Field Poll found that 73 percent of Californians favored a moratorium on use of the death penalty.

The question of deterrence is clouded by the infrequency with which the death penalty has been applied. In a move to expedite cases (some have been pending for a dozen years or more), the state supreme court ruled in 1993 that inmates who claim their constitutional rights have been violated are limited to one appeal. A second appeal is only allowed when the petitioner can show a "fundamental miscarriage of justice" has occurred.[6] This has proved less than effective as is shown by the many years (an average of 15) most of those on death row spend there. Among the more notorious, Stanley Tookie Williams, founder of the violent Crips street gang whose execution took place just short of 25 years after his conviction for multiple murders.

## Two Systems of Sentencing

A change made in 1977 in the way convicted criminals are sentenced has helped add to the overcrowding problem. Until that year California operated under a system known as indeterminate sentencing. That means that a judge would impose "the sentence required by law," typically five years to life. With time off for good

---

[6] *In re Clark.*

**TABLE 12.1     Illustrations of Prison Sentencing Under Three Strikes Prior Law Versus Current Law**

| Scenarios | Crimes Committed | | Time to Serve in Prison[a] | |
|---|---|---|---|---|
| | New Offense | Prior Offense[b] | Prior Law | Current Law |
| **No Prior Offense** | | | | |
| Any felony with: | | | | |
| • No prior felony | Burglary of residence | None | 2 years | Same |
| **Second strike Offense** | | | | |
| Any felony with: | | | | |
| • One prior serious/ violent felony | Burglary of residence | One prior burglary of residence | 4.5 years | 10.4 years |
| **Third Strike Offense** | | | | |
| Nonviolent/nonserious felony with: | | | | |
| • Two prior serious/ violent felonies | Receiving stolen property | One prior assault on a peace officer, and one prior burglary of a residence | 2 years | 25 years to life |
| Serious/violent felony with: | | | | |
| • Two prior serious/ violent felonies | Robbery | One prior burglary of a residence, and one prior robbery | 7 Years | 25 years to life |

[a]Assumes the offender (1) receives typical prison sentence for the new offense, (2) receives sentence enhancements for prior offenses, and (3) earns maximum credits from participation in work/education programs.
[b]Assumes prior offense resulted in a prison sentence.

behavior, a person serving such a term could be released in 20 months. If the prisoner proved uncooperative or violent, the time behind bars could be extended indefinitely. The rationale behind this system reflected the rehabilitation school of thought. Good behavior, such as participating in projects beneficial to society and education programs, would be encouraged by rewarding it with shorter time served.

Liberals opposed indeterminate sentencing, saying it was unfair to send someone to prison with no idea of how long the individual would be there. Conservatives disliked it because they felt it could be used as a safety valve by which overcrowded facilities could be relieved of pressure by releasing those who might still be a threat to society.

These objections, together with the public demand that government "get tough" on crime, led to the adoption of determinate sentencing in 1977. This system, which applies to over 90 percent of criminal offenses committed in the state (first degree murder is an exception), ensures that convicted criminals will serve a specific time behind bars. It is grounded in the belief that prisons are not very good at rehabilitation and better suited to punishment and keeping society safe from dangerous felons. In theory, determinate sentencing meets the concerns of both liberals and conservatives. In practice, there have been some problems. Knowing that their terms could not be extended no matter how much trouble they caused has led to a quadrupling of prison violence over a six-year span. Short of conviction for an act committed in prison (which is difficult to obtain given the reluctance of prisoners to inform on their fellows), nothing can be done to extend their stay. Also disquieting are some notorious cases in which those convicted of truly horrible crimes have been turned loose, their sentences having been served, with no assurance they will not commit like crimes again. In one instance a man who picked up a young hitchhiker, raped her, and cut off both her arms below the elbow, leaving her to bleed to death, was released despite a loud public outcry and no indication he felt any remorse. The determinate sentencing law required he be set free after serving eight years and four months in prison. Polly Klass's abduction and murder in 1993 raised again the issue of whether violent—and unrepentant—offenders should be released or made exceptions to the determinate sentencing law.

## The Gun Control Debate

There are few issues that generate as much heat as the subject of gun control. There are passionate defenders on both sides of this issue. And questions of constitutionality are deeply intertwined in the debate. Both those wishing to limit guns and those opposed to them cite the Second Amendment to the United States Constitution to legitimize their positions. The language of the amendment is deceptively simple: "A well regulated militia, being necessary to the security of a free state, the right of a people to keep and bear arms, shall not be infringed."

Proponents of the right to have guns emphasize the last part of the amendment that focuses on the right to bear arms while those favoring limits on guns note that a "well regulated militia" is cited in the amendment as the reason to have guns and no one could possibly describe the millions of Americans with guns as "well regulated." Those opposed to regulation cite what they see as a "slippery slope," saying *any* limit is only the opening wedge for those who would deny the people the right to hold any guns at all. In seeking more restrictions, those on the other side deny that is their intent, but urge specific laws, policies, and/or programs be implemented to make guns safer to use and more difficult for criminals to obtain. To which the National Rifle Association responds, "If guns are banned only criminals will have guns."

In California there have been several events, either in the state or outside of it, that have led to legislation designed to make guns less available. A ban on specifically identified semi-automatic assault weapons was passed in 1989 following a school yard massacre in Stockton. Five children were killed and 29 injured in that shooting spree. More recently, concerns over two types of weapons has emerged. The first are so-called "junk guns" or Saturday Night Specials. These are popular among youth gangs and are considered of poor quality and dangerous to the shooter (as well as the target) because of the potential for structural failure. California is home to companies that manufacture 80 percent of these junk guns that cost as little as $10 to produce and sell on the street for as little as $69.

Those who defend such weapons maintain that the very fact they are inexpensive makes them the weapon of choice for the law-abiding but poor members of society. Banning them would only leave these people more vulnerable to the criminal element than they already are. Despite opposition, the Los Angeles County Board of Supervisors voted to ban the sale of Saturday Night Specials within the county and shortly before the board acted the city council of Los Angeles voted to limit handgun sales within its jurisdiction to one per person per month. This was in response to reports of "straw purchasers" who can legitimately buy guns, buy large numbers of them and sell them to those not legally entitled to have them such as juveniles and convicted criminals.

The laws on semi-automatic weapons do not, across the board, outlaw them, but they do limit ownership to those who already have them. If someone leaves the state or dies, the weapon must also leave the state, be destroyed, or given up to law enforcement officials.

The law on cheap handguns was designed to insure they would not misfire, a form of consumer protection. Two types of tests must be passed, one involving dropping the weapon to show it will not go off in the process and the other which tests by firing the weapon 600 times with a failure rate of more than six misfires or any in the first 20 shots.

None of this impresses those who hold strongly to the right to bear arms. The National Rifle Association believes firmly that the best approach to the problem of abuse of weapons is to crack down on those who misuse them. They maintain the answer lies in strict enforcement of existing laws, which, they say, have been allowed to lie unused. They point to the Columbine case and note the two young men involved broke as many as 19 laws. And they repeat their mantra: guns don't kill people; people kill people.

Pressures of another sort emerged at the beginning of the twenty-first century. In April 2006 the prison population reached a record 169,154. Both space and personnel were stretched tight. More prisons were urged with many holding double the prisoners they were planned for, and as many as 2,000 prison guard positions were vacant. Overcrowding and inadequate staffing promised increased violence. Then there were backlogs at the courts to contend with. It has long been said justice delayed is justice denied and population growth with its attendant increase in crime has also strained the state's court system. Since 1980 the population of California has grown 50 percent while the number of trial court judges has grown just 20 percent. The result: a swamped system that is able to process cases more slowly than it should, according to seasoned observers. The law says that there are time limits for consideration of cases. If not treated, charges must be dropped. A case in point is Riverside County where, for the second year in a row in 2005, all civil trials were postponed for five weeks to deal with criminal cases. Riverside County's population has grown by 20 percent since 2000 with just one new judge added. The Judicial Council found need for 355 more judgeships in the state, but legislative action has not been forthcoming as 2006 dawned.

## REVIEW QUESTIONS

1. Which of the minority groups discussed are making the greatest advances in political power? Why are they more successful than others? (pp. 226–235)
2. What actions by voters stimulated increased activism on the part of Hispanics in the 1990s? (pp. 232–234)
3. The gay agenda saw both defeats and victories in the 1990s and into the 2000s. Explain. (pp. 234–235)
4. What evidence is there that California schools have been providing less than a quality education? How does the debate over quality relate to affirmative action, bilingual education, and social promotion? (pp. 236–239)
5. What has been the effect of "Three Strikes and You're Out" legislation? How has it been modified by the courts? (pp. 245–247)
6. What are the principal arguments presented by the two sides in the gun control debate? (pp. 249–250)
7. Explain the nature of the pressures on the state's court system. What are the consequences if it's not dealt with? (pp. 250–251)

## SELECTED WEB SITES

There are many sites covering the range of issues discussed in this chapter. A few of the more valuable would include those listed below.

Information on the penal system, data on prisoners, and prison overcrowding may be found on the Department of Corrections site at www.cdc.state.ca.us. Several sites are devoted to education including the state Department of Education www.cde.ca.gov, and the home school association www.hsc.org. The Superintendent of Public Instruction also has a site at www.goldmine.cde.gov/executive. Information on higher education is available as well. For the University of California, the site is www.ucop.edu/vcophome/webinfo.html and for the state university system it is www.calstate.edu/tierz/system.html. The California Postsecondary Education Commission's site is www.cpec.ca.gov.

For data on the prison system, go to the Department of Corrections web site at www.doc.ca.gov.

For information on immigration and other social issues, go to the list of state agencies and departments at www.ganymede.org.articles/agencies.html and click on the appropriate site.

# SELECTED REFERENCES ————————

Anderson, Nick, "Study Lays Out Problems State Faces," *Los Angeles Times,* December 30, 1999.

Anon., "Final Report on Proposition 227," Department of Education, Sacramento, 2006.

Anon., "Policy Puzzle: Leveling the Educational Playing Field Proves Tricky," Public Policy Institute of California, San Francisco, 2005.

Arax, Mark, "A Return to the Goal of Reforming Inmates," *Los Angeles Times,* June 1, 1999.

Brinkerhoff, Noel, "Lock 'em up," *California Journal,* February 1999.

*California Journal,* June 1993 issue, has several articles on aspects of education in California.

*California Tomorrow,* "Crossing the Schoolhouse Border," San Francisco, 1988.

Fox, Sylvia, "Testing, Anyone?" *California Journal,* September 2001.

Guthrie, Julian, "School Districts Taking Different Approaches, Getting Different Results," *San Francisco Examiner,* August 1, 1999.

Hamm, Theodore, "The Death Penalty," *California Journal,* August 2002.

Jepsen, Christopher, and Steven Rivkin, "Class Size Reduction, Teacher Quality and Academic Quality in California Public Schools," *Public Policy Institute of California,* San Francisco, 2002.

Johnson, Hans P., "Illegal Immigration," Public Policy Institute of California, San Francisco, 2006

Keysworth, C. L., *California Indians,* New York, Checkmark Books, 1999.

Maharide, Dale, "Did 1992 Herald the Dawn of Latino Political Power?" *California Journal,* January 1993.

————, *The Coming White Minority: California, Multiculturalism and America's Future,* New York, Vintage Press, 1996.

Morgan, Kathleen O'Leary, and Scott Morgan, eds., Lawrence Kansas, *California Crime in Perspective,* Lawrence, Kansas: Morgan Quinto Press, 1999.

Patringenaru, Ioana, "Tribes Come of Age," *California Journal,* October 1999.

Reyes, Belinda I., Hans P. Johnson, and Richard Van Swearingge, "Holding the Line? The Effect of the Recent Border Buildup on Unauthorized Immigration," *Public Policy Institute of California,* San Francisco, 2002.

Scott, Steve, "The New Legislature," *California Journal,* January 1997.

Shuit, Douglas P., and Patrick J. McDonnell, "Calculating the Impact of California's Immigrants," *Los Angeles Times,* January 8, 1992.

Sullivan, Andrew, "*Same Sex Marriages Pro and Con,*" New York, Random House, 2004.

Sweeney, James P., "The Fallout From Indian Gaming," *California Journal,* September 2001.

Taub, J. S., "Gay Politics," *California Journal,* November 1993.

Vanzi, Max, "Holstering His Guns," *California Journal,* March 2000.

Walters, Dan, *The New California,* Sacramento: California Journal Press, 1992.

York, Anthony, "Latino Politics," *California Journal,* April 1999.

Warren, Jenifer, "Packed Prisons Brace for New Crush," *Los Angeles Times,* April 22, 2006.

Wilkie, Dana, "Three Strikes . . . Out?" *California Journal,* November 2002.

————, "The Battle Over Legal Immigration," *California Journal,* August 1998.

Epilogue

# Reforms for the Twenty-First Century

As California moves into the twenty-first century, it faces many challenges, some new and some ongoing. A number of these have been discussed in these pages. Crises involving water supply and quality, transportation, air pollution, education, and racial relations are joined with energy and AIDS and illegal immigration to cite just a few.

There are, in addition, issues of governance. After all, much of California's governing structure was established in the latter part of the nineteenth century and modified by reforms enacted by the Progressive Movement of the early twentieth. A commission authorized by the state legislature studied various proposals for "modernizing" the state government and other suggestions have been put forward by elected officials and academics over the years. What follows is a summary of some of these proposals.

- Change the ways in which we elect our governor and lieutenant governor so that they run as a ticket, as do the president and vice president. This would avoid a situation, which has occurred often in the past, where the governor is of one party and the lieutenant governor of the other.
- Amend the state constitution so that when the governor is outside the state he retains his powers and the lieutenant governor does not become acting governor as he does now. This would presumably assure policy and programmatic consistency that has, on occasion, been lost when the governor has been out of the state.

- Make those offices that are primarily technical in nature appointive rather than elective. The commission recommended this be done with the Superintendent of Public Instruction, the State Treasurer, and Insurance Commissioner. Others, noting the controversy over the role of secretary of state in the conduct of the 2000 presidential election in Florida, have added that office to the list.
- Adopt a unicameral (one house) legislature. This would, proponents claim, be more efficient as well as save money through elimination of the duplication inherent in the present two-house system.
- Though highly unlikely, a small group of academics has proposed the state move to a parliamentary form of government under which the governor would be chosen by the legislature. This would insure that the executive and legislative branches would "march to the same drumbeat," avoiding the deadlocks seen where there has been divided control.
- The budget should be adopted by simple majority vote rather than the current two-thirds majority required. A different, though similar, proposal would drop the vote required to 60 percent.

In response to the many years when the state budget has not been passed by the time mandated by the state constitution, approve an amendment that would have the legislators and governor forfeit their pay for the period following June 30 when a budget has not been adopted. (They are not paid now but receive their salaries for this period once the budget has been adopted.)

Some of these ideas have gone nowhere in the time since they were proposed. Others have been explicitly rejected by the voters as with the requirement for approval of the state budget be lowered from the current two-thirds. One area considered by many to be a top priority if gridlock was to be ended in Sacramento also was turned down by voters at the 2005 special election, taking the power to redistrict away from the state legislature. The proposal in that election was backed by virtually every newspaper in the state and still lost. Does this mean Californians are satisfied with the way things are done, governmentally, in the state? Polls consistently indicate they are not. Yet the changes proposed never seem to quite meet the desires of the voters. What *do* they want?

There are other ideas that have been put forth, including ones dealing with direct democracy that have been discussed in Chapter 5. All are worthy of discussion. What is your opinion on these? Are they feasible? Desirable? Why or why not? Give them some thought.

# Index